Migration and Freedom

Migration and Freedom

Mobility, Citizenship and Exclusion

Brad K. Blitz

*Professor of International Politics and Deputy Dean,
School of Law, Middlesex University, UK and Senior Fellow,
Global Migration Centre, The Graduate Institute, Geneva,
Switzerland*

Edward Elgar

Cheltenham, UK • Northampton, MA, USA

Published by
Edward Elgar Publishing Limited
The Lypiatts
15 Lansdown Road
Cheltenham
Glos GL50 2JA
UK

Edward Elgar Publishing, Inc.
William Pratt House
9 Dewey Court
Northampton
Massachusetts 01060
USA

A catalogue record for this book
is available from the British Library

Library of Congress Control Number: 2014937778

This book is available electronically in the ElgarOnline.com Social and Political Science Subject Collection, E-ISBN 978 1 78195 584 0

ISBN 978 1 78195 583 3

Typeset by Columns Design XML Ltd, Reading
Printed and bound in Great Britain by T.J. International Ltd, Padstow

Contents

Acknowledgements

This book is the product of many people who gave up their time and provided advice, assistance and much hospitality over almost ten years. When I began this project, I never imagined that I would conduct more than 160 interviews in five countries to piece together personal stories of relocation and adjustment.

Some parts of this book were published previously as articles and are reproduced here with permission. Chapter 4 is developed from an original 2005 article, '"Brain Circulation", the Spanish Medical Profession and International Recruitment in the United Kingdom', *Journal of European Social Policy*, 15/4 (2005), pp. 363–79 (doi: 10.1177/0958928705057279), copyright SAGE Publications Ltd. An earlier version of Chapter 5 appeared as 'Fractured Lives and Grim Expectations: Freedom of Movement and the Downgrading of Status in the Italian University System', *Bulletin of Italian Politics*, 2/2 (2011), pp. 123–40 (http://www.gla.ac.uk/media/media_191022_en.pdf). The journal was re-launched as *Contemporary Italian Politics* and the article is reproduced with permission, copyright Taylor & Francis. Chapter 6 grew out of an article first published as 'Refugee Returns, Civic Differentiation and Minority Rights in Croatia 1991–2004', *Journal of Refugee Studies*, 18/3 (2005), pp. 362–86 (doi:10.1093/refuge/fei036), copyright Oxford University Press. Chapter 7 is based on the article 'Decentralisation, Citizenship and Mobility: Residency Restrictions and Skilled Migration in Moscow', *Citizenship Studies*, 11/4 (2007), pp. 381–402 (doi:10.1080/13621020701476277), copyright Taylor & Francis. Finally, Chapter 8 developed from a 2006 article, 'Statelessness and the Social (De)Construction of Citizenship: Political Restructuring and Ethnic Discrimination in Slovenia', *Journal of Human Rights*, 5/4 (2006), pp. 453–79 (doi 10.1080/14754830600978257), copyright Taylor & Francis.

The research conducted in Italy could not have been completed without the assistance of David Petrie of the Association for the Defence of Foreign Lecturers in Verona, John Young in Milan and Linda Lappin and Kim Manzi in Orta and Viterbo. These lettori welcomed me into their homes and shared their pioneering tales of intra-European mobility and the many disappointments they faced. I owe a particular debt to David for inviting me to Verona in 1995. I was a doctoral student and had just stumbled across the lettori problem during a conversation with Hugh McMahon, MEP in the European Parliament. For almost 20 years I have followed David's struggles and indefatigable commitment to achieve justice for lettori.

The research on the Spanish doctors in England was assisted by my former student, Shannon Nutting, who travelled to Madrid and conducted interviews on my behalf. I am also grateful to Lissa Perteghella and Victoria Rubini of the British Embassy Madrid and to the doctors, National Health Service and Department of Health staff who agreed to be interviewed in County Durham. I am especially grateful to Dr. José Garcia Miralles, who was instrumental in providing access to research participants in the UK.

In Russia, I must thank Galina Nowopaschina, without whom this research project would never have got off the ground and who offered contacts, planned meetings and provided interpretation and delightful company during my visit. I would also like to express appreciation to the members of Nelegal and the Moscow Helsinki Group, as well as several activists who provided information and assistance in support of this research project. Dmitry Valenty at the British Council and Dr. Alexander Routchine at Moscow University for the Humanities also provided logistical support and welcomed me to Moscow.

The research in Croatia was facilitated with the assistance of several organizations and individuals. I would like to express my appreciation to the former OCSE and UNCHR staff in Zagreb, Sisak, Knin and Vukovar; Croatian government officials; and several human rights defenders, including Tin Gazivoda in Zagreb; Ljubomir Mikić of the Centre for Peace, Legal Advice and Psychosocial Assistance in Vukovar; and Charles Taubner and his colleague Sasha of The Coalition For Work With Psychotrauma and Peace, also in Vukovar. I am also grateful to former OSCE staff Anton Hristov, Jeroen Jansen, Olga Roberts, Momir Vukmirović, Jasmin Mahmić and to my superb interpreter, Sandra Popović.

My colleagues in Slovenia have been among the most welcoming any researcher could wish for. I am especially grateful to Jelka Zorn for her friendship, advice and tireless work on the erasure and to Neža Kogovšek Šalamon, another remarkable defender of human rights. These two women and their colleagues at the Peace Institute set me on course for what has become a defining project in my career and one which has opened the door to many subsequent studies. I must also record my appreciation to members of the Association of the Erased for their interest in this study and willingness to participate in it. I owe a particular debt to Matevž Krivic and Jasminka Dedić, who connected me to many of the research participants, helped to arrange interviews and offered much useful information. Admir Baltic and Drazena Peric acted as my superb interpreters and also provided translation of key documents. Colleagues in the research and the human rights communities also informed my visits and provided me with a wealth of interesting material. I thank Borut Grgic, Miran Komac, Igor Mekina, Aldo Milohnić, Boris Novak, Neva Miklavčič Predan and Mitja Zagar for spending many hours briefing me on Slovenian domestic politics.

Several friends and colleagues reviewed early versions of the case studies in this book and commented on presentations and previous articles. Others provided a keen ear as I batted ideas across. I am grateful to Othon Anastasakis, Barrie Axford, Richard Black, Adam Blitz, Maurizio Carbone, Joshua Castellino, Daniele Conversi, Anastasia Christou, Tom Cushman, John Eade, Matthew Gibney, Judith Glover, John Gold, Annie Hughes, Linda Kerber, Eleonore Kofman, Maureen Lynch, Jim Newell, Kalypso Nicolaidis, Peter Nyers, Margaret Okole, Miguel Otero-Iglesias, Judith Pallot, Laurent Pech, Magnus Ryner, Rosemary Sales, Caroline Sawyer, Nigel Walford, Helena Wray and Roger Zetter. Colleagues at the Centre for the Study of Migration and Social Care at the University of Kent; Centre for the Study of Global Governance at the London School of Economics; and associates at South East European Studies at Oxford (SEESOX) and the Centre for Migration Policy and Society at the University of Oxford also provided insightful comments on earlier versions of some of the chapters. In addition, I benefited from presenting this work to the European Council Working Group on the Western Balkans (COWEB) in Brussels. Former research assistants Dan Ozarow and Donna Sherrington provided great help and directed me to new material which informed this study and I think made it considerably better.

I also received funding and assistance from several universities, the support of which was essential to this project. I wish to record my appreciation to Roehampton University, Oxford Brookes University, Kingston University, Middlesex University and the Refugee Studies Centre, University of Oxford.

The editorial team at Edward Elgar, Tim Williams, Emily Mew and John-Paul McDonald, have been a delight to work with and were more than indulgent as I underestimated just how long it would take to pull this project together. I am most appreciative to them, and to Edward Elgar, which continues to produce such engaging books. In addition, I should record a special note of thanks to Tempa Lautze and Diane Wardle, who read and re-read every chapter of this book and provided invaluable editorial assistance.

Finally, there are some other people without whom – or in spite of whom – this book would never have been written. Gail and David, Dawn and Michael, took more than a parental interest in my work and have, in different ways, been among my most enthusiastic cheerleaders. My wife Hayley braved the Russian winter, endured personal illness, sudden car failure and tolerated my absences on many occasions, all in the name of academic research. It was Hayley who initially led me to some of the most exciting case studies following a review of an article in the *Financial Times*, and my research has benefited from her support in countless ways. She has been the most consistent source of encouragement and insight over the past 12 years and it has been great fun investigating the world with her. And finally, to Romilly, the little girl who saw Daddy sitting at the computer, endlessly typing away, and for whom the world is one big discovery. Romilly has been the most wonderful distraction throughout the course of this project and it is to her that this book is dedicated with love.

Table of cases

Council of Europe

European Union

International Law

Slovenia

Table of legislation

1.   Migration and freedom

Freedom of movement: 'the first and most fundamental of man's liberties'.
(Cranston 1973, *What are Human Rights?*, p. 31)

INTRODUCTION

There are an estimated 214 million international migrants and approximately 740 million internal migrants in the world today.[1] In spite of these global migration flows, there is no guarantee of the right of freedom of movement, and most migration takes place against a backdrop of both official and unofficial controls. International migrants seeking to establish themselves even temporarily in a new setting must confront numerous state restrictions in the form of visas, fees and quotas, not to mention proof of resources, residency, employment, identification and other regulations. Even internal migrants find their mobility constrained by governmental requirements that may curb their opportunities to settle in new surroundings. In addition to state controls, migrants also face many administrative and social obstacles as 'newcomers', 'outsiders' or 'foreigners', and are frequently denied entry to protected spaces, above all in the housing and labour markets, further discouraging them from establishing new lives elsewhere.

This book considers some of the above challenges. The starting point is a re-examination of the right of freedom of movement. The concept of freedom of movement and its relationship to migration has received little comprehensive treatment among academics, yet it underpins much of what we expect as individuals living in liberal states. Hannah Arendt, who mistrusted states and saw them as sources of antagonism and the violation of human rights, also believed that the free movement of people was the bedrock for both human existence and democracy – without free movement we would be confined to slavery (Alonso-Rocafort 2009). Arendt's argument aligns with the views held by ancient Delphic priests (Moses 2006), for whom the right to come and go and be protected against detention was one of the four fundamental elements of freedom (Westermann 1955). More recently Satvinder Juss has advanced a sophisticated argument that draws upon historical and legal sources to suggest that without freedom of movement, other rights and universal values including 'mutual aid', 'hospitality' and 'good faith' are precarious, as is global stability (Juss 2004, pp. 289–90). The aim of this book is to explore such assertions by investigating the experiences of migrants and in so doing assess the pretentions of international and national provisions regarding rights to freedom of movement.

Legal foundations for the free movement of people include the American Declaration on the Rights and Duties of Man that first linked rights to nationality, residency and movement under Article VIII (International Conference of American States 1948). Some eight months later, the right to freedom of movement was explicitly elaborated in Article 13 of the 1948 Universal Declaration of Human Rights which states that: 'Everyone has the right to freedom of movement and residence within the borders of each State. Everyone has the right to leave any country, including his own, and return to his country' (UN General Assembly 1948). Subsequent bodies of international law, including UN conventions and regional conventions, have affirmed the right to free movement alongside other human rights protections,[2] thereby giving greater weight to claims that freedom of movement should be seen as a gateway right.

We note one important caveat: the scope and application of the right to freedom of movement. International law establishes provisions for international migration under certain conditions (e.g. the right to seek asylum); the principle of freedom of movement, however, has generally been accepted to apply within a state's borders, where it remains the prerogative of sovereign states. Arguments for restricting freedom of movement between states include claims over the preservation of sovereignty, where non-citizens are considered a potential threat to the state's resources and ideological foundations. According to the sovereignty-based argument, immigration controls are justified to defend borders and to protect interests that may be upset by the entry of large numbers of foreign nationals. This is a crude version of the argument, and we note that in practice several categories of foreigner have been identified as beneficial to the state and have been admitted (e.g. migrant labourers, professionals and students). Nonetheless the relationship between freedom of movement, the rights of non-citizens and the host state remains highly contested.

INTERNATIONAL LAW AND THE TREATMENT OF FOREIGNERS IN HISTORY

International law acknowledges that the rights of foreigners do not include full participation in the host state, but such participation has generally been understood to apply to political rights. Non-citizens enjoy all human rights irrespective of citizenship status just as do formal citizens, unless exceptional distinctions serve a legitimate state objective (Weissbrodt 2008). Nationality itself is not therefore a basis for discrimination. International law specifically records that nationality laws must be consistent with general principles of international law with respect to non-discrimination against non-citizens as affirmed in the 1923 decision by the Permanent Court of International Justice (1923) and Article 1 of the 1930 Hague Convention on Certain Questions Relating to the Conflict of Nationality Laws (League of Nations 1930). Yet the degree to which migrants may actually participate remains a grey area, and many non-citizens are excluded from a range of civic activities in the host state and struggle to see their human rights protected. Citizenship remains a common basis for differentiating between groups and for allocating state entitlements.

Furthermore, while citizenship may be acquired by means of naturalization in most states, thereby offering a route to greater participation, it is far from straightforward. Successful naturalization is conditional upon the applicant addressing specific criteria, often residency qualifications and language and citizenship tests. Naturalization is granted at the discretion of the state, and we note that most states still privilege ethnic and ancestral claims, which themselves are often a proxy for nationality preferences (Bauböck and Wallace Goodman 2010). Moreover, many naturalized citizens still do not enjoy the full range of rights afforded to those who acquired citizenship at birth.

Sovereignty-based arguments have been extensively amended, refashioned and challenged. Almost all states now permit some non-citizens to enter, even if only temporarily (Gibney 1988a), not to mention the large numbers of additional 'illegal' or irregular migrants that test the state's abilities to police its borders. The presence of these non-citizens has been cited as a reason for rejecting the idea that sovereignty is either an objective or a fixed concept that may reasonably be called upon as a basis for determining entry to the state. Further historical claims of cosmopolitanism and extensive flows of migrants across politically defined jurisdictions lend support to claims that sovereignty is neither a just nor accurate basis for exclusion. We note Amos Hershey's essay published in 1911 on the international relations of Antiquity in which he identified considerable inter-state and inter-tribal life, for example in his discussion of the Greek practice of Proxeny whereby a citizen selected by the city-state hosted foreign ambassadors at his own expense, in return for honorary titles. Hershey calls attention to the Proxenos Alcibiades who represented Sparta at Athens (Hershey 1911). Subsequent archaeological evidence has also affirmed the presence of migrants as traders, military personnel, servants and slaves in a profoundly cosmopolitan order.

Other historical studies of the Ancient world depict a complex picture of the mobility and associated rights of foreigners, which was at times open and receptive and yet preferential and ordered. Roland de Vaux's account of resident aliens (the gerim) in Ancient Israel illustrates such ambiguity. He notes that in Ancient Israel identity and belonging were not simply the result of tribal ancestry but were defined by an active territorial connection. The gerim thus included not only foreigners but landless Levites and lone Israelites, all members of the House of Israel (De Vaux 1997), who tended to be grouped with the poor, widows and orphans. While the gerim enjoyed fewer religious rights than the Israelites, they are recorded in biblical passages as having equal status in civil and criminal law.[3] They also enjoyed certain economic and social rights in that they were permitted to collect fallen fruit and olives and to participate in the tithe in the third year and in the produce of the Jubilee (De Vaux 1997).

While evidence of migration in Antiquity substantiates claims of cosmopolitanism, it is important to qualify both the rights to migration and settlement in Antiquity. Hershey advises that many other groups in Antiquity tolerated foreigners and admitted them into their territory, calling attention to the liberality of Indian Brahmans and recording that the Egyptians exchanged letters, presents and embassies and even forged marriage alliances with Kings of Mitanni, Assyria and Babylonia. Yet there were social divisions between such groups. Juss recalls that the presence of non-citizens in the Ancient Greek polis was even more complex in that the Hellenic world introduced multiple categories of status, distinguishing 'citizens' from 'barbarians' and later subdividing these into citizens, naturalized aliens, public guests, domicile aliens, non-domicile aliens and strangers (Juss 2004). While non-citizens could enter and enjoy the right of asylum, aliens were required to have patrons. Romans embraced naturalization within the Empire where foreigners were protected under the 'Jus Gentium'. Outside the Empire such rights did not apply. Nonetheless Hershey informs us that such toleration and openness had a lasting influence on subsequent European traditions, fashioning medieval universalism that he claims permitted considerable freedom of movement for specified classes of travellers (Hershey 1911). Yet it is important to stress that counter-claims could equally be found in Antiquity. Hershey records that Carthaginian merchants placed cruel restrictions on trade with foreigners and closed off the sea to some categories of foreigners. Arguably we can find evidence of both cosmopolitanism and mercantilism in Antiquity.

In the Medieval period, the place of foreigners and the rights to migration featured in royal policy but again with several inconsistencies. Many enjoyed no freedom of movement; serfdom was commonplace, armies were composed of indentured soldiers and Jews were expelled from England, France, and eventually Spain and Portugal. During Spain's Golden Age Spaniards were discouraged from leaving the country as economic skills were hoarded and mercantilism was embraced as central to the imperial state (Sznajder and Roniger 2009). Yet foreign merchants were permitted entry to these European kingdoms. Historical texts again provided further insights into the place of foreigners, suggesting some toleration of the right to migration, while the right to free movement was curtailed. The Magna Carta of 1215 (Runnymede Charter), and later the 1225 and 1297 versions of the Magna Carta, guaranteed the safety and right of entry and exit of foreign merchants; at the same time foreign-born knights, who were seen as a threat to the kingdom, were banished. The Magna Carta also records the place of bonded labour in its discussion of 'villeins' (peasant tenant farmers) who enjoyed no freedom of movement and feature in the document only in so far as they should be protected from crippling heavy fines that deprived them of their livelihood.[4] The right to migration was therefore not understood to apply as a natural right but rather was defined by association with economic activity, which was sharply delineated. Thus while foreign merchants generally enjoyed considerable rights of passage, other categories of persons were tied to the land or saw their mobility determined by their service in the military or to royal or aristocratic households.

The emergence of the nation-state in the 17th and 18th centuries provides the context for much discussion over the idea of sovereignty and its relevance to subsequent discussions over border management and freedom of movement. In his account of the development of the passport, John Torpey argues that immigration control was not intrinsic to the idea of the state but rather was the introduction of surveillance mechanisms, above all the passport, which was used to legitimate the state's authority (1998). Until that point, there was considerable evidence of freedom of movement that, even if it was not always defined as a formal political right, was treated as a natural right (Dowty 1989; Moses 2006; Whelan

1988), at least in Western Europe where the practice of serfdom had been banned. Juss developed this line of argument, making the bold assertion that there was an 'unbroken line of international morality that favoured the right to free movement' and that was not damaged by the emergence of the nation-state but continued during its ascendancy (Juss 2013, p. 11). Such claims may be informed by a closer analysis of the intellectual development idea of sovereignty and the state.

SOVEREIGNTY, THE STATE AND MIGRATION

The notion of sovereignty is attributed to Jean Bodin, though many claim Machiavelli introduced the term in his discussion of the state and the concept of 'lo stato' in *The Prince*, where he provides that public power may be separate from both ruler and ruled. In his *Six Books of a Commonwealth* (1576), Bodin set out a less contested definition derived from his claim that an orderly Commonwealth depended on the creation of a central authority that possessed unlimited power. Bodin's definition was later to be described as ruler sovereignty and had no bearing on the relationship between migrants and the emerging state, except in as far as such rights were derived by the ruler (Bodin 1992).

Since Bodin the idea of sovereignty has been expressed as the ultimate source of state power, de jure authority, limited governance, de facto power and influence. Common to all these notions is the separation of sovereignty into internal and external sovereignty, which raises important questions over the delineation of mobility rights. Internal sovereignty has traditionally designated the separation between ruler and ruled, providing one basis for determining membership. External sovereignty emphasizes territorial boundaries and political control over a defined area.

In his now classic work entitled *Sovereignty*, Hinsley (1986) argued that sovereignty is a theory or assumption of power, a theme repeated in much of the literature of the state (Ionescu 1974; Vincent 1987). Hinsley's definition supports the idea of 'state sovereignty', for which he finds considerable precedent. He traces the modern notion back to the period of Justinian rule when the idea of power and authority entered the vernacular. Vincent (1987) similarly argues that the vocabulary for sovereignty came into effect at this point through the introduction of the terms 'potestas' and 'auctoritas', which denoted official power and influence or prestige, respectively. The division between rule by a single central authority and the role of the public was further defined in the concept of 'lex regia' in the Justinian compilation of Roman Law, 'Corpus iuris', which provided the basis for rule by law, where people transferred their powers to the emperor. It is precisely this division and transference of authority that some claim makes the idea of sovereignty relevant. For David Held, such notions of sovereignty should be seen more as a form of legal authority or entitlement (1989).

The above definitions have been contested by post-modern theorists and others who argue that sovereignty marks a site of political struggle and not a fixed concept (Weber 1995). The term is no longer coextensive with the idea of the unitary state, nor does it relate to political ideas developed in the 16th and 17th centuries; furthermore, such arguments are at odds with empirical observations regarding the inter-state movement of people, which challenges statist ideas of political power (Deutsch 1978; Rosenau 1974; Weber 1995). Karl Deutsch, for example, argues that in order for sovereignty to be meaningful, it must be equated with the centralization of power, the monopolization of information and the concentration of decision-making authority.

> An even more essential characteristic of sovereignty is the absence of any recognized input channel of controlling or overriding information from outside the system. In the theory of sovereignty no outside organizations, as well as no preferences or values, may be permitted to interfere with the working out of the internal decision probabilities of the system. (Deutsch 1969, p. 108)

Thus for Deutsch the development of international and interdependent relations dealt a blow to the idea of state sovereignty.

Others have suggested, however, that the idea of de jure sovereignty is more relevant. Rather than stress the idea of state unity, they advocate reconceiving sovereignty as limited power, following Locke's conclusion in the *Two Treatises of Government* (1993) that sovereignty, although executed by the sovereign and the state, resides with the body politic (Middleton 1969; Schwarzenberger 1969; Stankiewicz 1969). Both Kavanagh and Spiro (1974), for example, dismiss Deutsch's transactional argument against sovereignty, maintaining that trends in interdependence have not destroyed constitutional independence. Held (1989) similarly suggests the term can be recast, provided one acknowledges five key gaps that complicate the usage of the term 'sovereignty', not least because they include reference to inter-state migration. These are: (i) shifts in the world economy; (ii) the development of regional trading blocs that influence the actions of states; (iii) the expansion of international organizations and regimes; (iv) the development of international law; and (v) the end of domestic policy as a result of transnational movements. In spite of these gaps, he notes that states retain ultimate sovereignty in that they alone reserve the right to go to war.

Contrary to the claims made by both Torpey and Juss about the permissiveness of liberal thought, several counter-precedents can also be found in the development of moral and political philosophy. We note, for example, the relevance of Rousseau's work for communitarian theory, much of which is opposed to the free movement of people and relaxation of immigration controls. While Rousseau believed sovereignty was retained by the people, he reached a different conclusion from Locke and explicitly discounts any possible division between political rule and society. In 'The Social Contract' he writes, 'Sovereignty cannot be represented for the same reason that it cannot be alienated; its essence is the general will and cannot be represented – either it is the general will or it is something else; there is no intermediate possibility' (Rousseau 1987, p. 141). The conclusions that follow from Rousseau's account are logically opposed to the idea of an individualized right of freedom of movement as set out in national constitutions and more recently in international law.

During the past 20 years political scientists have included population concerns alongside their studies of territory and authority in their treatment of sovereignty; the rights of migrants are not, however, well defined in this body of writing (Biersteker and Weber 1996). Scholars may interpret the origin of freedom of movement as a concept, but its intellectual connection to the idea of the state and its relevance to the multiple definitions of sovereignty most clearly enter the picture in historical accounts of late 19th and early 20th century discussions over nationality and citizenship. Notions of mobility rights developed independently for the most part from writings on the state, sovereignty and political authority.

INTERNAL MIGRATION AND ASSOCIATED FRONTIERS OF INEQUALITY

If, as Torpey argues, immigration controls and the institutionalization of the passport served primarily to legitimate the state's authority over migration policy, we note that the right to internal migration has also been subject to state interference. Although the relationship between the driving forces for such intrusion is notably different from the context Torpey describes, the impediments experienced by internal migrants nonetheless also raise questions about the pretentions of citizenship and the normative assumptions of international law. A central premise of this book is therefore that the idea of free movement within states is also contested by the number of state-sanctioned controls that apply in varying degrees to immigrants and domestic migrants, formal citizens and non-citizens and many categories in between.

In practice, the distinction between the mobility rights of those within the state and those seeking to move between states is also in dispute. Consider, for example, the case of skilled migrants. Recent data from the OECD record that the most qualified among them have a wide choice of destination countries and are found across the globe, as illustrated in Table 1.1. The table presents the image of a globalized pool of talent. Following the completion of the European Single Market in 1992 and the Uruguay Round in 1994, a global trading regime, the product of which is represented in Table 1.1, was created. What is not visible is the complexity of flows of highly skilled migrants, including short- and long-term migrations, return flows and multiple relocations between advanced states and developing regions, though these are recorded elsewhere.

Yet these global flows of highly skilled migrants are not unrestricted but rather are still shaped by political forces, as illustrated in the use of preferential immigration policies to restock labour and in international recruitment drives that are aimed to attract specific categories of migrant (see Lavenex 2006). Moreover, such flows are not unlimited. There are caps on the numbers of highly skilled that may be admitted into any host state. Several countries have followed the US lead of setting quotas for skilled migrants (e.g. Australia and Germany), while many other advanced states rely instead on a points-based system which rewards applicants for certain qualifications, such as level of education, language competency, knowledge of the prospective country of settlement and local family ties to the host state. Countries that have adopted this model include New Zealand (1987), which adopted a mixed approach of quotas and points; Australia (1988); Hong Kong (2006); France (2007); and the United Kingdom (2008).Other countries have introduced de facto points systems, basing entry qualification upon similar criteria but without actually counting up 'points'. Under such immigration schemes, skilled migrants must demonstrate proof of language proficiency, residency requirements and health checks, and might also be subject to age restrictions.

Skilled migrants, once admitted, face additional challenges that are not immediately obvious. For example, highly skilled migrants do not necessarily have the freedom to leave their employment while retaining their immigration status in the host state; rather (as is practised in the United Kingdom) their jobs may be 'pegged' to their place of sponsored employment. Consequently immigrants do not necessarily enjoy as much flexibility in the labour market, as internal relocation is complicated by administrative requirements, including the need of further sponsorship

Table 1.1   Foreign-born professionals in the OECD

Country of birth / Country of residence	Africa	Asia	Europe	North America	Oceania	South and Central America and Caribbean	Other and unknown places of birth	All countries of birth
Australia	27,572	115,224	185,319	16,798	43,996	7300	54	396,263
Austria	1086	3210	29,100	1353	189	729	–	35,667
Belgium	17,001	2178	36,584	608	–	–	8927	65,298
Canada	–	–	–	–	–	–	–	–
Denmark	849	3214	11,796	1369	172	519	–	17,919
Finland	465	815	6720	540	105	165	–	8810
France	145,889	30,448	76,128	6130	755	8189	–	267,539
Greece	3802	2281	24,627	3696	2351	419	–	37,176
Hungary	334	973	21,497	436	41	191	–	23,472
Ireland	2259	4398	27,558	2835	1218	279	501	39,048
Luxembourg	367	334	10,143	237	21	103	35	11,240
Mexico	194	1126	6902	8062	76	9810	16	26,186
Netherlands	5271	17,656	44,597	–	–	23,502	31,618	122,644
New Zealand	5946	10,890	29,775	3330	9207	444	–	59,592
Norway	–	–	2065	–	–	–	15,627	17,692

Poland	474	1500	21,714	327	48	201	420	24,684
Portugal	34,700	1396	13,593	1254	103	6340	–	57,386
Spain	10,647	4162	43,548	3616	496	40,800	–	103,269
Sweden	2220	11,000	42,725	2345	380	3500	–	62,170
Switzerland	4006	5207	60,913	4552	637	3527	1649	80,491
United Kingdom	84,125	118,790	126,728	29,553	30,376	19,486	2423	411,481
United States	–	–	–	–	–	–	–	–
OECD – total	347,207	334,802	822,032	87,041	90,171	125,504	61,270	1,868,027

Note: Data extracted on 23 July 2013 from OECD.stat.

and a second application for permission to work. Even highly skilled migrants who move within a state where they have the right to remain face the burden of providing documentation before they can establish their residence elsewhere, send their children to school or visit a doctor.

Displaced people, who in contrast to highly skilled migrants are among the least privileged, face multiple restrictions on both sides of the state border. Refugees and others in need of humanitarian protection are challenged at every stage of their migratory journey, even after success-fully navigating some considerable barriers. Before they reach the extremities of the Mediterranean or Andaman Sea, prospective asylum seekers must secure passage from their home state, which may entail paying smugglers or purchasing visas, documents and costly airline tickets and then skirting the watchful eye of immigration and asylum liaison officers instructed to deter their departure. The perils of seeking refuge in another state include the prospect of encampment in inhospit-able, crowded and often dangerous conditions; detention in the host state while applications for asylum are processed; then additional delays, uncertain procedures and potential legal challenges. During this time asylum seekers are normally denied the right to work even as they face other obstacles that undermine the chances of their successful integration into the host state.

Internally displaced people may face an even more precarious flight with fewer options of protection at the end. Often the only difference between the situation of the internally displaced person and the recog-nized refugee is that the latter has managed to cross an international border. Both may have experienced persecution as defined in the 1951 Refugee Convention, yet one remains in the state where the persecution was initiated. While asylum seekers may be held in a camp or centre, having surrended their autonomy to the UNHCR, Red Cross or a host government, internally displaced persons may similarly find their mobil-ity limited by their encampment, imposed curfews, formal and self-segregation, a lack of adequate housing and opportunities for employment – not to mention considerable threats to their personal security from armed groups associated with state or non-state actors. It is an incontrovertible fact that asylum seekers, refugees and internally displaced people lead unfree lives.

Other groups of international migrants, such as students and, to a lesser extent, retirees who have settled abroad, face a range of political and bureaucratic obstacles that also undermine their rights to mobility and settlement. Students seeking to study abroad may, for example, be subject to internal controls by their home state that may seek to discourage their exit for fear of 'brain drain'; this may take the form of fees or other requirements that must be satisfied before a student is entitled to leave. Host states may also place further restrictions on their entry, fearing that future graduates will remain in the country and may effectively displace nationals and force those with more favoured status out of the labour market. Like other categories of international migrant, they too face the burdens of fees, visas, financial guarantees and other limitations that set them apart from home students. State protectionism is an all too common response to the global politics of brain drain and brain gain alike.

Even within states the rights and entitlements of students vary considerably. In spite of attempts to promote internal markets in the European Union, for example, students in these regions experience different fee regimes based on their local place of residence. This applies even before one considers the possibility of intra-state mobility and out-of-state tuition. University students from Scotland who study at a Scottish university are currently exempt from tuition fees, unlike English students who wish to pursue their studies at another university in England. While students from neighbouring states may have the right to study in Scotland, the different fee regimes for home students versus non-home students illustrate further disparities that result from the exercise of mobility rights. Similar arguments may be made regarding access to reproductive rights in the USA or the European Union, where provisions vary from one state to another. Far from being unified, the market has become diversified, and people's entitlements are increasingly differentiated on the basis of local residency, among other criteria.

This book explores the relationship between mobility and citizenship. It re-examines the foundational claims of freedom of movement as a gateway right confined to intra-state mobility. In this context, freedom of movement is taken to apply to rights of entry and exit as well as the right to remain in one's own state. A central premise of this book is that the study of mobility illuminates the ways in which citizenship is understood and institutionalized within the state. By investigating the experiences of individual migrants, this book contends that we may gain a better understanding of the relationship between the political rights (in this context mobility rights) and social, economic and cultural rights that are at the core of personal liberty.

We note that successful migration is dependent on structural constraints, social barriers and individual factors, including ethno-national affiliations; age, sex, gender; educational level and linguistic ability; job status and occupational profile; social and professional networks; and residency. These constraints, in turn, serve to define a range of migrants whose personal identities, social and official status are often shaped by their degrees of access. Hence one may speak of various types of skilled or unskilled migrant, asylum seekers, refugees, displaced persons, students, tourists and expats who may identify as 'EU nationals', 'retirees', 'greencard holders', 'illegal' and 'irregular migrants' and 'trafficked persons', and so on.

The following observations are noted.

First, the ideas of freedom of movement and open borders are not identical. While free movement assumes open borders, the two are conceptually distinct. Opening up borders does not necessarily remove inequality or permit mobility. Furthermore, we note that the logic behind the open borders, communitarian and liberal nationalist arguments is overly dependent on push–pull models of migration, which fail to convey the context in which much migration takes place today. Immigration may be a livelihoods strategy but the idea that people move because of wage differentials between states or purely to improve their lot fails to acknowledge the complex interplay of autonomy, family and social networks, culture and other personal factors in the migration decision-making experience.

Secondly, there is an overriding statist bias in much discussion of migration that fails to recognize inequality within states. Although communitarians acknowledge diversity within states, their approach essentializes sub-national polities and ignores contestation between interest groups. There is an equal presumption that immigration policies are consistent, rational and effective, yet this is often far from true, as discussed below. The main exceptions to this are the transnationalists and critical economists and sociologists (e.g. the World Systems theorists) who believe that the world-system, namely the inter-regional and transnational division of labour, should be the primary unit of social analysis rather than the state. In order to capture such contestation, a more nuanced model is required.

Thirdly, and related to the above, the idea of borders is always assumed rather than questioned. Much of literature fails to recognize that, in some cases, borders are actively delegitimized or ignored. Here we may think of the many activists who assist those fleeing from Mexico to cross the border into the USA. Such subversion in itself raises a normative challenge to the exclusion of certain groups but even in the case of regular migration the erection of borders is not in itself evidence that borders prevent mobility. As Wendy Brown argues, even the walls dividing Texas from Mexico or South Africa from Zimbabwe may be little more than theatrical props which are frequently breached and blur the distinction between law and lawlessness they are intended to represent (Brown 2010). Borders demarcate jurisdiction of authority not necessarily mobility rights (Bauböck 2009, p. 10).

This book responds to the above-mentioned limitations by examining five central themes: (1) freedom of movement as a condition for action; (2) motivations for migration; (3) the relationship between open borders and freedom of movement; (4) the relationship between freedom of movement and democracy; and (5) the role of the state in promoting free movement. Rather than consider the well-charted issue of international migration, it explores the barriers to freedom of movement experienced by migrants inside the state. Borrowing Fitzgerald's (2006) recommendation for a neo-pluralist approach to understand inter-state migration, this study seeks to explore how competing interests *within* the state influence the ways in which – and the degrees to which – migrants access and enjoy their rights to mobility. The following chapters examine both conditions migrants face once they have moved and also the challenges introduced by the process of moving, including the problems of securing rights to residency, settlement, and associated social and economic privileges.

The setting for this study is contemporary Europe. There are several reasons for this choice of focus. First, of all the regions of the world, Europe has committed itself to the principle of the free movement of people. The right to free movement is enshrined in the EU's Treaties and has been affirmed in secondary legislation and in case law. A parallel body of European human rights law developed through the Council of Europe system also provides for the right to freedom of movement as set out in the European Convention on Human Rights (Protocol 4). Secondly, the afore-mentioned issues are of great political interest in contemporary Europe, where the status of migrants is the source of considerable debate regarding the identity of the liberal state and the degree to which it may admit or exclude non-citizens on the basis of immigration, asylum or security concerns. Thirdly, the European continent provides a diverse setting for analysis: it is the site of supranational development, regionalization and devolution; it enjoys a common system of external border controls, visa restrictions and anti-terror policies on detention and removal; and it remains a place of transition and a recent destination for the former states of Eastern Europe, the former Soviet Union and Yugoslavia.

This book begins with a review of the discourses on freedom of movement and the relevant institutional, legal and political context. The following chapter discusses the development of freedom of movement in European Union law and the European human rights law as developed by the European Court of Human Rights. This chapter sets the scene for the subsequent case studies which examine specific examples wherein migrants have tried to assert their rights to free movement.

The empirical basis for this study is the product of countless hours of field research with individuals in Croatia, Italy, Slovenia, Spain and the

United Kingdom. In addition this book includes a specific chapter on Russia, which serves as a contrast, as a state outside the European Union and one where there have been exceptionally stringent barriers to an individual's free movement within the state, not to mention restrictions on the right to emigration. The methodologies used include semi-structured interviews with migrants and their families, focus groups and further consultations with legal experts and human rights monitors. While qualitative research of this kind cannot claim to be representative, it is nonetheless informative and offers a window into the conditions facing people who may be overlooked in contemporary accounts of migration.

The first two case studies examine the experiences of professional migrants who have asserted their rights to freedom of movement within the European Union by relocating to another European Union member state. Chapter 4 describes the experiences of Spanish doctors who were recruited to work in County Durham in the North East of England. It draws upon interviews with the Spanish doctors and recruiters from the UK government to describe a set of initially positive outcomes where a select group of migrants have been able to establish themselves in the United Kingdom. It describes how their exercise of the right to free movement was facilitated by means of an Anglo-Spanish agreement between the Ministries of Health, which enabled professionals to assist their relocation. While noting the benefits of their move, this chapter also records how some doctors have become 'locked out' of their home country and 'locked into' the British system. It concludes with the doctors' assessment that societal and organizational barriers within the Spanish medical establishment may hinder the prospect of their return, thus limiting their mobility options in the future.

Chapter 5 presents a contrasting account of the challenge of freedom of movement within the European Union. It examines the difficulties language teachers from other EU member states have faced as they sought to work and settle in Italy. It describes how the pressure to open up the university system to foreigners resulted in a backlash against non-Italian language teachers, known as 'lettori', who had been working in the university system since 1989. Their plight formed the basis for four judgments by the Court of Justice of the European Union against the Italian universities, which it ruled had been guilty of nationality-based discrimination.

Chapter 6 examines the mobility options of returning refugees in Croatia, the newest EU member state, and describes the different fates of ethnic Serbs and Croats and their divergent reintegration experiences in post-war Croatia over the past 20 years.

Chapter 7 provides a contrasting example of a state where sub-national actors have frustrated the creation of a liberalized internal migration market. It describes the introduction of a 'registration' policy in Russia that requires migrants to inform the authorities when they move between cities. This policy carries over many aspects of the former Soviet 'propiska' system which controlled entry to Russian cities and determined access to a host of other social rights and scarce resources, including food and housing. Chapter 8 presents possibly the most disturbing account of where the right to freedom of movement, alongside a host of other fundamental rights in Slovenia, was revoked.

The final chapter revisits the normative claims of both European Union law and international law regarding the right to free movement as a foundational right. It reiterates the ways in which freedom of movement affects the enjoyment of social, economic and cultural rights and suggests that freedom of movement should therefore be considered in relation to the idea of personal freedom and hence citizenship.

NOTES

1. For a reliable account of current estimates, see United Nations Population Division (2009) and Bell and Muhidin (2009).
2. See also International Covenant on Civil and Political Rights (Article 12); International Convention on the Elimination of All Forms of Racial Discrimination (Article 5(d)(i)); Convention relating to the Status of Refugees (Article 26); Fourth Protocol to the European Convention for the Protection of Human Rights and Fundamental Freedoms (Articles 2 and 3); African Charter on Human and Peoples' Rights (Article 12); American Convention on Human Rights (Article 22).
3. De Vaux provides the biblical sources for his claims, noting that the gerim observed the Sabbath (*Exodus* 20:10, *Deuteronomy* 5:14) and the Day of Atonement (*Leviticus* 16:29); they offered sacrifices (*Leviticus* 17:8, for example) and participated in religious festivals (*Deuteronomy* 16:11, 16:14); and they observed the laws of purity (*Leviticus* 17:8–13). If circumcised, they could partake of the Passover sacrifice (*Exodus* 12:48–9).
4. See Treasures in Full: Magna Carta, http://www.bl.uk/treasures/magnacarta/translation/mc_trans.html (last accessed 13 January 2014).

2.   Investigating freedom of movement

> Personal freedom ultimately depends on how many doors are open,
> how open they are, and upon their relative importance in my life.
> (Isaiah Berlin, 1969, *Four Essays on Liberty*, pp. x–xi)

The literature on freedom of movement provides some glimpses into the relationship between migration, citizenship and personal liberty. Most relevant to this book are the theoretical and normative investigations into the rights of migrants and the obligations of states; historical and constitutional studies regarding the incorporation of migrants into the polity; and economic accounts of migration and the free movement of persons in the context of European integration.

THE RIGHTS OF MIGRANTS AND THE OBLIGATIONS OF STATES

Liberal political theorists writing on freedom of movement have been divided in their analyses of both the rights of migrants, above all international migrants, and the obligations on states to receive them. There are, however, significant differences in their treatment of mobility. At one extreme is the view held by Hannah Arendt that the right to free movement is foundational, not just for the expression of human rights but for human existence (2004). In her account, freedom of movement requires open borders since it is an indispensable condition for action that is one of the three fundamental activities of human existence. Action is achieved through labour (understood as livelihood-generating activities) and work (the act of constructing, building or producing), which entails reflection, a reality-affirming exercise. Action is therefore what defines us as human (since we alone can contemplate our existence). Any limitation on freedom of movement makes for a life without reflection (Alonso-Rocafort 2009). Freedom of movement is required for the practice of politics since democratic deliberation requires a plurality and this in turn demands the unfettered interaction of people. Related to this is her view that in the common space where people meet, ideas are shared and solutions found. Thus for Arendt, free movement is an essential building block in her theories of the human condition, which is expressly borderless.

Since Arendt, other scholars have advanced sophisticated arguments for free movement. We note, for example, that Rawls (2005) prioritizes free movement as an individual liberty and primary good that takes precedence over others. Similarly Amartya Sen (2001) discusses free movement in the content of his capabilities approach to development. Other scholars have advanced claims that, though grounded in rights-based claims to autonomy, present a less comprehensive approach than Arendt. For example, Arendt's belief in the paramount importance of free movement is echoed in contemporary writings on 'open borders', but with some clear changes of emphasis. We note in particular the work of Joseph Carens (1987), whose plea for unrestricted immigration is developed not from the perspective of actualization (or action and reflection in Arendt's account) but rather in response to inequality between states and the relative inequalities experienced by individuals housed within them. Restrictive immigration policies protect unjust privilege and deny poor, ordinary people the opportunity to build decent lives for themselves in more prosperous countries, according to Carens. Perhaps even closer to Arendt's argument is Satvinder Juss's (2004) interpretation of historical record and his insistence that freedom of movement is a foundational right which should be treated as a human right. Through a detailed discussion of both the premises of international law and the ways in which it has been misread – he claims, for example, that freedom of movement is effectively half a law since it protects the right to exit one's own country but not to enter another – Juss describes the limitations in the international system that he believes give rise to conflict and deprivation. As he writes,

> International instruments on migration make a distinction between two kinds of rights. The right to migrate and the right to seek asylum are technically different rights. One is voluntary, the other is involuntary. One is a matter of state practice; the other is a matter of international law. (Juss 2004, p. 296)

Yet opening up the borders does not in itself provide for the right to free movement. The removal of immigration barriers does not address the inequalities of opportunity, scarcity of resources and other obstacles that prevent those most in need of moving from low income to higher income states. For this reason some critics have argued that the logic of open borders offers at best a remedial approach to the problems of inequality between states where international migration is just one livelihoods strategy and means of protection among several others.

Moreover, the shift of emphasis from self-actualization and freedom in Arendt's account to basic protection under Carens' has allowed other scholars to revisit the relationship between migration, autonomy, nationality and citizenship (Owen 2010). For example, David Miller distances himself even further away from Arendt's maximalist claims for free movement and qualifies the duties of states towards migrants. Since states have created national 'homes', there is a legitimate basis for treating immigration as a special area of concern. People do not have the right to move or settle wherever they choose, however poor they are, argues Miller. Rather, all that should be granted is access to an adequate range of options, including choice of occupation, religion, cultural activities and potential marriage partners (Miller 2007, p. 207). States may therefore apply restrictions on freedom of movement provided they are grounded in the interests of discrete national communities: 'In general I do not see that public policy aimed at controlling internal migration within liberal states is forbidden by the principles of liberal citizenship, even if physical travel restrictions would be' (Miller 2007, p. 203). By framing the concept of mobility in the context of inequality (rather than freedom), the case for immigration control is reopened, even if it has not escaped criticism. For example, Owen writes:

> I find it hard to see why an account of global justice that seeks to take seriously the existence of national communities on the grounds of their intrinsic value, should propose rules of justice concerning freedom of movement that entail the de jure privileging of the value of national community over other sources of intrinsic value. Appealing to adequacy defined in terms of generic human needs is not an adequate answer here. (Owen 2010, p. 109)

The communitarian argument for controlling immigration similarly draws upon claims of legitimacy, a premise which Arendt fundamentally rejected. Michael Walzer, one of the most prominent communitarians, argues that selective immigration controls are an expression of communal interdependence where exclusion can be justified on the grounds that it 'serves to defend the liberty and welfare, the politics and culture of a group of people committed to one another and to their common life' (Walzer 1983, p. 39). Thus for both liberal nationalists like Miller and communitarians such as Walzer, freedom of movement is not an absolute or even foundational right but a right which must be balanced against many other claims, including those made by states and community interest groups. Yet how we deliberate between claims, and indeed which values we may call upon to advance such claims, remain contentious.

We note a modified version of the open borders argument developed by younger scholars aware of the long-standing divisions between the open borders and communitarian schools of thought. Adam Hosein (2013) takes issue with both Carens' (1987) and Miller's (2011) theses and suggests that democracy and universal values should drive arguments for freer international migration. Freedom of movement actively serves democracy by enabling people to share ideals, and build solidarity and mutual understanding. Similarly, Patti Lenard (2010) calls attention to the place of culture in the right to free movement and the right to remain. She argues that there are at least three situations where culture provides support for a freedom of movement that does not necessarily entail mobility: first, culture may be required to engage in one's cultural practices. For example, travellers and others require freedom of movement in order to carry on their lives; secondly, cultural claims may need to be fulfilled for freedom of movement to be exercised (e.g. in the context of the 'eruv' which delineates a boundary for Orthodox Jews or other minority national groups that seek sovereignty over specific territory); thirdly, freedom of movement may demand the freedom to stay put when that is demanded on cultural grounds or when one may need to stay on land in order to protect future access to culture. Lenard therefore advocates broadening the concept of freedom of movement but still insists on introducing other corrective policies. Although her approach satisfies some individual claims to autonomy, it comes at the expense of an unrestricted right to mobility. 'We [therefore] need to rethink freedom of movement so it includes freedom to stay and flourish in one's (cultural) homeland' (Lenard 2010, p. 643). Such responses illustrate that within liberal discourses, immigration is but one form of mobility (see Merriman 2012) and means of protecting rights.

A third line of argument has recently emerged which draws from the study of transnational migration and builds on the ideas of common space and community both within and between states. We note, for example, Étienne Balibar's (2009) *We, the People of Europe? Reflections on Transnational Citizenship*, which discusses the construction of a post-national European citizenship. The idea that interdependence results from free movement is also examined by Rainer Bauböck (2003) in his discussion of 'migrant transnationalism'. What is distinct about this approach is the recognition that migration impacts on conceptions of membership and rights in both the sending and receiving polity. Just as Neuman (1996) argues that the reach of the US must draw people into a framework of constitutional protections, Bauböck claims that the experience of transationalism forces us to rethink some normative assumptions of democracy and the way in which membership should be conceived. As a result of the multidirectional flows of migrants, he observes overlapping memberships between territorially separated and independent polities. In effect transnationalism exposes the gulf between nationality-based frameworks protection and broader ideas of citizenship that may extend beyond the territorial borders of the state. This disjunction creates a basis for a deeper cosmopolitanism, making borders effectively redundant. As Bauböck writes, 'borders are political, they demarcate jurisdiction of authority but do not necessarily determine mobility rights; for example, the internal borders of the USA or within the Schengen group do not deter migration even if they are politically significant' (Bauböck 2003, p. 10).

HISTORICAL AND CONSTITUTIONAL STUDIES

In contrast to the philosophical accounts for free movement and migration, there are several historical and constitutional studies which illustrate the vagaries of immigration policy development and at the same time build the case for freedom of movement to be treated as a foundational right. Focusing principally on Western Europe and the Americas, these studies present a more complicated picture in which immigration and emigration policy, constitutional decisions and the mobilization of competing interests define the rights to mobility in the nationalizing state.

As discussed above, one of the most original studies is John Torpey's (2000) *The Invention of the Passport: Surveillance, Citizenship and the State*, which shows how controls on identity and mobility were central to the development of the modern European state. In his account the passport and other means of identification are instruments of surveillance and control used to legitimate the state. As Torpey writes, 'states monopolise the authority to restrict movements of persons, not that they effectively control those movements' (p. 5). Moreover, state ineffectiveness regarding the regularization of mobility is not limited to immigration policy. As Alan Dowty (1989) discusses in his now classic text, *Closed Borders: The Contemporary Assault on Freedom of Movement*, states have also regularly restricted the right to emigration, though with varying degrees of success.

Tracing the history of emigration policy from classical slavery to medieval serfdom, to mercantilist edicts to mass expulsions and forced colonizations, Dowty argues that containment was above all used to consolidate power and build national belonging. His position is supported by other scholars. Mario Sznajder and Luis Roniger (2009) describe how, following the expulsion of Jews and Muslims from the Iberian Peninsula in the late 15th and early 16th centuries, Spanish rulers used the threat of expulsion and displacement to regulate and control subjects, often by sending the 'degredo' to the borders of the kingdom. Yet the development of policy regarding mobility has been far from consistent. Dowty and Torpey describe a liberal interlude between the 18th and 19th centuries when much of Western Europe (with the exception of France) lifted emigration restrictions. During this period there was almost complete freedom of movement for both labour and tourists (Turack 1968). The First World War saw the reintroduction of the passport regime that undermined not only the right to free movement but further contained many in need of protection. Dowty describes this situation as one of 'new serfdom', writing that 'most who moved did not want to, and most who wanted to could not' (Dowty 1989, p. 56). Again, such controls were ideological rather than effective.

Dowty's contention that limiting freedom of movement does not serve any legitimate social or national interest (1989, p. 223) invites further scrutiny. Historical research conducted by US constitutional experts has called into question not only the rationale for restricting freedom of movement but also the constitutional basis for a policy of containment. Gerald Neuman (1996) provides most notably a compelling argument for bridging the rights of those within the USA, normally covered by the US Constitution, and aliens and immigrants outside the USA. In *Strangers to the Constitution* (1996) Neuman argues that where the US tries to impose obligations on individuals, it simultaneously brings them within the constitutional system and should therefore afford them constitutional rights. To support his claim, Neuman notes that freedom of movement is specifically protected by the due process clauses of the 5th and 14th Amendments that concern the freedom from physical restraint (a negative freedom) and the right to go where one pleases (p. 126). Other scholars have since added to this the 1st Amendment, which they consider a gateway right to effectuating freedom of association and speech and the practice of one's culture (Wilhelm 2010).

Decisions made over the course of US history also provide a precedent for revisiting contemporary restrictions on rights to immigration. Neuman records that undocumented children, including the children of illegal migrants, were granted the right to citizenship at various points in US history and thus should not be excluded on the basis of the way in which they entered the country. Also the reconstruction Amendments (13–15), which corrected some of the most egregious inequalities during the

Antebellum period – including the denial of the right to freedom of movement to poor citizens and aliens, the banishment of citizens if they committed a crime and the denial of citizenship to African Americans whether slave or free as was previously permitted by *Dred Scott v Sandford*, 60 US 393 (1857) – also provide a strong basis for challenging restrictions on mobility rights on the grounds of immigration status.

Recent research on the right to inter-state travel, used by both the open borders and liberal national camps, introduces additional claims for treating freedom of movement as a foundational right. Neuman's assertion that inter-state travel has been protected by the Supreme Court on the grounds that it expresses the unity of the national territory and the equality of status among the citizens of several states, in addition to the human right of locomotion (Neuman 1996, p. 126), has been qualified by Kathryn Wilhelm, who argues that the Supreme Court has never actually declared that intra-state travel is a right retained by the American people (let alone an inalienable right), though there is case law to suggest that it should be a fundamental right. To support her argument, Wilhelm considers the pre-Civil War *Passenger Cases*, where the imposition of taxes upon alien passengers arriving into ports in New York and Massachusetts was declared to be contrary to the US Constitution and the rights to pass and re-pass through states were upheld.[1] She also offers the 1920 case of *United States v Wheeler* 254 US 281 293 (1920), where the Supreme Court held that all citizens were endowed with 'the fundamental right, inherent in citizens of all free governments, peacefully to dwell within the limits of their respective states, to move at will from place to place therein, and to have free ingress thereto and egress therefrom'. The decision in *Wheeler* has been further clarified by more recent rulings extending the right to travel[2] while acknowledging some restrictions permitted by states: for example, in the context of juvenile curfew ordinances; sex offender restrictions; employment residency requirements; drug exclusion zones; and custodial battles.

Studies from other federal systems highlight the role of sub-national groups and the conflict between centre and periphery, which undermines the presumption of statism and the effective monopolization of mobility rights. For example, in his analysis of Mexico's emigration policies from 1909 to 1996, David Fitzgerald (2006) describes how federal attempts to control the volume, duration, skills and geographic origin of emigrants to the USA have been unsuccessful due to the asymmetrical relationship between the two neighbouring states. In spite of governmental policy, Mexico's dependence on the USA in effect stimulated illegal migration that the government was then unable to control. Municipal governments meanwhile defied federal restrictions by using emigration as an 'escape valve' to alleviate local political and economic crises. Mexico's federal government was further weakened by 'bureaucratic balkanization' and corruption which prevent effective implementation of central government policies. Even when the Mexican government tried to encourage emigration to support the Bracero Agreements (1942–64) that provided 4.6 million contracts for temporary agricultural work in the USA, some Mexican states restricted the outflows of migrants by imposing fees to release braceros from their obligations to perform public work (e.g. build roads) in, for example, Oaxaca.

Mexico's efforts to control mobility flows were not limited to emigration. Rather the interventionist state used population policies to identify citizens through censuses and civil registries and keep track of them as they moved in order to police, tax, conscript and regulate the labour market. This was especially the case in the north, where links to central infrastructure were weak and where central government had hoped to redistribute labour, including migrants returning from the USA. Thus the case of Mexico presents a similar account to that described by Torpey wherein mobility and population policies were used as a means of legitimizing the state and in so doing shoring up nationalist ideologies. As Fitzgerald writes:

> The Mexico City government sought to legitimate the central state's growing control over peripheral regions and unify an ethnically stratified population around the common foreign menace of the United States. Emigration was threatening to the nationalist project because it symbolised to both foreign and domestic audiences Mexico's weakness vis-a-vis its neighbour. Mass emigration underscored the negative push factors in Mexico and positive pull factors in the United States. (2006, p. 264)

Yet in contrast to Torpey's findings from Western Europe, the Mexican experience exposes the limits of statist approaches to the development of both immigration and emigration controls. Rather, as Fitzgerald (1996) points out in his neo-pluralist analysis, the history of 20th century Mexico calls attention to the multiplicity of interests that are subject to contestation within the state (p. 286). It is these interests that determined the outcome of Mexico's contradictory emigration policy.

ECONOMIC ACCOUNTS OF MIGRATION AND FREEDOM OF MOVEMENT

As noted in the above discussions, economic factors and identities often determine one's rights to mobility. Even in contemporary liberal discourses on immigration, the idea of freedom of movement has been both defended and criticized according to economic values and social measures (e.g. poverty and inequality). Yet it is a curious fact of history that with few exceptions macroeconomists only recently turned their attention to migrants and the mobility of labour in their discussions of international trade. The writings of Jacob Viner (1937), one of the most distinguished international trade theorists of the 20th century, illustrate that while labour was treated as one of the essential factors of production, in no way is it substantively different from capital. Describing the effects of population growth as a result of immigration, he likens it to the influx of foreign capital and concludes that '[In this way] the international movements of labour and capital become assimilated to the ordinary processes of economic life, and may be regarded as the same in their general effect' (Viner 1937, pp. 187–8). Viner's later work on trade creation notes the limited interest in the analysis of migration, including the effects of immigration, on economic development:

> with the myriad long-run economic effects of the international migration of capital, or of labor, the theory of international trade has not dealt nor pretended to deal. While there is no doubt a valuable contribution still to be made by the theory of international trade in this connection, it seems to me that it is to the economic theorist, the economic historian, and other specialists, that we must mainly look for significant results in this field. Particularly in the field of immigration of labor, to whose vast specialized literature, as far as I know, no international trade theorist except Ohlin has made any contribution of consequence, it would probably sound like passing strange doctrine to the specialists in the field that they really were encroaching all the time on the legitimate boundaries of the theory of international trade. But it may be taken for granted that the specialists in industrial history or in immigration would welcome with open arms any genuine contribution to the analysis and solution of their problems which any specialist in international-trade theory has it within his power to make. (Viner 1937, p. xi)

Yet the passing reference to Ohlin underestimates the influence of his work and the emergence of a body of trade theory that discussed the place of immigration. With his doctoral supervisor, Eli Heckscher, Ohlin developed a general equilibrium model of international trade known as the Heckscher–Ohlin theorem. It predicted patterns of commerce and production based on the factor endowments of a trading region. According to this model, countries would tend to export goods that use abundant and cheap factors of production, including labour, and would import factors where there was a scarcity of supply. One of the core premises of the theory was the unrestricted flow of labour between sectors. Not surprisingly, as Chris Edwards tells us, the Heckscher–Ohlin theorem was exploited to justify both restrictions on labour migration and free trade in goods during a period of mass migration (Edwards 1985, p. 28). Shortly after the publication of the Heckscher–Ohlin theorem and Viner's influential *Studies in the Theory of International Trade*, the idea of the free movement of people entered economic debates through other approaches, above all labour economics and endogenous growth theory. These are briefly reviewed below.

It is important to note that migration theory, which includes economic debates over free movement, was forged during the industrial era and reflects the concerns of that period, notably the need for labour, and which were macro-sociological in nature. One of the emerging themes from the classical literature relevant to this study is a powerful critique against mechanistic explanations for migration in favour of multi-levelled analyses of flows and the decisions that encourage them (Zolberg 1989). Thomas Faist (2000) defines the three main levels of analysis that characterize studies of international migration and are offered as ideal-types. These are: the micro level, where individuals exert considerable autonomy which informs their decision to migrate and presumes free movement; the state level, where political, economic and cultural institutions influence mobility flows; and the meso level, where migration is affected by social and symbolic networks.

Until the 1970s migration theory was heavily influenced by approaches that focused on individualistic explanations at the micro level. It again presumed some freedom of movement where migration was the result of personal choices determined on the basis of the costs and benefits of moving and based on an individual's skill set (Massey et al. 1993). This approach gave way to more structural explanations in the 1970s when scholars placed greater attention on the inequalities produced by migration. This was often explained as a regional phenomenon with groups of people moving to areas where wages were higher; hence the growth of studies on 'brain drain'. Although the term 'brain drain' was coined by the Royal Society and first applied to migration from post-war Europe to North America (Cervantes and Guellec 2002), there was a surge of interest in the problems of human capital flight from the developing world to advanced economies. These structural explanations recognized that migration choices were differentiated on the basis of many formal

criteria, including education levels and nationality, and that such migration was far from free.

These macroeconomic theories represented an important departure
from the push–pull approaches associated with geographical writers and
first attributed to Ernest George Ravenstein in 1885. Where Ravenstein
similarly tried to describe trends in the absorption (countries of immigration) and dispersion (countries of emigration) of migrants, his approach
assumed free movement without formally qualifying who was able to
move. Half a century later, Samuel Stouffer (1940) emphasized the
importance of opportunities that affected the individual's preferences and
called attention to the possibility that people might exercise the right not
to move. Everett Lee (1966) later suggested that migrants experience
both incentives and disincentives between the country of origin and
where they are received upon arrival, describing a push–pull effect. One
of Lee's central findings, which is most relevant to this study, concerns
Lee's recognition that migrants enjoy different opportunities of access
and hence there is no universal right to free movement. The profile of
migrants who respond to push or pull factors varies considerably.
Migrants who are attracted to relocate as a result of pull factors in the
place of destination (e.g. higher wages) tend to be positively selected
(e.g. by age, education, skills or motivation) and thus also include highly
skilled individuals. By contrast, those responding primarily to push
factors in the place of origin tend to be negatively selected and include
forced migrants such as refugees as well as low-skilled economic
migrants.

The push–pull approach to migration has been a central feature in the
academic study of migration for 40 years but has nonetheless generated
several important criticisms which are relevant to our discussion of
freedom of movement. Scholars note that the approach is far from
universal in application – why is it that migrants in some regions opt to
leave but not in others where conditions are objectively as bad, if not
worse? Some claim that the approach is simply too rigid: the push–pull
model ignores the historical context in which migration takes place
(Zolberg 1989). A similar complaint is the lack of attention placed on the
political system. According to Zolberg, one pivotal reason why migration
theory cannot explain why the vast majority of the world's population
stays put is due to the primacy of the sovereign state, whose boundaries
are upheld by international law. For political scientists, the nature of
international migration is best explained in the context of a system of
interacting states where the potential mobility of labour is restricted by
competing interests. This includes both receiving and limiting the flows

of migrants to satisfy labour needs on the one hand and domestic political interests on the other (e.g. anti-immigrant opinion).

Several other commentators have argued that the push–pull approach simply does not take into consideration the significance of governmental policies on immigration and other structural conditions at origin and destination that shape migration (Boyd 1989; Kritz, Lim and Zlotnik 1992; Portes and Rumbalt 2006). The push–pull model also fails to account for individual differences in migration choices, and perhaps most important, no longer captures the empirical reality of migratory movements, especially in a highly globalized world. Mahroum (2001), for example, claims that other factors such as taxation, studying abroad, quality of work and openness in communication influence the decisions of migrants to relocate overseas.

There is in addition a considerable body of economic writing on the challenges of 'brain drain' that emerged in response to neo-classical models that treated the movement of labour as a positive action for the sending countries with no adverse effect on the welfare of those left behind (Ul Haque 2007, p. 5). As noted in the above discussion, many states did object to the departure of their own nationals and put in place barriers to deter their exit. Such political challenges were not, however, immediately recognized in the economic literature until the 1970s and early 1980s, when several economists identified 'brain drain' as a major impediment to the development of the sending states and found that the out-migration of skilled people directly lowered economic growth in source countries (Bhagwati and Hamada 1974).

In the 1980s a new branch of economic thinking, associated with endogenous growth theory, painted an even more pessimistic picture supporting controls on emigration. Since endogenous growth theory emphasized the development of human capital (Romer 1986, 1990) and innovation for growth (Grossman and Helpman 1991), the main problem with 'brain drain' is not simply the removal of skills but the polarization that it creates within source countries (Straubhaar and Wolburg 1999). In this model 'brain drain' reduces the wages of the unskilled population while increasing the wages of remaining skilled workers and thus creates greater inequality, which in turn sows the seeds for exclusion and poverty to take root (Lowell 2002).

More recent economic theory has re-examined the motivation for migration and in so doing has re-examined the primacy of wage differentials as activating reasons for migration (Alonso 1976; Cain 1976; Stark 1993). Several researchers have adapted neo-classical economic models of the labour market and have drawn contrasting conclusions about why people migrate and under what circumstances (Harris and

Todaro 1970; Sjaastad 1962; Todaro 1980). Todaro and Harris (1970) created a long-standing framework for understanding patterns of rural–urban migration where the decision to migrate is not based on wage differentials, as suggested in push–pull and classical economic formulations, but rather on the expected income differentials between rural and urban areas. This helps to explain why migrants are prepared to move to areas of high urban unemployment.

Since Todaro and Harris other scholars have recognized limitations with earlier cost–benefit models of migration, and rather than treat migration as the aggregate of individual choices, have drawn upon empirical research on the role of families and networks that both facilitate and encourage migration (Massey et al. 2005; Zolberg 1989). According to the new economics on migration, individuals act within family structures and households not only to maximize their expected income but also to minimize the risks to their economic well-being. One way of doing so is by diversifying the allocation of family labour by sending relatives to different locations (Massey et al. 2005, pp. 14–15). As Light and Bhachu (1993) record, migration introduces the possibility of exploiting a region's competitive advantage: 'international migration is especially effective because international borders create discontinuities that promote independence of earnings at home and abroad. Good times abroad can match bad ones at home, or vice-versa' (Light and Bhachu 1993, p. 2). Thus even the idea of individualized free movement needs to be reconsidered.

Linked to the above approaches, a wave of critical migration theories emerged from Marxist analyses focusing on the dynamics of production and the reproduction of labour (Castells 1975; Castles and Kosack 1973; Piore 1979). This literature responded to the changing nature of Western industrial states and considered the role of exploited unskilled and low-skilled migrants who filled marginal niches as well as large sectors of the economy. The dual labour market theory's emphasis on the dynamics of international recruitment and the underlying logic of the state as a recruiter of short-term labour and as an international operator that can exploit the global pool of talent to meet national demands recalls that mobility is often constrained by political decisions.

According to dual labour market theory, the economy is divided into primary and secondary sectors that broadly relate to high status/low status occupations. Historically, the secondary sector was characterized by short-term employment relationships with little or no prospect of internal promotion and wages were determined by market forces. Those who occupied this sector consisted of low or unskilled workers in support roles or manual or service industries (e.g. clerks, manual labour, waiters, etc.). Michael Piore's work on the dual labour market and specifically migration from underdeveloped rural areas to industrial societies has contributed to our understanding of brain drain. In his ground-breaking *Birds of Passage: Migrant Labor and Industrial Societies*, Piore (1979) argues that emigration from rural areas to advanced states is generated by forces inherent in the nature of industrial economies. His work has been linked with the concept of brain drain, since he forcefully challenges the claim that the out-migration of people from poor regions is beneficial to both sending and receiving societies and questions whether migration enables individuals to develop skills necessary for the emergence of an industrial labour force in the home country (Piore 1979, 1983). His conclusions have been supported by Saskia Sassen, who discusses the polarization of labour markets and creation of upper and lower circuits of capital and argues that many migrants are locked into poorly paid jobs in receiving states where economic conditions preserve established occupational hierarchies, most notably in service industries (1990). The relevance of this body of writing for our understanding of freedom of movement lies above all in the growing evidence of inequality of opportunity between migrant groups sustained by selective and hierarchical immigration policies.

An additional body of critical writing that informs our understanding of labour economics and freedom of movement can be found in the application of World Systems theory. Rather than focus on a two-level division between developed and underdeveloped states, World Systems theory assumes that migration is facilitated by cultural, linguistic, administrative and communication links, and results from imbalances between three distinct zones (core, semi-periphery and periphery). Migration is far from free and is associated with other social and political processes, including colonization/decolonization, trade (Petras 1981; Portes 1998; Sassen 1990; Wallerstein 2011) and the creation of state policies on immigration (Zolberg 1989).

FREEDOM OF MOVEMENT AND EUROPEAN INTEGRATION

Over the course of the 20th century the idea that people should be able to move freely from one state to another developed largely in response to protectionist policies and debates over the benefits of free trade and against the backdrop of inter-state conflict. Nowhere is this more evident than in Europe, where classical and neo-classical preferences for the removal of trade barriers, the creation of open competition and reliance on the market over political systems were enshrined in regional trade agreements, most importantly the EU Treaties. Although other customs unions and regional trading blocs have since emerged, the European Union remains the key arena where the free movement of persons is a fundamental principle. The development of the European Union is premised in part on the idea of the free movement of people. As Scott Davidson records, the European Union specifically calls upon member states to remove obstacles to the free movement of persons and services, providing a rationale for free movement which is both economic and human (Davidson 1987, p. 120). Much has been written on this topic and it therefore only requires a brief mention here.

Many scholars cite David Mitrany's *A Working Peace System* (1966) as the intellectual basis for the development of an integrated European area, based on the pursuit of welfare and the creation of peace. Karl Deutsch's writings – in particular his *Nationalism and Social Communication: An Inquiry into the Foundations of Nationality* (1972) – introduced a new element of public participation that is most relevant to the idea of free movement. Deutsch was a communicationist who studied the level of transactions between states. For him, European integration was not a process but rather a fact which could be measured by means of the integration between states. In this setting people were potential inputs and the cross-border flows were measures of success and potential indicators of 'we feelings', collective values and attitudes which signalled the decline of nationalism. In order to form an amalgamated community, functional linkages needed to be established, including trade and the free movement of goods, services and people; in addition large numbers of exchanges were required to develop the socio-psychological community. One important failing in Deutsch's model of integration is that while he believes that the movement of people may effect attitudinal change, he neglects the role of institutions that operate as part of the state apparatus, as noted by Marxist intellectuals and 'reproduction theorists' (Althusser 1968; Bourdieu and Passeron 1990; Bowles and Gintis 1976), and equally underestimates the pervasiveness of discrimination.

Much academic literature on free movement in the European Union has moved away from Deutsch's communicationist approach and instead has offered more instrumental accounts of the operations of the European Internal Market from the perspective of law and employment relations. Notable exceptions include Adrian Favell's (2011) study, *Eurostars and Eurocities*, which offers some refreshing empirical insights into the struggles and opportunities that face skilled migrants within highly specialized sectors. Also notable is Pécoud and de Guchteneire's (2007) edited volume, *Migration without Borders: Essays on the Free Movement of People*.

Elsewhere, the relationship between mobility rights and citizenship rights and the growing divide between those inside and outside the European Union have also attracted interest in equality studies, as well as legal and philosophical analyses regarding the rights of third country nationals. We note, for example, Linda Bosniak's *The Citizen and the Alien: Dilemmas of Contemporary Membership* (2008) and Sawyer and Blitz's *Statelessness in the European Union: Displaced, Undocumented, Unwanted* (2011), which describes how non-citizens who do not enjoy the rights of third country nationals attached to EU citizens navigate around the exclusions presented in 'fortress Europe'. We also note not only the problems of exclusion but of differentiation within Europe. Mau, Brabandt, Laube and Roos (2012) describe how border arrangements define greater mobility rights for some groups, while simultaneously restricting opportunities for others. Similarly Karanja (2008) documents that while Schengen offers the promise of freedom of movement to third country nationals within the agreed area, it includes both conditions for admission and an obligation to refuse entry under Articles 5(1) and 5(2), respectively. Thus although Schengen harmonizes visa policy, it further restricts freedom of movement and delineates mobility rights. This view is shared by McMahon, Cygan and Szyszczak (2006), who argue that while case law has stressed the relationship between free movement rights and the principle of non-discrimination, the Court's continued expansion of citizenship provisions places third country nationals residing in the EU at a disadvantage.

For those who now benefit from European citizenship, the markers of integration are found in the areas of residence, employment and social integration (Condinanzi, Lang and Nascimbene 2008). Yet these are precisely the sticking points which have historically undermined the development of the Single Market. As Joanna Apap (2002) records, the right to freedom of movement was linked to economic activity that brought with it clear lines of access and privilege. Just as Neuman (1996) argues that the right to free movement in the USA of the 19th century was based on one's financial status, Apap recalls a similar hierarchical relationship in Europe, with workers having more rights than students or retirees. Apap and contributors describe how during this period freedom of movement was undermined by problems over the transfer of unemployment benefits; timely recognition of qualifications for employment; transfer of retirement benefits; restrictions on family reunion rights; the rights of third country nationals; and persons dependent on social assistance.

Others have identified specific challenges to the free movement of workers as a result of specific directives and rulings of the Court of Justice of the European Union. Jan Cremers (2013), for example, criticizes the practice of the Posting of Workers Directive[3] (Directive 96/71/EC) that covers the million employees sent to another member state to work on contractual projects as a result of inter-company transfers and direct temporary recruitment by a placement agency. The idea behind this Directive is that labour standards apply in the country where the work is pursued rather than where the employment relationship began. In his 12-country study, Cremers found that the posting rules were counteracted by a combination of national level labour market regulation, lax implementation of regulations and relatively increased cross-border recruitment in the form of labour-only sub-contracting (2013, p. 202). He further claims that judgments of the European Court of Justice regarding the free provision of services[4] created a situation whereby foreign providers did not have to comply with provisions of national law as opposed to domestic service providers. Such differences have created a hierarchy within a unified economic bloc (pp. 210–11) and undermine the promise of free movement.

CONCEPTUAL FRAMEWORK

The above review provides the contextual architecture for a re-examination of the concept of freedom of movement set out in the following case studies of Croatia, Italy, Slovenia, Spain and Russia. A central premise of this book is that any examination of freedom of movement should explore the substantive aspects of the migration experience that inform our understanding of the relationship between mobility and citizenship. Freedom of movement is not simply a procedural right. As recorded in the above discussion of the writings of Arendt (2004), Carens (1987), Rawls (2005) and Sen (2001), an essential feature of mobility is the degree to which people are able to access the labour market, engage in productive work and enjoy protection from the state. If freedom of movement is a foundational right, as they claim, then the relationship between mobility rights and citizenship rights must be set out. This is especially problematic since, as noted by communitarian writers Miller (2011) and Walzer (1983), there are competing arguments for restricting migration to protect citizenship rights; hence their counter-argument against open borders.

In order to provide a basis for comparison, this book presents case studies that are examined through five key themes, outlined below.

- *Freedom of movement as a condition for action*: the philosophical writings discussed above emphasize the relationship between freedom of movement and access to other rights. This study examines Arendt's claim that freedom of movement is foundational and is central to action and therefore investigates the transformative aspects of freedom of movement. Key indicators include the exercise of mobility rights, access to work and the right to useful economic productivity (Arendt 2004; Rawls 2005; Sen 2001) as well as the right to protection as suggested by Carens (1987).

- *Motivations for migration*: the economic literature reviewed above identifies a shift away from classical and neo-classical accounts of migration that emphasize push–pull factors in favour of a multi-levelled analysis of migration, taking into account both structural and individualistic factors as well as specific state initiatives. In order to explore the relationship between freedom, mobility and citizenship rights, it is important to identify motivations for migration. We note that while migration is a decision, it is not necessarily a choice. We further recognize, as Lenard (2010) recommends, that the decision to remain should also be factored into any study of migration. Our examination therefore examines migration decisions through the lens of both opportunity and equality.

- *Relationship between open borders and freedom of movement*: the relationship between open borders and free movement is most pertinent in the context of the European Union where EU citizens enjoy considerable mobility rights. Yet, as discussed in detail in the following chapter, the rights to mobility and citizenship are not coextensive. In order to access one's rights to free movement, one must be economically active. Further, the rights of non-EU citizens are differentiated on the basis of their family status. Thus it is suggested that the degree to which migrants enjoy freedom of movement, and indeed citizenship in the European Union, may be informed by an investigation of the ways in which both EU nationals and non-EU nationals experience migration within the European Union.

- *Relationship between freedom of movement and democracy*: as noted above, liberal economic theory and early writings on European integration identify the movement of people with positive trends in social integration and economic development. This view is most pronounced in liberal theories of migration and international

relations, in sharp contrast to critical writings including World
Systems approaches that contest the positive aspects of migration
and call attention to structural inequalities, discrimination and lack
of opportunity. The following study investigates Hosein's (2013)
claim that freedom of movement serves democracy by enabling
people to share ideals, build solidarity and mutual understanding
and create a common space.

● *Role of the state in promoting free movement*: as the above review
records, the state plays a critical role in enabling migration and
settlement. Yet the state's desire to control migration under the
purview of sovereignty is, as Torpey (2000) writes, linked to a
long-standing commitment to surveillance and the control of certain
populations. Thus the following chapters seek to explore the state's
involvement in migration and the degree to which states facilitate
and effectively promote free movement. Critical issues of concern
are the ways in which states receive migrants and support and
enable recruitment campaigns that seek to attract both skilled and
unskilled labour.

The above themes are explored in the following chapters, which provide
a brief account of the research methods used, the ways in which
populations were selected, and the questions asked in interviews and
focus groups.

NOTES

1. The *Passenger Cases* were two similar cases taken together: *Smith v Turner*; *Norris v Boston*, 48 US 283 (1849).
2. See *United States v Guest*, 383 US 745, 757 (1966) and *Sáenz v Roe*, 526 US 489 (1999).
3. See http://eur-lex.europa.eu/LexUriServ/LexUriServ.do?uri=CELEX:31996L0071: EN: NOT (last accessed 13 January 2014).
4. *Ruffert* C-346/06 in 2008 and *Commission v Lux* C-319/06 in 2008.

3. Freedom of movement in Europe

Freedom of movement for workers shall be secured within the Community. Such Freedom of Movement shall entail the abolition of any discrimination based on nationality between the workers of the Member States as regards employment, remuneration and other conditions of work and employment.
(Article 45, Treaty on the Functioning of the European Union)

THE DEVELOPMENT OF FREEDOM OF MOVEMENT IN THE EUROPEAN UNION

The right to the free movement of persons is one of the four fundamental freedoms that underscore the Internal Market. From the inception of the European Economic Community, it was understood that the creation of a common European market would require that not only goods and capital would travel freely but also people and services. This idea was discussed at length in the 1956 Spaak Report on the General Common Market which gave way to the Treaty of Rome, establishing the EEC (Spaak, 1956). In Chapter 3 (regarding the free movement of labour), the Spaak Report considered the free movement of people in terms of restocking and re-allocating labour across a recovering post-war Europe.

Each State will increase annually the number of workers from other Member States which it will allow to be employed.

a) The basis for the increase will be:
  – either the average for the last three years of the number of new workers admitted in each country from other countries of the Community;
  – or 1% of the total number of wage earners for those countries which have in the past employed only a small number of foreign workers.

The rate at which the number of workers is increased can be slower to the extent that the base is large in a particular country: a scale reconciling these two factors should be established.

b) The European Commission will decide on the necessary protection measures in order to avoid an inflow of labour which would be dangerous for the standard of living or employment of workers in certain specified industries, without affecting the rights acquired by foreign workers.

c) Access of foreign workers to all jobs will be ensured by the progressive shortening for all occupations of the waiting period of five years applied by the countries of the OEEC before permitting a foreign worker to accept employment.

d) The European Commission will propose to the States measures for the progressive elimination of all discriminatory regulations (legal, administrative, or administrative practices) which, on the basis of nationality, reserve more favourable treatment for nationals than that accorded foreigners with regard to access to an independent profession or the practice of that profession.

This principle will also apply to regulations concerning entry and residence without prejudice to provisions governing public order and safety. (Spaak 1956, p. 19)

The logic of the Spaak Report influenced the design of free movement policy in the coming years. Although the Treaty expressed the founders' determination to 'lay the foundations of an ever closer union among the peoples of Europe', the free movement of people was initially treated as a negative freedom, defined by a concern to remove barriers rather than to promote mobility as a common European right. The wording of Article 3c of the Treaty of Rome (EEC Treaty) illustrates this point in that it specifically calls upon member states to remove 'obstacles' to the free movement of persons and services. At the same time, we note that the Treaty also sowed the seed for further development, since it set out important, though limited, social (e.g. equal pay for equal work for men and women) and legal provisions to enable the then EEC to issue legislation regarding social security.

Over the past 55 years the right to free movement has developed from a negative freedom linked to the labour market to a positive goal associated with the substantive citizenship rights of members of the European Union and the associated rights protected under the European Convention on Human Rights (ECHR). The ECHR, for example, prohibits countries from returning people to situations where they may face torture or inhumane treatment. For the first 30 years the idea of freedom of movement was largely developed in instrumental terms. The Single Market was to be created by means of the liberalization of labour and services that were described as factors of production, not unlike goods. Several commentators maintain that in spite of this logic, the framers of the European Union appreciated the political and socializing aspect that resulted from the free movement of people for the purposes of work. More than 25 years ago, Davidson argued that the right to free movement had been interpreted to apply to human as opposed to purely economic concerns (1987, p. 120). This sentiment has since been recorded in much case law, as noted by Siofra O'Leary:

> it is equally well known that the case law on the free movement of persons and services is replete with decisions whose reasoning derives as much from a desire to protect and respect the social and human consequences or demands of migration as it does from the aforementioned economic objectives. (O'Leary 2011, p. 505)

Nonetheless, there has been a consistent divide between those who may benefit from the right to free movement. As indicated in the Citizenship Directive, secondary legislation introduced by the Council, European Parliament and European Commission has emphasized the mobility rights of workers and the provision of services that cover an important but restricted sample of intra-European migrants.

One constant of the EEC's interpretation of the Treaty framework has been the restriction of free movement rights on the basis of economic and financial criteria. The most significant instrument that intended to facilitate inter-state travel was aimed at workers, who were seen as building the concept of a united Europe, as spelled out in Regulation 1612/68 and that has since been updated by Regulation 492/2011. Although Regulation 1612/68 recognized the rights of family members, and in effect protected the right to family unity, it could only be enforced through an economically active family member. Free movement was therefore to be restricted to workers defined as those in a subordinate employment relationship and the self-employed, who could demonstrate that they had sufficient resources so as not to be a burden on the host state.

Secondary legislation that aimed to promote the free movement of skilled persons was also drafted with economic criteria in mind. This is evident when one considers the ways in which the recognition of diplomas developed as a policy area by the Council and Commission. Until the introduction of specific legislation that addressed students in 1990, and following the development of a related body of case law, the free movement rights of the highly and semi-skilled could only be exercised if one was in pursuit of a professional job. For the 30 years between 1964 and 1994, the Council and Commission produced over 60 directives in which they interpreted the provisions of the EEC Treaty based on the mutual recognition of diplomas (ex Article 57(1)) to apply to specific professions. These directives applied to a select number of

individuals who benefited from the Commission's attempts at harmon-
ization across a handful of sectors and were consequently permitted to
pursue their professional activities anywhere in the member states, even
if their trade was not regulated everywhere. This approach to harmon-
ization proved especially burdensome and was subsequently abandoned
in favour of a system that featured the semi-automatic recognition of
diplomas that succeeded in promoting the right to free movement of
doctors (1993 Doctors' Directive) but saw few other successes.

In the late 1980s the European institutions developed a new system for
recognizing qualifications. This system was to set the tone for further
efforts to promote the free movement of skilled workers by liberalizing
professional services. Directive 89/48/EEC applied to nationals who were
fully qualified to practise a regulated profession in the European member
states and provided a general system for the recognition of higher
education and training of at least a three-year duration at a post-
secondary level. Unlike previous directives, it was neither sector- nor
profession-specific. This new system introduced the principle of mutual
respect that entailed neither blanket recognition nor the presumption of
equivalence but rather recognized an obligation to assess 'foreign'
qualifications thoroughly. States were nonetheless permitted to introduce
additional tests and other requirements such as adaptation periods, most
important of which was the requirement stating that one needed to be
economically active or seeking to be economically active in a profession.
This provision remained a staple of European Union law until 1990,
when students were given the right to residence. The introduction of
Students' Residence Directive 90/336/EEC therefore marked an important departure where the Council formally recognized that others might
also call upon their rights to free movement.

From the late 1990s and most notably between 2004 and 2005, there
was a shift in the treatment of mobility rights. New beneficiaries were
identified through sweeping provisions that gave greater definition to the
idea of European citizenship, included in the Maastricht Treaty (TEU)
(1992). Until that point European Union citizenship had largely been
considered a nominal complement to national citizenship with few
demonstrable benefits. Many who had questioned the significance of
European Union citizenship were, however, to find that it eventually grew
teeth. On the basis of European Union citizenship family members and
others were also to benefit from the right to free movement.

LEGAL PROVISIONS

The rights to free movement are set out in the 2010 consolidated version of the TEU signed in Maastricht in 1992 and the Treaty on the Functioning of the European Union (TFEU), formerly known as the EC Treaty, that was signed in Rome in 1957. The main provisions regarding the free movement of persons and the associated rights to social security and welfare are now included in:

- Article 18 TFEU that prohibits discrimination on the basis of nationality;
- Articles 20 and 21 TFEU that set out the rights associated with European Union citizenship, including free movement rights;
- Articles 45–48 TFEU that deal with the free movement of workers and social security coordination;
- Articles 49–53 TFEU that relate to freedom of establishment for self-employed persons.

In addition to the above Treaty provisions, there is an important body of secondary legislation including:

- Regulation (EU) No. 492/2011 of the European Parliament and of the Council of 5 April 2011 on freedom of movement for workers within the Union that replaces Regulation (EEC) No. 1612/68 of the Council of 15 October 1968 on freedom of movement for workers within the Community.
- Directive 2004/38/EC of the European Parliament and European Council on the right of citizens of the Union and their family members to move and reside freely within the territory of the member states (Citizenship Directive).
- Regulation 883/2004 on the coordination of social security systems and its implementing regulation 987/2009.
- Directive 2006/123 on services in the Internal Market (the Services Directive).
- Directive 96/71/EC of the European Parliament and of the Council of 16 December 1996 concerning the posting of workers in the framework of the provision of services (Posting Directive).
- Directive 2005/36/EC on the mutual recognition of professional qualifications.

The member states have also signed the 2000 Charter of Fundamental Rights of the European Union, adding another dimension of rights with respect to asylum (Article 18) and prohibition against refoulement (Article 19). As a result of the entry into force of the Treaty of Lisbon, the Charter is now legally binding. EU institutions and member states are bound to comply with the Charter when implementing EU law. This provision is set out in Article 51 of the Charter. In addition to the above, mobility rights have been advanced through the European Court of Justice and feature as part of an important body of case law.

European Union law reflects the tension between the goal of advancing greater mobility and the concern not to endanger national welfare systems. This conflict has seen the Court define greater rights to mobility, reflecting a more integrationist interpretation of EU law. Where the Court had previously found that nationals of a member state may only invoke rights of entry and residence if they had already exercised their freedom of movement to carry out an economic activity in a member state,[1] in *Deborah Lawrie-Blum v Land Baden-Württemberg* (C-66/85, 3 July 1986) the Court ruled that restricting free movement to economic integration would be contrary to the broader objective of creating an area in which Community citizens would enjoy freedom of movement. In this ruling the Court signalled an important shift away from the economic logic described above. Labour was not simply to be understood as a commodity but rather as a foundation upon which fundamental rights were anchored.

The imperative of non-discrimination has also been a central feature of both secondary legislation and case law. The free movement Regulations 1612/68 (and now 492/2011) set out several provisions regarding the right to non-discrimination on the basis of nationality and the basis for equal treatment. Article 7(1) of Regulation 1612/68 provides that migrant workers enjoy equal treatment as regards remuneration, stability of employment prospects, promotion and dismissal. In addition to conditions in the workplace, states are required to treat previous periods of comparable employment worked by migrants as professional experience acquired in their state. Article 7(2) further entitles migrants to the same social advantages as national workers. These provisions were upheld in *Württembergische Milchverwertung-Südmilch AG v Salvatore Ugliola* (C-15/69, 15 October 1969), where the Court confirmed that the free movement of workers requires the abolition of any discrimination based on nationality between workers of the member states, including employment, remuneration and other conditions of work and employment. The Court further ruled in *Giovanni Maria Sotgiu v Deutsche Bundespost* (C-152/73, 12 February 1974) that all covert forms of discrimination were also prohibited.

Yet while seeking to reduce the potential for discrimination on the basis of nationality, Regulation 1612/68 restricted the provision of free movement rights on the basis of occupational status in that it was aimed at those who were 'economically active', understood to apply exclusively to workers and self-employed persons. The Court subsequently clarified the meaning of economic activity in *D.M. Levin v Staatssecretaris van Justitie* (C-53/81, 23 March 1982), where it explained the concepts of 'worker' and 'activities as an employed person' and stated that member states must not interpret these definitions restrictively. The Court, however, informed that the rules on free movement also apply to part-time workers and low paid workers as well. In *Deborah Lawrie-Blum v Land Baden-Württemberg* (C-66/85, 3 July 1986), the Court further defined a worker as: 'Any person performing for remuneration, work the nature of which is not determined by himself for and under the control of another, regardless of the legal nature of the employment relationship.' This definition is offered in contrast to self-employed people, who do not enjoy a subordinate employment relationship.

In both *Levin* and *Lawrie-Blum*, the Court reiterated that work must be 'genuine and effective', a condition which applies to all, including those on temporary contracts and those working fewer hours (e.g. au pairs and trainees). The Court subsequently clarified what was understood by a genuine and effective link. In *Gertraud Hartmann v Freistaat Bayern* (C-212/05, 18 July 2007), the Court considered the rights of a frontier worker who worked in one state but resided in another. The Court rejected the idea that residence requirements were a means of demonstrating an effective link and hence were not an exclusive basis for determining access to social advantages in the host state. Other factors of integration were also to be assessed. In C-213/03 2007, *Wendy Geven v Land Nordrhein-Westfalen* [2007] ECR I-06347, the Court ruled that work, which constituted a substantial contribution to the national labour market, should also be regarded as a valid requirement for the status of migrant worker. The Court had recognized in *Antonissen* (C-292/89) that by restricting free movement rights to those in active employment, job seekers had been excluded. It therefore expanded provisions to include those seeking employment, on condition they provided evidence that they had a genuine chance of being engaged.[2] The ruling also reiterated the obligation that the host member state may not discriminate and that such migrants should receive the same level of assistance as non-migrants from the national employment office. In *Commission v The Netherlands* (C68-89, 30 May 1991), the Court also confirmed that nationals of member states have the right to enter the territory of other member states in the exercise of their freedoms, including the right to provide services.

There are additional distinctions between the rights enjoyed by workers and the self-employed which warrant discussion. While workers are able to access their free movement rights on the basis of work, self-employed persons must, by contrast, demonstrate that they have sufficient resources and medical coverage in order to reside in the host state. This distinction, although limited to select bands of workers, nonetheless reflects another concern among the member states – namely their fear of 'social dumping' and 'welfare tourism', and their insistence that the self-employed be self-sufficient. This remains an area of tension. The Citizenship Directive later qualified under Article 8(4) that states may not lay down a fixed amount that they regard as 'sufficient resources' but must consider personal situations on a case-by-case basis. The self-employed still, however, faced several temporal restrictions regarding their rights of establishment and access to services and assistance from the host state, in addition to special transitional restrictions governing EU citizens from new member states (e.g. Croatia).

The Court's interpretation of the Treaty provisions and secondary legislation further deepened the contradiction between the non-discriminatory provisions and an exclusivity of mobility rights. On the one hand the Court pressed to expand the right to equal treatment – for example, in the case of *John O'Flynn v Adjudication Officer* (C-237/94, 23 May 1996), where the Court ruled that the principle of freedom of workers also applied to social allowances and made clear that states may only distinguish between nationals and foreign workers if their reasons for doing so are objective and proportionate; otherwise, this could be regarded as a form of indirect discrimination. Similarly, in the *Viking*[3] and *Laval*[4] cases, regarding whether collective action could be used to resist what some may view as 'social dumping' within the EU, the Court affirmed the right to strike and ruled that the economic objectives that underpinned the right to free movement needed to be balanced against the objective of improving living and working conditions. On the other hand, while these decisions were of great importance for the development of EU industrial relations, they also highlighted the conditional nature of the ways in which rights may be accessed and that the principal beneficiaries of free movement were still defined according to their economic status.

Other case law has clarified the rights of equal treatment, entry and residence, and return. In the case of *Singh* (C-370/90, 1992), where a British woman married to an Indian national moved to Germany and then attempted to return to the UK with her husband, the Court ruled that the category of migrant applies even when returning to one's home state.

Attempts to discourage migrants from returning, in this case by breaking up a family, were considered unlawful.

Students have long benefited from the right to free movement and a guarantee of equal treatment. In *Françoise Gravier v City of Liège* (C-293/83, 13 February 1985), the Court ruled that member states may not require an EU national from another member state to pay registration fees as a condition of access to vocational training if such fees were not imposed on nationals from the host state. Since then the logic of equal treatment has expanded considerably. In *Rudy Grzelczylk and Centre public d'aide sociale d'Ottignies-Louvain-la-Neuve* (C-184/99, 20 September 2001), the Court confirmed that member states were not permitted to discriminate against EU citizens who had exercised their free movement rights (in this case, a student). In *Grzelczylk*, the Court ruled that a student could enjoy the benefit of a social advantage, provided they did not become a burden on the resources of the host state, while recognizing that any potential strain on resources should be balanced against openness and solidarity in cases where one enjoys a temporary right of residence. More recently there have been some notable interpretations of the Treaty provisions by the Court with some radical consequences for students seeking to study in another member state. In *Morgan v Bezirksregierung Köln* (C-11/06, 2007), concerning a German national who sought a grant to study in the United Kingdom, the Court established a right to export student grants and loans.

The rights of sportspeople to move within the European Union have also received greater attention by the Court. Sport is increasingly a paid activity and the demand for athletes and others in the growing market for sport has generated several cases where the Court has been called upon for clarification. The Court has struck down nationality restrictions in the cases of *Walrave*[5] and *Gaetano Donà v Maria Mantero* (C-13/76, 14 July 1976) as well as in subsequent cases. It has also addressed the issue of transfers between clubs, affirming the right of professional players to move freely in the European Union.

The parallel development of European citizenship further expanded and clarified the free movement rights, including the rights to residence and establishment enjoyed by EU nationals. These rights were decoupled from the economic logic described above. In 1998 in a ground-breaking decision the Court ruled in the case of *Maria Martinez Sala v Freistaat Bayern* (C-85/96, 12 May 1998) that nationals of a member state can rely on their European citizenship for protection against discrimination on grounds of nationality by another member state. Siofra O'Leary explains the significance of this decision:

First it exploded the notion that the introduction of Union citizenship was little more than a cosmetic exercise which left essentially unaltered the existing legal framework governing the free movement of persons. Secondly, it decoupled the application of the aforementioned principles of free movement and non-discrimination from the need to exercise an economic activity. Thirdly, and regardless of the Court's protestations to the contrary, Martinez Sala indicated that Union citizenship could have a significant impact on the material scope of application of EU law or, at the very least, on what situations were henceforth to be deemed to be governed by EU law and therefore falling within the material scope of the latter. (O'Leary 2011, p. 500)

The rights of European citizens were detailed in the citizenship provisions of Article 21 TFEU as derived from Article 20 (ex Article 17 TEU) that states that European citizenship is held in addition to national citizenship and is provided by the member states and warrants additional civil and political rights normally associated with the rights of sovereign states, including rights to mobility:

2.   Citizens of the Union shall enjoy the rights and be subject to the duties provided for in the Treaties. They shall have, inter alia:

(a)   the right to move and reside freely within the territory of the Member States;
(b)   the right to vote and to stand as candidates in elections to the European Parliament and in municipal elections in their Member State of residence, under the same conditions as nationals of that State.

Article 21 TFEU that sets out the free movement rights for EU citizens and specifies their rights to move and reside within the Union has been complemented by the Citizenship Directive 2004/38/EC that repealed the existing free movement directives, including those discussed above. It left in place an amended Regulation 1612/68 (and its implementing Directive 1408/71) and enlarged the scope of beneficiaries to include not only citizens of the European Union (nationals of the EU member states) but also their dependants and under certain circumstances other family members.

The Citizenship Directive reiterates and expands upon Treaty provisions, including respect for private and family life, freedom to choose an occupation and the right to engage in work (TEU Articles 6–9). It provides all European Union citizens and their family members the right to enter another member state as well as the right to reside there for up to three months on the basis of a valid ID card or passport, irrespective of

their employment status. European Union citizens acquire an uncondi-
tional right of residence after five years' uninterrupted legal residence.
These provisions are set out under Article 7 of the Citizenship Directive:

1. All Union citizens shall have the right of residence on the territory of
   another Member State for a period of longer than three months if they:

   (a) are workers or self-employed persons in the host Member State; or
   (b) have sufficient resources for themselves and their family members
       not to become a burden on the social assistance system of the host
       Member State during their period of residence and have comprehen-
       sive sickness insurance cover in the host Member State; or
   (c) – are enrolled at a private or public establishment, accredited or
       financed by the host Member State on the basis of its legislation or
       administrative practice, for the principal purpose of following a
       course of study, including vocational training; and
       – have comprehensive sickness insurance cover in the host Member
       State and assure the relevant national authority, by means of a
       declaration or by such equivalent means as they may choose, that
       they have sufficient resources for themselves and their family mem-
       bers not to become a burden on the social assistance system of the
       host Member State during their period of residence; or
   (d) are family members accompanying or joining a Union citizen who
       satisfies the conditions referred to in points (a), (b) or (c).

It should be noted that the definition of a family member is wide and
includes those in registered civil partnerships, where those are legally in
force in member states.

The extension of the above rights has been complemented by developments in the European Economic Area (EEA) and neighbouring states,
where the same rights have largely been extended to nationals of the
EEA, including Iceland and Lichtenstein. Swiss nationals may also
benefit from the right to free movement within the European Union as a
result of two separate agreements.

In terms of social policy, the Directive clarifies the meaning of
solidarity that was included in the TEU provisions concerning labour and
industrial-related rights such as social security and health care (TEU
Articles 20–26). The Citizenship Directive provides European Union
citizens not only with the right to travel to another member state to seek
employment but also the right to receive the same benefits from the
national employment office as nationals. The Citizenship provisions also
permit European Union citizens to benefit from the coordination of social
security where previous periods of work, insurance or residence in other
countries are aggregated and may still count towards their pensions and
other entitlements. Most importantly EU citizens residing in other

member states may receive social security. These rules cover contributory benefits (such as child benefit), attendance allowance, disability living allowance for carers, and non-contributory benefits such as jobseekers allowance, State Pension Credit and disability living allowance. The Directive also provides an additional source of protection in that it permits citizens to retain the status of worker or self-employed person even after their work is ended.

The notion of equal treatment, reaffirmed in Directive 2004/38, has been extended to family members of EU citizens, including third country nationals who have a right of permanent residence. Family members also have the right to work in the host state and send their children to school in the same way as nationals. The children of migrant workers have the right to educational grants and other assistance, though this is not the case for self-employed people, whose family members may only access these benefits after a five-year period of residence in the host state. The Court has subsequently reaffirmed the right to family unity, most notably in the case of *Metock*,[6] where the Court had previously ruled that the condition that third country nationals must have been lawfully resident in the European Union in order to access their free movement rights was incompatible with the aims of the Citizenship Directive. Overruling its previous decision in *Akrich* that upheld the states' competence to regulate a third country national's first entry into the European Union, the Court found that such barriers to family reunification could undermine the right to free movement of EU nationals. Thus, as a result of its ruling in *Metock*, the Court has shown that European Union citizenship is not merely an ideological token but an enforceable basis of law.

CONFLICTS AND CONTRADICTIONS

The idea of the Single Market applies no longer just to workers and self-employed persons but also to people who enjoy various types of economic status. Further qualifications to the principle of freedom of movement have been partially addressed by the substantive development of European citizenship through the Citizenship Directive and Court rulings, but the distinction between economically active and non-active citizens remains a source of division; we note as well a division between older member states (pre-2007) and new entrants that are subject to transitional arrangements. Several categories remain outside the scope of these provisions: non-economically active people (with no family link to an EU economically active citizen) who fail to meet the test of self-sufficiency (e.g. the ill, elderly and unemployed); and non-EU nationals who cannot derive rights on the backs of family members.

One glaring point of inequality concerns the restrictions to the mobility rights of European Union citizens from new member states. Both the Treaty of Accession of 2003 and the Treaty of Accession of 2005 include temporal provisions which set out transition periods before workers from the new member states are able to enjoy full rights to freedom of movement. Individual member states may restrict the right to work of EU citizens from the acceding states for up to seven years from the date that their home state joined the European Union. In the case of Bulgaria and Romania, this period expired at the end of December 2013. Croatian citizens of the European Union, however, have been denied the full/free movement rights afforded to other European nationals until 2020 and must apply for work permits in other EU member states. Although migrants who are subject to these transitional arrangements are entitled to equal treatment with national workers, once they are legally employed in another EU member state, the use of such transitional arrangements introduces the spectre of protectionism and the denial of access to key social assistance and services.

Moreover, states are still permitted to treat nationals and European Union citizens differently when they may demonstrate a justified distinction (i.e. any restriction must be objectively justified) and member states' actions must be determined to be in pursuit of a legitimate public interest and also proportionate. This applies to areas which may be considered basic rights by large sections of the European population and include, for example, affordable education and decent housing (Chalmers, Davies and Monti 2010). These areas are a source of potential division. The case of *Förster* (C-158/07) illustrates this point. Förster was a German national who had been denied study finance because she was economically inactive and had not been a resident in the Netherlands for five years. In this case the Court ruled that the Dutch authorities were permitted to deny her the funding that would have been available to Dutch nationals. This was not a matter of nationality-based discrimination but rather a conclusion that she had not satisfied the criteria for integration – in this case, the residence test. As Chalmers, Davies and Monti write, 'for a foreigner, it takes time or work to integrate, but for a national, it does not' (2010, p. 459).

Yet, there are many other instances where the Treaty framework establishes provisions which enhance the rights of European citizens and create a new basis for differentiation. The cases of *Hartmann* and *Morgan* demonstrate that those who seek to exercise their rights to free

movement may benefit, for example, by the receipt of grants and loans
for educational purposes; however, such provisions do not apply to
non-migrant citizens. Arguably, in order to benefit from EU law one must
be a migrant.

The Commission has also found that the free movement provisions are
not sufficient to promote mobility. In spite of the above-mentioned
developments in European Union law, it recognizes that the numbers
benefiting from the exercise of free movement rights are low by
comparison with the inward migration of third country nationals into the
European Union. Eurostat records that only 2.3 per cent of EU citizens
reside in another member state and that almost two-thirds of migrants
come from countries outside the European Union. Despite the progress
made there are still legal, administrative and practical obstacles to the
exercise of free movement rights. Commenting on the European Year of
Workers' Mobility in 2006, the Commission noted that:

> in addition to the legal and administrative obstacles on which recent efforts
> have generally focused (e.g. recognition of qualifications and portability of
> supplementary pension rights), there are other factors that influence trans-
> national mobility. These include housing issues, language, the employment of
> spouses and partners, return mechanisms, historical 'barriers' and the recog-
> nition of mobility experience, particularly within SMEs. (European
> Parliament/Legislative Observatory 2010, pp. 2–3)

The above barriers have not, however, deterred significant numbers of
third country nationals from migrating to the European Union.

The treatment of non-EU nationals in EU law has been briefly
discussed in the context of third country nationals who are in a family
relationship with an EU citizen. However, the application of EU law goes
considerably further and exposes great divisions on the basis of citizenship. Third country nationals may enjoy a right to enter or reside in the
European Union in that they have acquired a particular status (e.g. as the
spouse or dependant of a European Union citizen, as a student or as a
refugee). These categories are nevertheless both limited and restricted,
and many third country nationals seeking to enter the European Union
will not enjoy such status. These restrictions are the result of both history
and design.

Just as the idea of European Union citizenship was being developed at
Maastricht, there was a parallel effort to define a common and restrictive
approach to immigration and asylum within the European Union. Such
developments took place on the heels of the Schengen agreements of
1985 and 1990. Though outside the European Union, these agreements
bound most of the then 15 EU member states (with the exception of the

United Kingdom and Ireland) by means of an international agreement that allows the abolition of internal border checks and establishes a common external frontier. Schengen also provides a common visa system (currently in effect) as well as the development of a common asylum and immigration policy. In addition to the expansion of Schengen, the European Union member states constructed a common policy of border management, immigration and asylum as established in Articles 77–79 TFEU.

Under Article 77 the TFEU provides that the EU will refrain from controlling entry and carrying out checks on all people crossing the internal borders of the EU and further declares (under Article 78) its ambitions for a common asylum policy:

Article 78

1. The Union shall develop a common policy on asylum, subsidiary protection and temporary protection with a view to offering appropriate status to any third-country national requiring international protection and ensuring compliance with the principle of non-refoulement. This policy must be in accordance with the Geneva Convention of 28 July 1951 and the Protocol of 31 January 1967 relating to the status of refugees, and other relevant treaties.

The TFEU also provides for the fair treatment of third country nationals residing legally within the member states and seeks to combat illegal migration and human trafficking. These provisions have been included in the Area of Freedom, Security and Justice (AFSJ), a series of policies that have been attached to the TFEU under Article 67.

Chalmers, Davies and Monti (2011) note the contradictions inherent in the AFSJ. They argue that the AFSJ should be thought of as contributing to sustaining a particular way of life for its citizens. In this context the above free movement rights should be considered alongside the development of asylum, immigration and security policies. They write that migration policy is paradoxical, since it both affirms the contributions that migration may make to sustaining the European Union and simultaneously treats migration as a threat to its very security. The risk of removals and denial of rights to non-European nationals who cannot demonstrate that they are lawfully present in the European Union presents a less than harmonious image (Sawyer and Blitz 2011).

As to the treatment of refugees and asylum seekers and the protection of the rights of refugees, subsidiary and humanitarian protection has been extensively documented elsewhere. More relevant to our study, however, is the introduction of Directive 2008/115/EC on Common Standards and

Procedures in member states for Returning Illegally Staying Third-Country Nationals (Returns Directive) that sets a new standard in migration policy within the European Union. The Directive compels member states to issue a return decision and in effect prompt the departure of any third country national staying illegally in its territory, unless the state is prepared to offer authorization for 'compassionate, humanitarian, or other reasons'. In this context illegality does not mean a third country national has broken the law; only that they may have breached the terms of their entry to the member state (e.g. not having a valid document or sufficient means of support). This provision has been used to remove significant numbers of foreigners. Chalmers, Davies and Monti (2010) maintain that both in practice and in law, the Directive does not prohibit states from breaking up families or sending sick and vulnerable people back; it only requires member states to respect the principle of non-refoulement as set out in the 1951 Refugee Convention. Other scholars note that even the prohibition against refoulement has not been upheld (see Blitz 2007).

THE EUROPEAN CONVENTION ON HUMAN RIGHTS

In addition to the development of European Union law, there is an important body of European human rights law that has been developed through the Council of Europe and in particular the European Convention on Human Rights. Although the two bodies of law developed independently, further to the Lisbon Treaty entering into force on 1 December 2009, the EU has established a legal basis for acceding to the ECHR. The European Union member states have drafted an agreement to accede to the European Convention on Human Rights that will be finalized shortly (see European Commission 2014). Accession of the European Union to the ECHR will strengthen the protection of human rights in Europe by ultimately submitting the EU and its legal acts to the jurisdiction of the European Court of Human Rights (ECtHR). This development is especially significant and builds on a series of political steps that have sought to bring these two bodies of law closer together. The 1997 Treaty of Amsterdam first called for respect for the fundamental rights guaranteed by the ECHR, and the Court of Justice of the European Union has since sought to include principles of the ECHR into European Union law.

The proposed accession of the European Union to the ECHR has great significance for the protection of the rights of migrants. Under Article 1, the ECHR protects all those within the territory of signatory parties, regardless of nationality or citizenship. The Convention speaks of the rights of all people and does not mention foreigners as regards rights to migration. The only explicit mention of migration is in Protocol 4, which guarantees the right of freedom of movement within the territory, providing that one is legally present.

Article 2 – freedom of movement

1. Everyone lawfully within the territory of a State shall, within that territory, have the right to liberty of movement and freedom to choose his residence.
2. Everyone shall be free to leave any country, including his own.
3. No restrictions shall be placed on the exercise of these rights other than such as are in accordance with law and are necessary in a democratic society in the interests of national security or public safety, for the maintenance of ordre public, for the prevention of crime, for the protection of health or morals, or for the protection of the rights and freedoms of others.
4. The rights set forth in paragraph 1 may also be subject, in particular areas, to restrictions imposed in accordance with law and justified by the public interest in a democratic society.

In addition to the above protocol, we note that other provisions in the ECHR regarding the prohibition against torture, inhuman or degrading treatment or punishment (Article 3) and the right to respect for private and family life that offer foreign spouses protection from state intrusion are subject to some conditions.[7]

The provisions in ECHR Articles 3 and 8 have been used to develop an important body of case law regarding migrants' rights, above all in cases of expulsion. Two pivotal cases which set the standard for protecting the rights of migrants are the ECtHR decision in the case of *Abdulaziz, Cabales & Balkandali v UK* [1985] Ser A. 95 and the 1988 case of *Berrehab*. In the case of the former, the United Kingdom had introduced legislation that restricted the possibility for settled women to bring foreign husbands to live with them in the UK. Men were not subject to this particular restriction. The ECtHR found this law discriminated on the basis of gender and ruled that it was contrary to the Convention. In the case of *Berrehab*, where the Dutch government attempted to expel the Moroccan father of a Dutch child who resided with its Dutch mother, the ECtHR ruled that any such action would be a breach of an individual's right to family life.

More recently the ECtHR ruled in the controversial case of the radical cleric Abu Qatada (who had been detained under the UK Anti-terrorism, Crime and Security Act 2001) that the United Kingdom was not permitted to return him to Jordan to face terror charges.[8] In *Othman (Abu Qatada) v the United Kingdom* (8139/09), the Strasbourg Court considered whether or not the defendant would receive a fair hearing

(Art. 6) and also whether or not he would be ill-treated if he were returned to Jordan (Art. 3). Although the Court found that deportation would not constitute a violation of the ECHR, it decided that there was a real risk that evidence used in the trial had been obtained by torture and therefore his removal from the UK to Jordan would violate his human rights to a fair trial. Although the cleric was eventually returned to Jordan, as a result of this decision the British government was forced to engage in an active diplomatic effort with the Jordanian authorities to address the above problem and ensure that upon his return to Jordan the defendant would enjoy a trial that met the standards of evidence as set out by the ECHR.

CONCLUSION

The above analysis records that while labour has been regularly treated as a factor of production, the notion of European citizenship has been steadily developed since 1992. Migrants who were initially identified as inputs in the creation of an integrated European economy are now considered to be social actors with families and a growing set of rights and entitlements. The right to free movement that had been explicitly elaborated with particular emphasis on economic and financial conditions and was restricted to a proportion of the European population has proved to be a more expansive right.

Arguably the idea of European citizenship that was heralded at Maastricht has been the key catalyst for such change. We note that while the policies regarding the mutual recognition of diplomas were developed over 40 years and have since enjoyed some degree of success, the beneficiaries were primarily workers and selected professionals – a fraction of the European population. The conditions attached to the policies permitting free movement have been partially mitigated by the interpretation of Regulation 492/2011 (formerly 1612/68) that promises to protect the rights of family members under the banner of non-discrimination, as well as case law and the Citizenship Directive 2004/38.

The role of the Court has overwhelmingly pushed the rights of migrants by clarifying EU law in its rulings and through the expansive development of case law as witnessed in the *Lawrie-Blum* case regarding part-time workers and the *Hartmann* case regarding frontier workers. We also note the Court's insistence on equal treatment in matters of immigration (e.g. in *Singh*) which may further impact the right to family unity and education. The case of Morgan further presents a test of how people will draw upon their rights in a global market for education. The focus above all on citizenship that was first highlighted in *Martinez Sala* and developed through the Citizenship Directive and TFEU now promises greater protection for third country nationals, as evidenced in *Metock*.

The Charter on Fundamental Rights, by which states are bound when implementing EU law, as well as the Court's efforts to define states' obligations with respect to the European Convention on Human Rights, have elevated the place of migrants' rights in the evolution of the European Union. The anticipated accession by the European Union to the European Convention on Human Rights will signal an even greater advance in human rights protection as the ECHR will have a direct effect on states and thus on the European populations housed within them. To date the decisions of the Strasbourg Court have protected non-nationals against expulsion from EU member states. The accession of the European Union to the European Convention on Human Rights will no doubt raise further questions about the ways in which member states may return third country nationals and to what extent they will go to make this happen.

The development of European human rights law is one further example of the increasingly supranational nature of migration policy in both the European Union and in the Council of Europe system. This supranationalism is more complex within the European Union. The development of a substantive European citizenship and the further elaboration of rights to mobility for EU citizens, their family members and others, concepts of sovereignty and the role of the state as a defender of its internal and external borders need to be revisited.

NOTES

1. See C-35 and C-36/82, *Elestina Esselina Christian Morson v State of the Netherlands and Head of the Plaatselijke Politie within the meaning of the Vreemdelingenwet; Sweradjie Jhanjan v State of the Netherlands* (27 October 1982).
2. See C-292/89, *The Queen v Immigration Appeal Tribunal, ex parte Gustaff Desiderius Antonissen* (26 February 1991).
3. C-438/05, *International Transport Workers' Federation and Finnish Seamen's Union v Viking Line ABP and OÜ Viking Line Eesti* (11 December 2007).
4. C-341/05, *Laval un Partneri Ltd v Svenska Byggnadsarbetareförbundet, Svenska Byggnadsarbetareförbundets avd. 1, Byggettan, Svenska Elektrikerförbundet* (18 December 2007).
5. C-36/74, *B.N.O. Walrave, L.J.N. Koch v International Cycle Union Association, Koninklijke Nederlandsche Wielren Unie and Federación Española Ciclismo* (12 December 1974).
6. Full reference is C-127/08, *Blaise Baheten Metock and Others v Minister for Justice, Equality and Law Reform* (25 July 2008).

Migration and freedom

7. Article 8 provides for protection from state interference unless it is law and is necessary in a democratic society in the interests of national security, public safety or the economic well-being of the country, for the prevention of disorder or crime, for the protection of health or morals, or for the protection of the rights and freedoms of others.

8. *Othman (Abu Qatada) v the United Kingdom* (Application no. 8139/09), [2012] ECHR 56.

4. Spanish doctors in the United Kingdom

> There are a lot of people waiting for jobs and you lose contacts, you lose your contract, the hospital, everything. There are very few possibilities in Spain, so if you go away, you haven't any real opportunities to go back to Spain again.
> (Spanish male doctor, 5 November 2003)

INTRODUCTION

The social factors that affect the movement of professionals in the European Union and the reliance on medical recruitment schemes to fill gaps in the British National Health Service (NHS) are explored in this chapter. The field research was initially conducted during summer and autumn 2003 (and subsequently supplemented by means of further desk research). The aim was to gather information based on the experiences and motivations of Spanish professionals who were employed or who were seeking employment within the NHS. This research took place during a period of active recruitment by the Department of Health and access to informants was largely subject to NHS channels.

Focus groups and in-depth interviews were held with practising doctors from Spain who identified as general practitioners (GPs) and sometimes former hospital specialists (also known as 'specialty and associate specialist' (SAS) doctors) in Madrid, London and County Durham (n = 12); interviews were also conducted with NHS managers and recruiters (n = 10). Further interviews were held with doctors licensed in other EU states, including one doctor from Germany and another from Italy. Participants were self-selected and included candidates who responded to invitations to interview that were offered at Department of Health-sponsored recruitment fairs and information briefings in London and Madrid in June and July 2003; other participants were recommended to the research team. Semi-structured interviews were used to draw out motivations for relocation and to gather background information on the nature of the Anglo-Spanish agreements and the way in which they were being implemented by Department of Health recruiters. Three focus groups were held with Spanish doctors and included: (1) young GPs, (2) recent arrivals, and (3) former hospital specialists. The aim was to gather further knowledge regarding key issues, including job satisfaction, the availability of jobs for trained doctors and personal motives for relocation. The data from interviews and focus groups were sorted thematically and explanations for migration were then ranked based on the impact they had on primary activating factors. The doctors in this study were on average 28–35 years old and had been working for at least three years. Some of the specialists who were returning to primary care in the UK were in their late 30s and early 40s. There was a relatively even mix of men and women. The majority of interviewees came from urban centres, including cities and towns in Northern (Barcelona, Zaragosa), Central (Madrid) and Southern Spain (Murcia, the Balearic Islands). Most of the participants came to the UK alone, but some who settled in Northern England arrived with spouses and children.

REASONS FOR PROFESSIONAL MOBILITY

As discussed in Chapter 2, there are many reasons for personal and professional mobility. Data gathered from the International Passenger Survey (Office for National Statistics 2013) suggest that employment-related factors remain one of the principal reasons for migration between developed states and the UK (see Figure 4.1). Professionals and technical workers constitute the majority of new arrivals (International Labor Organization 2010). The conditions under which individuals review their employment and personal status and formulate arguments for relocation, however, are less clear.

Human capital, with its emphasis on the potency of wage differentials, goes part way towards explaining the movement of professionals from one state to another. Yet relocation is also encouraged and facilitated by political processes rather than by individual decisions – above all the need to counteract skills shortages (Salt 2005). The expansion of recent governmental policies (e.g. the creation of the UK's highly skilled migrant programme in 2002 that enables eligible migrants to enter the UK to seek and take up work for a 12-month period) supports Salt's claim. We further note the growing competition between source countries over the pool of talent and the need to manage migration flows. State and regional policies act in this setting as 'lubricators' that facilitate the movement of skilled professionals into the desired sector (Iredale 2001). One feature of the global recruitment market is the degree to which the

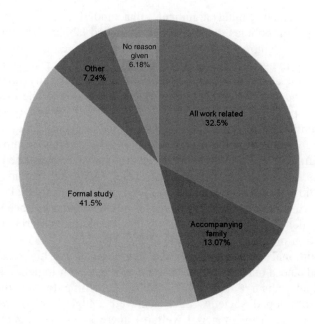

Figure 4.1 Reasons for long-term migration to the UK

highly skilled job seeker may choose among various options. According to Doudeijns and Dumont:

> Against a background of keener competition between the OECD countries, skilled migrants are in a position to compare the terms on offer in potential host countries. Those may relate to working conditions and remuneration but also to non-wage benefits (extra-professional environment, accommodation, provision for families). (Doudeijns and Dumont 2003, p. 18)

In practice, although many countries have attempted to match demand for employment with the supply of jobs, the rationale for such programmes has been overwhelmingly based on short-term priorities and several have produced mixed results. In their review of the UK's international recruitment of health professionals, for example, Young et al. (2010) concluded that intensive recruitment was not a sustainable solution to the UK's workforce shortages even though it was achieved without major disruption to the NHS service. Similar experiences have been noted elsewhere and OECD data record significant labour shortages for certain skilled professionals in spite of active governmental programmes and recent recruitment drives (OECD 2002).

The human capital arguments that underlay most state-sponsored immigration policies that are aimed at skilled labour reflect a bias which is partially contradicted by the statistical evidence on migration flows, above all the growing trend in return migration that may be motivated by non-financial factors such as acculturation and family concerns (Cervantes and Guellec 2002; Findlay 1995; King 2000). The insistence also on the primacy of economically defined pull factors (such as wage differentials) is at odds with evidence of the large-scale migrations which highlight the centrality of push factors. Salvatore's seminal study of migration from Southern to Northern Italy demonstrated that push factors, above all unemployment, carried far greater explanatory weight than did pull factors as the driving force in his analysis (Salvatore 1977). In the case of re-entrants, the logic of human capital has been challenged by evidence of return driven by non-economic criteria such as the attraction of home (pull factors) (King 2000).

Additional explanations for the migration of the highly skilled from one advanced state to another can be gleaned from Inglehart's studies on post-materialism (1971, 1977, 1990). According to this theory, when more developed societies have achieved a high level of personal and economic security (material welfare), there is an ideological shift away from satisfying basic human needs to satisfying personal and social needs such as freedom, self-expression and quality of life. In Inglehart's view, the spread of post-materialism would take place as previous generations died off. Post-materialist values would be disseminated from the centre, where there is the highest concentration of material welfare, to the periphery (Abrahamson, Ellis and Inglehart 1997; Inglehart 1971, 1977, 1990). The spread of post-materialism would therefore be driven by elites and be directly related to social status. Those most likely to hold post-materialist values are young, well educated and economically well-off. Juan Diez Nicolas introduces an amendment and points out that the issue of social status should be reviewed as social position, taking into consideration access to information and the proximity to decision centres (Diez Nicolas 1996). His research on changing attitudes in Spain confirms that those who enjoy greater social privilege and are closer to decision centres are more likely to exhibit post-materialist values (Diez Nicolas 1996, p. 154), and that this may be evidenced by an increased trend towards the pursuit of personal satisfaction.

THE MEDICAL PROFESSION IN BRITAIN AND SPAIN: PROSPECTS FOR RECRUITMENT

The arrival of European doctors in the 1990s signalled a new phase in the history of international medical recruitment in the United Kingdom. Previous waves of immigrants from India, Pakistan and the Caribbean found jobs as doctors, nurses and other hospital specialists from the 1950s onwards, and new migrants from different source countries have only recently replaced them. The shift away from Asian doctors to larger numbers of European doctors has its origins in a series of EC directives, as discussed in Chapter 3. In spite of the EU's commitment to promote free movement, the number of doctors moving to England from within the European Economic Area (EEA) remains relatively low at just over 6 per cent (British Medical Association 2012) (see Table 4.1). Given the relatively low numbers of doctors relocating from within the EEA, it is helpful to review the push and pull factors that influenced European doctors to take advantage of policies aimed at recruiting an additional 10,000 doctors into the NHS by 2005 (Department of Health 2002).

Status and Reputation

The British medical profession has a number of attractive features compared with other European systems, not least of which is its reputation within British society. The National Health Service is a comprehensive service that is largely cost-free at the point of use. Over the past decade NHS net expenditure has increased from £57.049 billion in 2002–3 to £105.254 billion in 2012–13. The NHS also features a diverse and cosmopolitan environment. In 2012 the NHS employed 146,075 doctors, 369,868 qualified nursing staff and 37,314 managers. A substantial number of these medical staff received their licences outside the UK.

Until recently the UK's medical sector was revered as a site of considerable professional autonomy in which doctors created and trans-mitted knowledge, selected new recruits and set standards. For this reason, Julia Evetts maintains that self-regulation through peer review has been the characteristic method of social control (Evetts 2002, p. 346). In relation to other European countries, the British medical profession enjoys considerably more autonomy, even though this privilege appears under threat from new corporatist practices and increasing levels of external evaluation imposed by the government. In spite of the intrusion of government, doctors remain a self-selected group, distinguished from

Table 4.1   UK medical workforce by country of qualification

	Total	UK		Rest of EEA		Outside EEA		Unknown
		Number	%	Number	%	Number	%	
All medical staff	150,061	101,317	69.50	8701	6.00	35,678	24.50	4372
All hospital grades*	57,028	34,921	62.70	4031	7.20	16,752	30.10	1326
Consultant	43,010	29,140	69.90	2906	6.90	10,239	24.20	725
SAS grades (inc. associate specialist, staff grade/ speciality doctor, other grades)	14,018	5781	43.10	1125	8.40	6513	48.50	601
All training grades	57,618	38,968	71.30	3044	5.60	12,621	23.10	2990
Registrar group	42,463	27,135	66.10	2578	6.30	11,339	27.60	1415
Financial year 2	7850	6088	81.60	331	4.40	1042	14.00	389
Financial year 1	7181	5651	94.20	128	2.10	224	3.70	1179
GPs (excl. retainers)**	35,415	27,428	77.60	1626	4.60	6305	17.80	56

Notes:

* Does not include Wales or Northern Ireland.
** Does not include Scotland or Northern Ireland.

other professions by their relatively low numbers. The density of doctors as measured against the general population of the UK (2.8 per 1000; OECD 2013) is lower than the OECD average (3.2 per 1000; OECD 2013) but is consistent with trends across the European Union (see Figure 4.2). The lower density of doctors relative to Spain (4.1 per 1000;

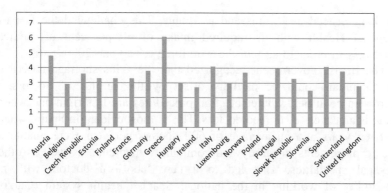

Figure 4.2   Density of doctors per 1000 in EEA (2011)

OECD 2013) gives rise to claims that medicine is an exclusive profession
– a factor that is attractive to some foreign nationals in search of status.

Job Availability

A significant pull factor is the availability of jobs in the UK. Although
the United Kingdom has been hovering around the EU average in terms
of health spending (and is currently just above the European average at
9.4 per cent GDP), the British health sector has become a booming
market for international recruits. There are several explanations for this,
the most important being the increase in population and the shortage of
skilled professionals to fill positions. Roger Chapman identifies the
following factors that have contributed to the skills shortage: the lack of
GPs in some poor regions and urban areas where doctors may be
required to work out-of-hours, attend to large lists of patients and where
there is little community support; on top of these factors, the difficulties
of achieving access to secondary care for patients. Staff shortages in
highly specialized areas (e.g. psychiatry, radiology, anaesthesiology) have
left visible holes in the NHS (Chapman 2000). An additional handicap is
the change in lifestyles of medical professionals at both ends of their
careers. There has been a marked trend towards flexible and part-time
work among more senior GPs as well as an increased shift towards
private practice. Younger doctors also appear even less committed to
careers in general practice within the NHS. A 1998 report by the British
Medical Association noted that only about 19 per cent of junior doctors
planned a career in general practice (Chapman 2000). The drop in
numbers has led to a shortage of up to 800 doctors in general practice,
while approximately 7500 GPs have chosen alternative medical paths,

working instead as locums and assistants. This challenged the Department of Health with its required intake of 50 per cent of medical graduates in order to sustain the workforce (Chapman 2000, p. 6).

The British government recognized that the skills shortage described by Chapman could be partially offset by the surplus of doctors in European countries, where selection procedures are less rigid and where there is an excess of trained doctors. This is most evident in Spain, where just ten years ago an average of 600 doctors per year were unable to secure placements in family and community medicine, as well as other medical specialties. This led to a new 'pool' of doctors with no possibility of working in the national Spanish health system (Garzon 2014).

In addition to the surplus of trained graduates, there are a number of structural impediments that have prevented Spanish doctors from obtaining secure employment. According to Lissa Perteghella, an officer in charge of medical recruitment in the British Embassy in Madrid, many health services in Spain use contractual labour where doctors work for three months at a time so that the employers can avoid paying social security (interview with L.P., 17 June 2003). The use of a recruitment system where education and experience are converted into points that determine entry and promotion within the medical sector has also been cited as a further barrier to the mobility of doctors within Spain's internal market (interview with L.P., 17 June 2003).

Public Investment and Spending

Recent trends in public spending also put the British medical system in an advantageous position, relative to its European neighbours. Funding improved significantly under New Labour, with more than £5 billion invested since 2001 (Department of Health 2003b), though funding then fell remarkably with the arrival of the Conservative government in 2010. During the 2000s the increase in staff, pay and construction of new hospitals was reflected in a higher degree of satisfaction shown by the British public when compared with Europeans in Germany, Ireland, Spain, Italy, Portugal and Greece (OECD 2013). The picture in Britain therefore contrasted with patterns of retrenchment in Spain, where medical unions challenged new policies of regionalization and restructuring, and in Germany, where the introduction of the Cost Containment Act in 1999 preceded a programme of dramatic structural reforms (Lipp 1999).

RESEARCH CONTEXT

During the millennial decade, the UK Department of Health established a number of routes to attract European doctors to the NHS, including direct recruitment into consultant and GP positions as well as entry into supervised positions, allowing the doctors to become better acquainted with the British system (see Department of Health 2003a). The three main mechanisms used by the Department of Health were a global recruitment campaign for individual applications, targeted recruitment campaigns aimed at specific countries, and special arrangements. These are briefly described below.

The Global Recruitment Campaign was launched in September 2001 and aimed to attract doctors interested in working as GPs or consultants. It targeted shortage specialties and specialties where significant expansion was planned to meet NHS targets. It was managed by TMP Worldwide that had produced a database of potential recruits. TMP Worldwide worked with the International Recruitment Team in the Department of Health, advertising in the international medical and national press and organizing seminars in specific countries.

Specific Targeted Recruitment is an ongoing policy conducted by means of a government-to-government agreement or agreement with appropriate professional bodies in relevant countries. The Department of Health initiated two important campaigns – one with Germany, conducted through the German employment service, and another in Spain, where the Spanish Ministry of Health and the British Embassy in Madrid coordinated the recruitment drive. The Spanish campaign had its origins in the North West of England, where the local international recruitment team initiated the pilot programme for Spanish doctors.

Special arrangements include the NHS International Fellowship Scheme, launched in January 2002 with the intent of recruiting experienced consultants from outside the UK to two-year positions in the NHS. Fellowship posts are selected from funded vacancies or consultancies created through expansion plans. The employing Trust pays the salary and ongoing costs of the fellow, and the Department of Health pays from central funds for the cost of the national recruitment process, relocation expenses, accommodation and pension that is given at the end of the fellowship.

The Managed Placement Scheme, another ongoing policy, aims to attract doctors at the consultant level who are interested in working in the NHS but would like to experience living and working in England before applying for a substantive post.

Some Trusts prefer to work with commercial agencies to attract consultants rather than to use the above-mentioned schemes. In June 2002, when the study first began, some ten recruitment agencies signed up. These ad hoc recruitment campaigns have proved particularly effective in regions that have a specific draw for certain groups of doctors. In South East London, for example, the proximity of the Eurostar and Channel Tunnel enabled the Trust to attract and retain French GPs (A.M.D., interview with the author, 19 September 2003).

INVITATION TO COUNTY DURHAM

The doctors interviewed in this study had already arrived in the North East of England, in County Durham, a region underserved by NHS staff and exhibiting many of the problems associated with the former Northern mining towns. Today the population of County Durham is 505,000 (Office for National Statistics 2013), with the largest settlements being in Darlington (100,000), Stockton on Tees, which spills over into the neighbouring county of North Yorkshire (190,000), Chester-le-Street (53,000), Derwentside (87,000), Durham (94,000), Easington (95,000), Sedgefield (88,000), Teesdale (25,000) and Wear Valley (63,000) (Office for National Statistics 2013). At the time of the interview there were six Primary Care Trusts (PCTs) in Durham, Chester-le-Street, Derwentside, Darlington, Sedgefield and Easington.

These Spanish and other European doctors came to this area because of the initiative of one long-standing doctor who had trained in Spain but settled in the UK in 1989. Dr José Ramon Garcia Miralles, now a GP at Tyson and Partners in Chester-le-Street, Co. Durham, was born into a medical family and studied at the University of Zaragosa. His father, sisters and brothers-in-law were all doctors. He had spent every summer holiday throughout his medical training as a visitor in the UK and described his decision to move to the UK as a natural progression. He told how his Spanish university did not make it easy for him to study in the UK, so he sent hundreds of letters to hospitals and as a result worked in Birmingham, Nottingham, Dublin and Sheffield over a six-year period. He stated that whereas in Spain doctors were revered, he did not receive any special treatment in the UK, making him feel welcome: 'a normal bloke – a member of a team' (interview with Dr. José Miralles, 13 October 2003).

In 2000 the Strategic Health Authority of Co. Durham and Teesside conceived the idea of recruiting from abroad. To further the scheme Dr. Miralles was called upon to design a proposal to present to the UK

Department of Health. He next moved into the role of medical advisor for the Department of Health on international recruitment and offered to facilitate peer support meetings for newly arrived doctors. While recruitment was initially driven by the Department of Health, he noted that this caused a bottleneck. The recruitment effort was later franchised out within the regional Workforce Development Confederation. This permitted Miralles and colleagues to establish direct links with medical institutions in Spain, including Aragon and Catalonia, the sites for subsequent recruitment drives. From 2001 Co. Durham began to receive recruits from Spain, who committed to stay for between one and three years. Arrivals were housed in university or hospital accommodation for a few weeks before transferring to rental properties.

RELOCATING FROM SPAIN TO NORTHERN ENGLAND

Participants gave multiple answers to the question: what made you consider moving to the United Kingdom? A mix of answers citing push and pull factors resulted, although push factors carried greater weight and focused on occupational and economic barriers to advancement in Spain. Participants tended to stress a number of the following four reasons for their relocation: (1) structural factors, (2) professional development, (3) personal development, and (4) financial considerations.

Structural factors were discussed in the context of the barriers to employment in the Spanish and other European medical systems, although they were often mentioned in connection with UK-specific pull factors, including the opportunity to work in English and experience living abroad. The participants interviewed cited lack of professional opportunities, difficult working conditions and the instability of their jobs as among the most important reasons behind their decision to relocate. The structural obstacles varied considerably: for the Spanish consultants and GPs, the lack of job security (driven by the practice of three-month contracts), a general dislike of private practice, and the fact that young, recently trained doctors are frequently forced to choose between working out-of-hours for extended periods or as locums, added to personal and professional frustration; for the German consultant, the issue was more one of age and his current status in a system that was undergoing adjustment and where fewer opportunities were available for middle- and senior-level specialists; for the Italian, it was the nature of work within general practice that presented structural problems.

The complaints made by the Spanish doctors and specialists were remarkably consistent and focused on the oversupply of well-trained doctors. A young Spanish doctor from Barcelona, who attended a job fair in the United Kingdom, claimed that the Spanish system was not working because there were simply too many doctors and that after years of looking for permanent work she had been forced to look outside of Spain. She described her situation as 'normal' and argued that the only way ahead was to leave:

> They don't give you the opportunity [of work elsewhere], they oblige you. Every country wants Spanish doctors except for Spain. It's terrible. And they prepare good doctors. After that they tell you there's no work, go abroad. The only doctors working in Spain are old, and they haven't any interest in doing anything. The only thing they want is retirement. (Female doctor, Pelton, Co. Durham, 5 November 2003)

Her colleagues noted that for those who chose to remain in Spain, the only option was to accept whatever was offered. One recent arrival to England claimed that since there were so many doctors, even locum posts were in demand and one needed to accept whatever was offered simply to remain on the books (which is what she had done before her move). 'If you don't work out-of-hours, you have to work as a locum with a mobile and be on call 24 hours. You have to say yes because if you say no, they won't call you anymore' (Spanish female doctor, 5 November2003). The situation was just as precarious for the Spanish consultants. A surgeon specializing in facial reconstruction spoke about the attrition rate of highly trained specialists forced to leave the public sector for private practice. Out of his graduating class of 50 specialists, only eight were working in a public hospital.

The demanding nature of shift and contract work was not, however, limited to the Spanish participants. Similar experiences were recorded by doctors from other countries. One young Italian doctor claimed to have worked seven days and four nights a week over three years. Shifts over 84 hours were poorly remunerated; he took home less than 1500 Euro per month. The nature of payment was also precarious, and he claimed not to have been paid at one point for a period of ten months. Although he sued his employer, he claimed it would take 15 years before he saw any money paid back to him (Italian doctor, 5 November 2003).

Alternative medical routes were also limited by the shortage of places and the degree of competition among qualified doctors. A senior German neurologist added that the main problem for him was the hierarchical way the German medical system was structured, where a consultant was treated more like a department chair. In spite of the supply of highly trained doctors there were few posts available to experienced specialists. One GP questioned the degree to which competition for jobs outside of general practice could be described as fair and spoke extensively about the prevalence of nepotism in his medical system. '[Working in a] hospital is not an option because you have to be the son or the relative of a doctor who already works there' (Italian doctor, 5 November 2003).

Professional development was another major factor motivating doctors to seek employment within the NHS. Opportunities for practice and skills development, in contrast to the professional barriers mentioned above, were frequently listed as strong pull factors. Several GPs noted that the limited job market back home made continuity of care particularly difficult, even though the principle of following up with patients was considered to be a fundamental tenet of primary care. Other professional traditions, such as the fact that consultants did not correspond with patients, were seen as disadvantaging both doctors and their patients. The fact that in Britain doctors maintain a relationship with their patients was an important draw for them. One Spanish doctor described how she reached her decision to relocate, based on professional considerations.

> I was working as an out-of-hours doctor and mainly it was holidays and weekends and one evening every two or three days. So it was quite hard being out of home and then I found it very difficult to have any continuity, having follow-ups with the patient which I think is one of the main rules of primary care. So I thought being an emergency doctor was very interesting but it would not let me learn much more from the patients because I would never know what was the treatment, the diagnosis when they were at hospital so I thought I would rather go to any country where I could have this follow-up. (Spanish female doctor, 5 November 2003)

Training and development were also identified as positive reasons for commitment to the NHS. The mere act of moving would provide some with additional professional development, as remarked by a young GP: 'If you change your country and other ways of working, you can improve your skills' (young female doctor, Pelton, Co. Durham, 5 November 2003). One gastroenterologist from Barcelona spoke about his desire to improve something within his specialty. This prompted him to attend a recruitment fair. The Spanish participants in particular noted that there are many opportunities for training in the UK and that it is easy to find information regarding professional development. By contrast several commented on the barriers that prevented them from enjoying further training in Spain. These barriers included bureaucratic procedures with lengthy application forms and the need to send passports and driving licences to various agencies. Such hurdles deterred doctors from seeking opportunities for professional development in Spain (in contrast to the UK, where several participants were enjoying regular access to further training). Cultural differences with regard to training and personal development were further highlighted by an Italian GP, who noted that not only does British society appreciate continued professional development but so do medical peers and colleagues. In Italy, by contrast, a doctor is often criticized for this by colleagues who claim that they have been shown up.

In spite of the differences described above, the Spanish participants commented that the British and Spanish systems were quite similar and this eased their transition in the United Kingdom. In terms of being a GP, the management of patients and basic professional protocols are very similar. Several added that the Spanish system is based on the UK public system and most doctors were familiar with British medical journals because they are used in medical schools. One doctor from Italy spoke of the additional benefits of working in the United Kingdom and the lure of serving in a 'non-Latin' system, one that was GP centric:

> I always wanted to work in a place where medicine could be practised based on evidence and where our profession is not strictly ruled by the market and by patients' expectations. In Italy, there are too many doctors and some of them have to strictly follow the market route. I used to say that they have to wash the patients' cars and scratch their backs. In Italy, they constantly try to double-cross you. So you are always thinking, *where's the catch?* In England, there's no catch. Trust is a thing that is given to everybody, unless they prove they are not worthy of it. (Italian male doctor, 5 November 2003)

Attitudinal differences between patients and doctors and even within the medical community were frequently mentioned by the participants who felt more welcome in the United Kingdom than in their home environment. Improved professional status, such as being taken seriously as a doctor, was reflected in improved personal status. The Italian doctor noted, 'I wanted some respect from the country I worked for, and I found this in England. England is a place that grants me trust' (Italian male doctor, 5 November 2003). The fact that British patients were described as polite and were less likely to challenge the doctor's authority directly or switch GPs when their requests for unnecessary prescriptions were turned down (as they frequently did back home) contributed to the doctors' sense of being respected within their new communities, which they appreciated. Other doctors recognized that although GPs enjoyed greater respect, they also had additional responsibilities. The potential for litigation and claims brought against doctors was far greater in the UK than in their home countries, and this contributed to additional worries for some GPs.

For others the personal gains were described in terms of new experiences. One psychiatrist, who arrived in Britain before the recruitment programmes were created, spoke about how he was led by his desire for adventure, flexible work and personal autonomy over his career: 'I just came with the idea of completing a specialty, coming and going back [and forth to Spain] and having the capacity to decide which is important for me to preserve. Spain did not offer that' (Spanish psychiatrist, 5 November 2003). His views were in part shared by a new arrival who spoke of his long-standing desire to have an experience abroad that was satisfied in part by his relocation to the North of England: 'Basically my first motivation was to go abroad because I think this is a very good experience for me both personal and professional' (Spanish male doctor, 5 November 2003). Another Spanish doctor commented that it was about 'personal improvement' (young male doctor, Pelton, Co. Durham, 5 November 2003). His colleague, who practised complementary medicine, added that, by moving, he thought he could improve his family's 'general condition', which was not simply limited to professional opportunities. The combination of better working conditions, a change of lifestyle and a country where he could improve his English made the UK a 'good opportunity' (Spanish father, Pelton, Co. Durham, 5 November 2003). The notion that personal motivations could encompass several, non-material factors was reiterated by another contented colleague, who had two school-age children and who, together with her self-employed husband, was able to settle quickly into English life.

Being able to work in the English language was regularly cited by interviewees as an important factor that contributed to their decision to relocate and to their choice of country. Some participants had explored opportunities in Scandinavia, France and Portugal but preferred Britain. Although it had some obvious professional benefits (e.g. the fact that much medical research is published in English), the desire to work in an English-speaking country was often expressed in purely personal terms. One female doctor commented that she and her colleagues had been studying English for years 'so I think it is more like an exam coming here and being able to manage on your own without any help from teachers or anybody else. It is more about personal satisfaction' (young female doctor, Pelton, Co. Durham, 5 November 2003). Her colleague, who had a long-standing interest in English culture, Celtic mythology and 1970s English rock music, spoke about the lure of the English language and how it reflected a tradition of honesty, which he valued. 'With English, you usually say what you mean and that reflects English personality.' In contrast, he noted that:

Italian, Spanish and French are quite complicated languages and are very delicate. They are just like wood. You can carve wood but you have to be very careful because one wrong hit can spoil the whole block, and you have to start from scratch. English is like metal. You can mould it. You can do everything with it. It is not as complex as Italian but has a different hue that Italian lacks but it is pretty straightforward on the other side. (Italian doctor, 5 November 2003)

Financial considerations, although not the most important of factors, were nonetheless mentioned by participants as influencing their decision to relocate to England. Most of the participants interviewed, with the exception of a German specialist, earned between 1500 and 2000 Euro per month in their home countries. One Spanish surgeon mentioned that he only earned 2000 Euro a month, and that was hardly sufficient for his family. For those with families the issue of pay came up more often. Others noted that even though they could earn more than £50,000 working as GPs and were living in an inexpensive part of England (County Durham), the cost of living was still exceptionally high.

TO STAY OR TO RETURN?

Most participants arriving since 2001 were undecided about the length of time they intended to spend in the UK. Several GPs commented that although they never felt as if they made a commitment to emigrate, they also had no fixed plans regarding return. One female doctor suggested that the geographical proximity of her native country to the UK put her in the position of not having to make hard decisions regarding permanent settlement and loosening her ties to her homeland. She added that 'some think it is brave to leave things behind, friends and family, but you can go back to visit every few months or they can come to visit' (young Spanish female doctor, 5 November 2003).

A number of Spanish doctors living in North East England took steps to become more established by buying flats and houses, but these were not necessarily seen as long-term measures. With the exception of consultants with families, who stated that they were planning on settling permanently in the United Kingdom, most participants were open to the idea of return.

When questioned about their views regarding the prospect of return, however, a number of participants commented that by taking up a post in the United Kingdom, Spain would be 'finished'. One young doctor currently working in Galicia but who was considering relocating to the

United Kingdom claimed that by 'moving to Britain you are closing your doors to Spain'.

In returning to their home countries, the vast majority believed that they would face similar conditions to what they had left behind and, in this sense, it would signal a backwards step. One young doctor from Spain described the lack of options there and how working in the UK had raised his professional and personal expectations:

> If I go back, job conditions will be the same, maybe worse because I spent time here and therefore lost contacts. So I have the impression that it won't be easy for me to go back to Spain, and I would not be happy to go back and do what I did before. And it would be even harder, having spent time here. I don't think things are going to change. (Young Spanish male doctor, 5 November 2003)

Instead, he held out the possibility of relocating to a third country such as the United States or Australia.

Others found little reason to go back and take up jobs in the Spanish system. For the doctor who planned on working in the growing field of complementary medicine, the most sensible option for him was in private practice. He admitted that he had 'no expectation to go back to Spain to work for the public sector, not because it is a difficult issue but because I wouldn't enjoy that in Spain' (newly arrived doctor, Pelton, Co. Durham, 5 November 2003).

PERCEPTIONS FROM HOME

The way in which their peers back in their home country reacted to the doctors' decisions to relocate also affected their views regarding the possibility of returning and reintegrating back home. For some the decision to relocate to the UK had been greeted by their colleagues with jealousy, which was not always healthy:

> Some colleagues think I am an idiot and a traitor, but there is another group who want to know how I did it because I can work as a doctor, be paid as a doctor and have respect. And there are five of these to one of the other. (Italian doctor, 5 November 2003)

The above doctor reported that by relocating he had made himself an outsider. Others commented that they were greeted more as pioneers who were considered brave for trying to establish a new life abroad.

COMPARATIVE ADVANTAGE

For highly skilled professionals, there are several factors that must be considered in addition to those suggested by the human capital theory – for example, comparative advantage. While the need for skilled medical staff has created global competition and an international recruitment market for doctors and nurses, Doudeijns and Dumont (2003) note that the individual also has a degree of bargaining power and may choose between competitors. In addition to the financial gains made by some doctors, most of those interviewed noted that by moving to the United Kingdom they were able to enjoy greater job security as well as professional and social status than in their home countries. This contributed to their own personal satisfaction.

AUTONOMY AND ADVENTURE

The statements offered by participants regarding their desire for adventure and search for personal fulfilment affirm Diez Nicolas' conclusions regarding the value shift towards the pursuit of personal satisfaction among well-educated Spanish elites (Diez Nicolas 1996). All of the participants mentioned their desire to work in an English-speaking system and experience living in the United Kingdom or another country in positive terms. Although this was not the most significant factor pushing them to seek employment in the NHS, it was nonetheless a contributory factor. The issue of autonomy, however, should not be understood only in individualistic terms. Indeed there are several important social gains that also relate to the doctors' quest for greater autonomy and the belief that this could be achieved in the more decentralized British system.

ADDRESSING THE SOCIAL CONTEXT

The most encouraging campaigns to recruit doctors have developed the combined package approach, involving both government and private agencies that have been particularly successful at attracting foreign nurses (Buchan 2002). Incentive-based approaches involving national and foreign ministries, medical professional bodies and local recruiters as well as specialized agencies have managed to attract and retain doctors in key communities such as South East London and North East England. The relocation of foreign doctors to these parts has taken place against a backdrop of considerable administration and planning, including tailor-made induction programmes and contracted accommodation services and weekly support group meetings. This fact supports Salt, Findlay and Appleyard's finding that micro-level considerations are a central feature of successful professional migrations and a key to retention (1989).

THE PERSISTENCE OF STRUCTURAL BARRIERS

Although doctors were able to improve upon their financial position and were able to acquire new skills by relocating to the United Kingdom, for almost all of the participants this was not a free choice that they had embraced willingly. Most of the participants saw the possibility of working in the United Kingdom less as an opportunity and more as a necessity, if they wished to continue in their field of expertise. Such decisions, however, had important implications for those doctors who contemplated the prospect of return.

CONCLUSION

This chapter exposes a number of obstacles to the promise of free movement within the European Union. While the doctors interviewed are among the most mobile and their mobility is in no short measure due to long-standing efforts to promote the free movement of doctors across the European Union by means of special directives and bilateral agreements, other factors may complicate this goal. We note in particular the availability of work, problems related to age, and the social context of both sending and receiving states. As described above, both the situation in Spain and the employment climate in the UK had a significant impact on participants' levels of satisfaction, both professional and personal. Few participants could actively envisage returning to their home country, given the state of the Spanish medical system.

This chapter suggests in addition that human capital explanations for professional migration need to be revised to take into consideration important push factors such as underemployment and job scarcity. Although the doctors in this study chose willingly to relocate to the United Kingdom and expressed some of their reasons for moving in terms of their individual preference to work abroad and in an English-speaking environment, the overwhelming factors influencing their decision to leave Spain were structural. In the words of one young doctor, the system obliged her to seek work abroad. The pull factors of personal satisfaction and self-fulfilment that are suggestive of post-materialism may be considered contributory factors behind the doctors' decisions to migrate, but they are nonetheless of secondary importance in this study.

Finally, this chapter shows the significance of occupational type and job specialization as factors influencing the prospect of free movement. The situation of the Spanish doctors stands in marked contrast to the young Spanish nurses who are able to come to the United Kingdom on a time-limited contract, earn credit towards their training and return to Spain at a higher rank. Such leap-frogging is possible in highly graduated types of employment – not in general medical practice. Ironically for the Spanish GPs, whose search for autonomy was repeatedly stressed in interview, the relatively flat structure of their profession, in contrast to the hierarchical nature of the nursing sector, appears to be a deterrent to their readmission into the Spanish medical sector.

5.   European language teachers in Italy

Now in this whole process, I do not officially appear. My name is not on the exam
commission, and someone else signs the register, the 'verbale'. We used to sign
the verbali, but not anymore, since signing it would be support in court to our
claim for teacher status. But we're not; we're watermelon pickers.

(Language teacher, Central Italy, 27 June 2007)

INTRODUCTION

The right to freedom of movement is one of the cornerstones of the
European Union and is associated with the prohibition against discrimination on the basis of nationality (TFEU Art. 18). For over 50 years these
provisions have been central to the ambition of creating a European
union of peoples and have been reaffirmed in the Treaty on the
Functioning of the European Union in the context of EU citizenship and
the rights of workers as discussed in Chapter 3. Together these provisions
set out the legal basis for European nationals to travel and settle in other
European states.

While the scope of EU anti-discrimination provisions has grown over
recent years to include matters of race, age and sex (European Union
Agency for Fundamental Rights 2010), nationality remains a contentious
issue within the workplace. The Court of Justice of the European Union
(CJEU) has on numerous occasions concluded that EU nationals have not
been treated fairly when they have competed for jobs outside their home
states, even after many years of residence. Recent judgments issued by
the Court illustrate that this is not simply a problem for recent members
but also for some of the founding member states,[1] a fact also acknowledged by other EU institutions (European Commission 2007). This
chapter examines a well-documented case of nationality-based discrimination in Italy in order to explore the challenges of exercising one's rights
to free movement and to consider the long-term effects such discrimination has on the victims.

The context is the situation of 'lettori', the non-Italian foreign
language teachers in Italian universities, who claimed they had been
victims of nationality-based discrimination and who have been vindicated

by the findings of the CJEU that has issued multiple rulings against Italian state institutions.[2] In spite of these rulings, however, the occupational, social and economic status of the lettori has deteriorated over the past two decades, prompting further questions regarding the degree to which nationality-based discrimination can be mitigated through legal channels. This chapter explores the ways in which discrimination has been expressed and institutionalized, to the detriment of the lettori, most of whom are EU nationals. It begins by reviewing the history of the lettori struggle before national courts and the CJEU and subsequently examines the impact of the non-enforcement of European rules regarding non-discrimination. It charts the social distance created between the lettori and their Italian colleagues in the workplace.

The empirical basis for this chapter is a series of semi-structured interviews and focus groups with lettori conducted over a two-year period from 2005–7 with additional telephone interviews in 2009, 2010, 2011 and 2013. The sample (n = 22) included British (English and Scottish), Irish, French, German, Spanish and non-EU nationals. Interviews were conducted in Brussels (2005), Edinburgh (2006), Verona (2006) and Central Italy (2007). In order to locate participants the author relied on contacts established from interviews conducted in 1995 and 1996 (see Blitz 1999) and on contacts provided by the Association of Foreign Lecturers in Italy. Respondents were asked about their current employment status and the legal issues it posed; about difficulties they had encountered in securing alternative employment; in providing for their children's education; in dealing with government and public bodies; and about how change in their occupational status affected them in terms of their home life, work, social life and position in the community.

HISTORICAL CONTEXT

The Creation of the Lettori

On 11 July 1980, as part of an attempt to reform the Italian university system, a number of professional categories were created by means of a new education Act and presidential decree (DPR 382).[3] One of these categories was the class of lettori. Article 28 of DPR 382 made it possible for foreign nationals to be admitted to the university system as temporary teaching staff with annual contracts renewable for a maximum of six years. These nationals were hired to carry out specialized duties, including teaching their mother-tongue language. The 1980 law also distinguished between non-Italian lettori (listed under the heading of 'professori a contratto' and governed by private law) and Italian academics, who were treated as public servants. The lettori had no rights to benefits, social security, national health insurance or pensions and were considered to be 'autonomous workers'. The law also established maximum salaries for lettori equivalent to those of associate professors 'alla prima chiamata', amounting at the time to 1,000,200 Lire, or about 517 Euro a month. Most lettori taught approximately eight hours per week and conducted exams. For this reason their work was implicitly recognized as a form of instruction.

Unlike Italian academics the lettori did not need to be successful in a competitive entrance examination (concorso) to work in the university system, though they did need to pass annual competitive selections. Partly for this reason, by their very presence they challenged the hierarchical structures within the university sector. As a consequence, university finances became increasingly stretched in the 1980s, and disagreements between the lettori and university professoriate and/or administrations surfaced, coming to a head in 1993 when large numbers of lettori went on strike, following attempts to cut their salaries and reduce their duties by ousting them from examination commissions.

By February 1993 the European Parliament had been alerted to a string of complaints filed by David Petrie, President of the newly formed Committee for the Defence of Foreign Lecturers, who argued that Italian universities were discriminating against non-Italian teachers and were undermining the provisions of freedom of movement as stipulated by the then Article 48 of the EEC Treaty (now Article 45 TFEU). Even though in several instances local groups of lettori had successfully gone before local employment tribunals to obtain redress for wrongful dismissals, the processes of appeal in Italy ensured that universities could fight these decisions and prolong disputes (to the detriment of the lettori). Petrie decided for this reason to approach European institutions. This was the start of a major battle between the Italian state and the European institutions, notably the European Parliament, Commission and Court of Justice. At its heart was a dispute over the more favourable treatment and protection given to those on permanent contracts (contratti a tempo indeterminato). Since the terms of employment of lettori were governed by private law, they were not immediately eligible for such contracts, in contrast to Italian nationals working within the university system.

The bid to secure 'tempo indeterminato' was initially fought through national courts, as lettori appealed against sackings and reductions in salary. On 29 April 1987 the lettori won the first round when a local employment tribunal in Verona declared that the plaintiffs should be treated as regular employees and that health insurance and pension contributions had to be paid on their behalf by the University. A year later, on 13 August 1988, the Pretura di Verona issued an injunction ordering the University to guarantee the employment status of the plaintiffs for the year 1988/89. The same tribunal ruled on 26 October 1991 that the contractual relationship between the lettori and the University was to be considered as indeterminate in terms of time and could not therefore be limited by annual contracts, a ruling later upheld by the Corte di Cassazione. However, in spite of these rulings, the struggle over tempo indeterminato did not result in a comprehensive settlement, and so the ECJ was asked to step in.

In the case of *Pillar Allué and Carmel Coonan* (C-33/88), known as *Allué I*, the ECJ ruled that tempo indeterminato should apply. The Court's ruling noted that there was a conflict between EC law and Italian law, since only non-Italians seemed to be affected by time-limited contracts.[4] Four years later, on 2 August 1993, the ECJ ruled that it was illegal to issue time-limited contracts to non-Italian nationals, except under certain circumstances.

The non-enforcement of the *Allué* rulings eventually brought the Italian state into conflict with the European Commission, which claimed that since the rulings had yet to be introduced into domestic law, infringement procedures remained in place. Lettori in Verona were denied during this period the right to apply for temporary teaching positions on the grounds that they had never passed the 'concorsi'. They again were forced to take legal proceedings against the University. Lettori in Naples were 'sacked' on 15 July every year, spending five, six or seven months without work before being rehired.[5] In March 1995 lettori in Bologna argued that they were still being discriminated against[6] in spite of the ECJ's rulings in the *Allué* cases.[7]

Change in Status and Fragmentation of Lettori

A particularly important development took place on 21 April 1995, when a decree was passed and subsequently converted into law (21 June 1995) officially abrogating Article 28 of DPR 382. The decree (DPR 236) abolished the position of lettore, replacing it with a category consisting of employees who were to be called 'collaboratori ed esperti linguistici' (CELs, or linguistic experts). CELs were to be employed on permanent contracts but new conditions were introduced with respect to incoming foreigners, and the decree merely offered the ex-lettori precedence in selection procedures for the new post. The net result of this decree was that foreign teachers throughout Italy were forced to work longer hours for less pay and lower status. An estimated 223 lettori in the Universities of Bologna, Naples Federico II, Naples L'Orientale, Salerno and Verona declined to apply for the new posts of CEL and were fired (David Petrie, letter to Professor Enrico Decleva, 18 February 2010).

The changes in the law produced essentially three groups: (1) lettori who had been employed under DPR 382 but refused the new CEL contracts; (2) ex-lettori who had been employed under DPR 382 but then opted for contracts as CELs under the 1995 legislation; and (3) new CELs who had never been employed under anything but the 1995 legislation. One might include an additional category of the very few non-Italians who benefited from changes in the concorsi system that was now open to foreigners. The treatment of the former lettori therefore differed widely across Italy, depending on the nature of the contracts signed between them and individual universities. Some universities created new job descriptions for the lettori without their agreement, while the ex-lettori were no longer permitted to carry out teaching duties.

Further judgments by both Italian and European Courts challenged the legality of Law 236 and its implementation. On 14 January 1999 the Venice Regional Tribunal, following principles laid down by decision ECJ C-90/96, ruled that three British teachers were illegally prevented from having their applications considered for a teaching post. The Court ruled on 26 June 2001 in *European Commission v Italy* (C-212/99) that the Italian state had failed to uphold its Treaty provisions and that the selection process for linguistic collaborators failed to safeguard the acquired rights of the lettori.

The lettori did eventually win the right to the minimum salary of tenured researchers from the first day of their employment, following the introduction of Law 63 of 5 March 2004 that was upheld by the European Court in Luxembourg (C-119/04). The question of equal treatment was not addressed until the Court issued another decision in the case of a Belgian citizen, *Nancy Delay v Università degli studi di Firenze and Others* (C-276/07), where the Court ruled that:

> if national workers are entitled, under domestic legislation, to reinstatement from the point of view of increases in salary, seniority and the payment by the employer of social security contributions, from the date of their original recruitment, former foreign-language assistants who have become linguistic associates must also be entitled to similar reinstatement with effect from the date of their original recruitment.

The mechanism by which the lettori were reclassified was not, however, limited to their status under Italian law. For more than a decade, university management and administrators introduced policies and procedures designed to further segregate the foreign language teachers from the remainder of the teaching staff and discourage them from working in these public institutions. These procedures and their effects are discussed below.

EXCLUSION AND INVISIBILITY

Interviewees described the incremental effects of their exclusion, which was punctuated by two distinct phases; in the 1980s they were removed from examination commissions, and then, following the introduction of Law 236 in 1995, their duties were reduced and many were formally reclassified.

> In June, everything exploded. I had a job which from every point of view interested me and from one day to the next, there was a meeting. I was told you will no longer offer courses on civilization but a beginner's language course. Therefore they had created a course for which I was not even competent to teach and knew nothing about. From that point on, I was pushed aside. (French woman, Verona, 21 June 2006)

Respondents explained that lettori had in the past enjoyed the status of teaching staff and been official members of exam commissions, recognized as such by means of the official registers students were required to sign before handing in their written exams. The change in their job titles that came with the new law, however, brought with it a marked deterioration in status. As one language teacher noted, the title of 'collaboratore' was also used for cleaning ladies (woman in Central Italy, email to the author, 21 June 2010). Some participants explained that their hours also changed: 'I have always worked 700 hours [per year]. You are now telling me I'm not a teacher and have to do this job in 450 hours. It's not possible' (British woman, Central Italy, focus group, 12 October 2007).

Several interviewees noted that following their removal from exam commissions, they were still responsible for designing, administering and marking written exams as well as examining students orally. One woman explained that there was no actual change in examination procedures, but the lettori were formally removed from all official documents that might attest to their role in any of the examination processes (teacher of English, Central Italy, email to the author, 19 June 2010).

> The new law listed our duties much more vaguely, established that we were only 'part-time workers' and no longer 'full-time', allowed us to work in other places and listed us among the *'tecnici amministrativi'* [which] equals office

personnel. By not specifying all our duties, it created an ambiguous situation in which it could be considered that our duties had changed, which they hadn't. (Language teacher, Central Italy, 27 June 2007)

Lettori were told that they no longer gave lessons within the classroom but simply held 'esercitazioni' (practice sessions). A teacher in Central Italy commented that 'one rettore [university rector] told a lettore that he could oversee language drills but not explain grammar'. She also noted that in some universities the 'docenti' took special care to emphasize that the exams done by the lettori were 'not real exams and [could not] be called exams' (language teacher, Central Italy, 27 June 2007).

Further efforts to set apart the work of the lettori from that of the professoriate were contained in a 'regolamento' (regulation) issued by the University of Viterbo that stipulated not only that the marks awarded by a lettore were not binding but also that any professor from anywhere in the university could override or ignore the mark given by a lettore. A seasoned teacher argued that the regulation was tantamount to saying that the final mark was at the discretion of the professor, who could choose to ignore the student's scores on the language tests, either to the benefit or detriment of that student (language teacher, Central Italy, email to the author, 19 June 2010).

PHYSICAL SEPARATION AND ARBITRARINESS

In order to maintain that the lettori were now CELs, several university managers and administrators contrived to keep the non-Italian teachers at considerable physical distance from the Italian professoriate. One described how he was no longer permitted to enter the University by the front door but did so in protest anyway, while his Italian colleagues avoided eye contact with him:

> But I do walk in the other door. I can get to the office by going through the front door, and I'll tell you, I don't look at my shoes. When I'm walking up the corridor, they look at their shoes. (David Petrie, Edinburgh, 25 May 2006)

Petrie also described his basement office, measuring four by six metres, which was to serve 13 members of staff. The European Parliament later commented on the office space given to the lettori: 'the basic human rights and democratic freedoms of fourteen foreign language teachers are being violated following eviction from their offices to a basement measuring six metres by four and through other forms of intimidations and legal filibustering' (European Parliament 1995). Others offered their own accounts of the cramped and insalubrious conditions where they were expected to work:

> We were given a mouldy chapel to do our lessons in my last year, where the echo was so bad it was impossible to understand when students spoke. Another room we were given was attached to the chapel and had poor lighting and no desks and there was no exit from that room without passing through the other, so that during your lesson, you had groups of students trooping through your class to get to the other classroom. (Language teacher, Central Italy, email to the author, 22 June 2010)

David Petrie described his relocation and his confined working conditions, using political terminology:

> What does apartheid mean? It means separate development. Now do you see yourself physically in a different building – yes or no? Yes. Do you see yourself divided by linguistic terminology ... do you see the Italians having their job description changed? Do you see them being told that they don't actually do exams, that they do 'tests' ... all of these things? Do you see yourself physically in a different space? These are all things which I say justifies the accurate use of the word 'apartheid'. And similarly with the idea of 'ghetto'; 'ghetto' is to do with the geography. We are literally in the basement, in the bunker, in the bowels of the faculty and there are separate entrances for us, to make sure that we do not embarrass the professors by walking in the wrong door. (David Petrie, Edinburgh, 25 May 2006)

Some of the accusations made by Petrie were also made by other participants who noted that they were at times instructed to remain out of sight. One woman claimed that this happened during a visit to the University by the Italian President, Giorgio Napolitano, writing that she considered the instruction 'an affront, a degradation, a de-qualification, a very low blow, after 23 years of service at that university!' (woman in Central Italy, email to author, 8 November 2007). David Petrie reported that he too was 'pulled out of his classroom the same morning a government minister was officially opening the university for the academic year' (David Petrie, email to the author, 22 June 2010).

CASUALIZATION

With the introduction of the first national contract in 1996 came a shift in government policy. According to one lettore, the government had never set aside sufficient sums to cover the contracts of lettori and as a result universities were allowed to cover the shortfall in salaries through a supplementary contract (trattamento integrativo) 'in accordance with productivity and experience'. This set the lettori further apart from other categories of worker, making them the only workers in Italy whose basic salaries were not stipulated in their national contracts. A new law introduced by the Berlusconi government has also subjected the lettori to a greater degree than other public sector workers to financial penalties (thanks to salary deductions) if they take sick leave. Absence from work due to illness can cost a lettore as much as 40 Euro for each of the first ten days of leave taken (J., telephone interview, 22 June 2010).

A further illustration of the ways in which policies and procedures have been used to justify reclassifying lettori and reinforce their exclusion in some universities is by the use of timecards. From the moment a lettore clocked in, they would be considered to be engaged in classroom activity, irrespective of whether or not they had already reached the classroom, needed to make photocopies in preparation for classes or needed to speak to students. One US-educated woman described a situation where, although time keeping was allegedly used to monitor the comings and goings of the staff, in practice the use of the timecard interfered with classroom teaching. Supervisors could add hours to or subtract them from timecards at will. The net result, in the perception of one 'lettrice' (a female teacher) was that she and her colleagues were 'working under a situation of blackmail'. She explained how she found herself threatened with disciplinary measures when, having not been provided with any information about the workings of the timecard system, she calculated her own hours. She explained that by taking a 30-minute lunch break then adding 30 minutes onto her day or by exceeding her required hours if she met with students, she accrued more hours than was permitted and was subsequently reprimanded:

> Here is an example. Some lettori opted to do long days of 8 hours. By law, all office workers doing 7 hours 12 minutes are required to take a lunch break of minimum half an hour, which in theory is automatically removed from the timecard tabulation by most electronic systems in use today in the public administration. In other words, if your working day is 8 hours and you don't leave the premises of your workplace, clocking in and clocking out for lunch, then you have to remain an extra 30 minutes because the timecard system automatically removes a half hour for the lunch break. In order not to have a thirty minute 'debt', you have to stay a half hour longer. Workers however also receive a meal ticket for the equivalent of 7 euros for each lunch break, which can be used to buy groceries at the supermarket.
>
> Immediately the question arose, are lettori who do 8 hours (or more during exams) required to stay an extra half hour, and are they entitled to a meal ticket? Nobody in the administration seemed to know the answer to this question. The timecard was applied this year [2007], and nobody could tell us

if we needed to stay extra or not. First they said we had to, then we didn't, and in any case we couldn't have a meal ticket, but they never put it down in writing, because they knew they would fall into contradiction. In the end those of us who stayed half an hour more ended up having too many hours on our timecard and were accused of insubordination!

But I forgot to mention the real problem of this timecard. Every month the worker receives the official tabulation of his hours printed out by the machine. He checks it and then takes it to the head of his office to sign. Only when signed is it an official document. Now whereas we had been receiving copies of the tab sheets, no one said a word that they needed to be signed in order to be valid. In other words, we were never given the official documents tabulating our hours that every worker has a right to see (and keep a copy of) every month. Nobody even bothered to explain the process. In March, seven months after the timecard was introduced, we discovered that our tab sheets were just pieces of paper that had no legal value, and the man in charge of the timesheets said, 'The boss can cancel out anything she wants until it has been signed.' We doubted this was true, but it illustrates the atmosphere under which we were working. So we asked for them to be signed. The union also made an official written request and did not receive a reply. That's when the real farce began. First we were told that they could not be signed since there were 'unauthorized hours' on our tab sheets. The administration then sent us a letter of reprimand saying that accruing unauthorized hours could be considered an act of insubordination. (After three counts of insubordination you can be fired.) They refrained from saying exactly how many hours they contested. Although we asked, they never replied. (Language teacher, Central Italy, 8 August 2007)

The use of the timecards also intensified the feeling among the lettori that they were 'shift workers'. One woman noted that with the timecard there was no possibility of making up lessons or even taking sick leave if you found yourself about to run over your stated hours. She added, 'They [the University] are paying less and getting more hours. It's slave work' (M., Central Italy, focus group, 12 October 2007). Her colleague explained how the introduction of timecards affected the quality of teaching and lowered morale:

the regulating of our schedule in such short units – five hours per day, which had to accommodate everything – four hours of lessons and one hour of whatever else – lessened the quality of our service to students. If you were in the middle of showing students their exam papers, or conferring with a student when your schedule was about to end, you just had to stop, pack everything up, and rush out and punch your timecard. Or subtract whatever extra minutes you did that day from your next day – so that lessons got shorter, as did exams, and we weren't as available to students. That is what the director of centro linguistico wanted: for us to gradually disappear. Since that time, three out of 12 lettori in my university have gone on unpaid leave for a year, and one has transferred to another university. (Language teacher, Central Italy, email to the author, 22 June 2010)

One additional worry concerned the security of pension entitlements. A respondent from Tuscany explained how the reclassification of lettori and the introduction of a new law in 2005 had substantially reduced their pensions:

> In 2005 a new law was introduced which said that state workers should not be in INPS [Istituto Nazionale per la Previdenza Sociale: the state pension institution for private sector workers] but rather the INPDAP [Istituto Nazionale di Previdenza per i Dipendenti dell'amministrazione Pubblica: the state pension institution for public sector workers]. Many universities registered the lettori without their consent with INPDAP. On 1 January 2008 Florence registered its lettori. Now the problem was that where INPS calculated pensions and severance pay on the entire income, INPDAP calculates on all but trattamento integrativo, in some cases 60 per cent of someone's salary. (J., telephone interview, 22 June 2010)

The lettori argued that by failing to base final pension calculations on the entirety of their salaries, they would be left in a precarious position. Lettori at the University of Bologna returned to court for this reason and others began to explore the possibility of bringing another case before the ECJ. Still others presented their grievances to their national governments. Writing to a House of Commons investigative panel, one female language teacher explained her situation and fears over her retirement:

> Over the past thirty years I have watched my salary go down rather than up. I have watched my work be rendered banal and uninteresting because the authorities were afraid that I would take them to court if I were 'too' professional. But take them to court I did and was awarded due recompense! I currently have another law suit pending against the University that I have been working in since 1988 and unless I am awarded what is due to me (i.e. the difference between what I was actually paid and what I should have been paid), I am facing a very poor retirement indeed. After thirty-two years of service, my take home salary for full-time employment as a lettrice is €921. My pension will be approximately two-thirds of that amount. (Anon. 1, submission to Free Movement of Persons Balance of Competences report, 10 August 2013)

FURTHER STRUGGLES

The lettori did eventually win the right to the minimum salary of tenured researchers from the first day of their employment, following the introduction of Law 63 of 5 March 2004 that was upheld by the European Court in Luxembourg (C-119/04). The question of equal treatment was not addressed, however, until the Court issued another decision in the case of a Belgian citizen in *Nancy Delay v Università degli studi di Firenze and Others* (C-276/07), where the Court ruled that:

> if national workers are entitled, under domestic legislation, to reinstatement from the point of view of increases in salary, seniority and the payment by the employer of social security contributions, from the date of their original recruitment, former foreign-language assistants who have become linguistic associates must also be entitled to similar reinstatement with effect from the date of their original recruitment.

Equal treatment was still not guaranteed across the Italian universities, and in July 2010 the lettori in Siena were in dispute with their University that, facing overwhelming debts estimated to be in the hundreds of millions of Euro, had reduced the pay of lettori by more than 60 per cent (J., telephone interview with the author, 22 June 2010). The lettori in Siena had been well protected under a 2006 contract that enabled them to receive the same level of pay as university researchers. Once that contract expired at the end of 2008, the University's Administrative Council and Academic Senate withdrew from the local agreement, one that had provided a significant supplement to the salaries of lettori through addition of the 'trattamento integrativo' (i.e. the University's contribution to their pay), and from 1 May 2010 approximately 45 lettori saw their salaries reduced to just 835 Euro per month. This arbitrary action was to set the scene for further abuses.

On 29 January 2011 a new Law 204 came into effect. Known as the Gelmini Reform, after the former Minister of Education, Maristella Gelmini, this law reinterprets Law 63 of 2004 and the related ECJ judgment and explicitly 'extinguishes' the rights of the lettori to have their claims adjudicated in a court of law. Art. 26 para. 3 of the Gelmini law restricts equal pay up to the level of associate professor from 1980 (when Law 382 was introduced) to the enactment of the 1995 law that created the category of linguistic expert. The Gelmini law explicitly states, 'From the date this present law comes into force, all pending court cases relating to these matters are forthwith extinguished', and in so doing has undermined both the primacy of European law and the right to judicial remedy.

RESISTANCE, RESIGNATION AND ADAPTATION

Respondents displayed mixed feelings regarding the ways in which they could address their situations within the university structure. Throughout the interviews both resignation and feelings that the odds were stacked against them were expressed.

> Lettoris' rights were trampled. They were forced to work more hours and managed to be accused of insubordination because they worked more hours. They were generally humiliated and clearly shown that the law works one way for Italians and another way for lettori. The general feeling is that since so many of us are seven to eight years shy of retirement, it's time to turn the screw another notch, and make life as unpleasant as possible so that we will quit before they have to pay us our full liquidazione [severance pay]. (Language teacher, Central Italy, 8 August 2007)

Respondents reiterated that they had been mistreated, and that was the reason why they initiated court cases. One language teacher joked:

> What have we done for you to hate us? We keep your clients active, year by year? They trust us – they know we're doing the job right. They could never do it like we do ... why did X and I start the court case? It was because we weren't getting paid properly. It wasn't a career advance! (M., Central Italy, focus group, 12 October 2007)

Others argued that the lettori problem was essentially of European-wide significance:

> I think the postscript as far as advising people working inside the European Union ... or specifically working in Italy ... the postscript is, don't. Don't. If the lettori are sorted out, they will be sorted out after 20 years of litigation. Has the Italian state changed, reformed? Will it change? Will it open up its doors? No it will not. And so therefore my advice to a young graduate, whether he was a dentist, a doctor or anything else, if you've fallen in love with a young Italian woman, don't go to work in Italy. (David Petrie, Edinburgh, 25 May 2006)

The above view was supported by respondents to the Free Movement of Persons Balance of Competences investigation and report of 2013. Several others noted that their experiences exposed the wider problem of promoting free movement and that Italy remained an exceptional state where labour standards did not apply:

> My experience in Italy would lead me to advise most young UK citizens not to migrate to Italy. Take casual employment, by all means, but do not expect

contractual obligations to be adhered to. Be especially wary of working for state institutions. Above all, heed the warning that I, as an impetuous youth, failed to act on. 'Italy differs from Northern Europe where corruption can be a significant fact of life. In Italy corruption is a way of life.' (Anon. 3, Submission to Balance of Competences investigation report, 10 August 2013)

Respondents in interview stressed the importance of seeking redress before the courts and identified the CJEU as the primary instrument for ending their disagreement with the Italian universities:

> In this case as foreign workers who 20 years ago came away with dreams of a unified Europe, which today is being realized and it's a Europe that's expanding, we would have expected a court of justice at any level … not to say at least a European level … to have upheld and protected the rights of those individuals who so strongly believed in it. You know we believe we're part of Europe. (Irish woman, Brussels, 18 July 2006)

Others mentioned the possibility of industrial action, speaking of the importance of working through the Confederazione Generale Italiana del Lavoro (Italian General Confederation of Labour, CGIL) and participating in strikes and protests against the general cuts in higher education and the attack on workers' rights (J., telephone interview with the author, 22 June 2010).

EXPLANATIONS AND EFFECTS

Earlier accounts of the lettori dispute suggested that it was explained by interest-group competition and long-standing traditions of patronage within closed, guild-like institutions (Blitz 1999). Yet several interviewees offered further cultural explanations that in their view better accounted for their mistreatment and degradation of status. One lettore argued that craftiness was prized in a context where the rule of law was often absent:

> Italians themselves, they divide themselves into two groups, the so called *furbo* and the *fesso*: *furbo*, which I guess you could say are sly, cunning sneaky, and the *fesso* are the chumps. And those are the two categories that Italians divide themselves into. And you can choose to be either one of those. So most people say well why a chump be, I'd rather be a sly fox. You know the rule of law doesn't really enter this equation at all. (S., Verona, 22 June 2006)

A number of lettori spoke of structural corruption. 'The state institutions are still based on power relationships and pay little regard to justice, merit or opportunity' (Anon. 6, Submission to Free Movement of Persons Balance of Competences report, 10 August 2013). Petty corruption within the institutions also played a significant role. One lettrice added that when Italian colleagues saw her in a different context, outside of work, they were often pleasant, but the workplace was dominated by a 'battle of the ranks' (language teacher, Central Italy, 27 June 2007).

Irrespective of the underlying causes, the reclassification of the lettori and the restructuring of the environment in which they work have carried a heavy price. Several respondents spoke of the development of painful physical conditions and the onset of depression. One Spanish man revealed a bad case of eczema that he linked directly to his employment, noting that when he was away from the University it was much better (Central Italy, focus group, 12 October 2007). He eventually left the University, opting to work as a school teacher.

A long-standing resident in Italy offered the following account of her own situation:

> Psychologically it was unbearable because I felt humiliated, then an enormous sense of having been cut out of everything which was now suppressed, destroyed, annihilated. I was in the midst of a crisis of humiliation when I had an asthma attack. We were in the basement bunker and our offices were being moved when I had a violent asthma attack. (French woman, Verona, 21 June 2006)

Another woman based in Southern Italy added that her and her colleague's employment situations had been the cause of considerable stress, adding that 'it [was] cropping up at night ... cropping up in our psyche'. She herself experienced many migraines, linked to tension in her jaw, and as a result was forced to wear a brace at night (Central Italy, focus group, 12 October 2007). Her colleague continued, 'Last year, I had problems sleeping. This year I had a problem with asthma' (M., Central Italy, focus group, 12 October 2007). When asked why she attributed her illness to her situation at work, she explained that 'you can only blow your top so much at work', so she like her suffering colleagues internalized the negative situation:

> I see it as a kind of suffocation and that is connected to my pathology and asthma. But I haven't had such bad asthma attacks as this year. The trigger was the end of the academic year, also at the end of August [just before I had to return to work]. It has affected my personal life with my partner. (M., Central Italy, focus group, 12 October 2007)

Others noted that financial pressures, as a result of their poor pay, worries over their pensions and the cost of legal fees, contributed to their ill health.

THE EFFECTS OF DISCRIMINATION

The above account reveals that the discriminatory procedures that first brought the Italian state universities into conflict with the European Union institutions did not end with the introduction of Law 236. The reclassification of the lettori as technical staff was instead considered a justification for mistreatment, giving rise to new legal challenges and personal struggles. The division of the lettori into the three groups described above resulted in differential pay arrangements and for many a marked demotion in terms of their occupational status. Neither Law 236 nor the introduction of new contracts, however, protected the lettori from abuse and harassment, even if the introduction of contracts set a financial parameter, in effect a baseline for their salaries. Reclassification of the lettori consequently corresponded with a rise in the number of local court cases, not to mention further litigation before the ECJ. More than 1000 cases have been filed in Italian courts.

The introduction of the Gelmini Reform in 2011 further disadvantaged the lettori not only by denying them access to courts but by revoking hard-won rights:

> After winning recognition for my status as university teacher (and pay arrears for 20 years), I have very recently seen this decision annulled (i.e. the appeal denied me access to due judgment), leaving me with the same basic wage of €1000 per month. I have been ordered to pay back my retirement benefit (€39,000) as this was also retrospectively denied, by the Gelmini law. Presently, I do not believe I can pay maintenance and mortgage payments so I may well need to move back to the UK or elsewhere. (Anon. 6, Submission to Free Movement of Persons Balance of Competences report, 10 August 2013)

The arbitrary use of this law to curtail an individual's access to legal remedies has generated a new wave of advocacy before the European institutions and national governments.

The story of the lettori in Italy has significance beyond the Italian university context. From the perspective of the enforcement of EU norms regarding freedom of movement and settlement, the issue reveals just how difficult it is to guarantee protection of these rights in the workplace and how quickly one's occupational status can change. All of the participants interviewed asserted that even though their titles changed from lettore to collaboratori ed esperti linguistici, the demands placed on them remained the same, if not greater.

The introduction of new terminology to reassign occupational roles also had the intended effect of creating greater distance between the non-Italians and other members of the teaching staff. New terms were accompanied by new procedures and rules, from restricting entry to certain buildings to exclusion from both pedagogic and formal activities to the physical separation of non-Italian teaching staff in cramped basement offices and unsuitable classrooms. Although many of the lettori interviewed contested their reclassification, they all agreed that the use of particular words and titles was significant in so far as it gave the university and their superiors a cover for what the lettori perceived as mistreatment.

Conflict with the university employers also had a noted effect on the lives of the lettori. The above accounts of stress following harassment, of financial worries and costly court proceedings and of an overall lack of control over one's working environment point to some of the costs for lettori of their employment. Others stated that their unacceptable situations could not be solely attributed to nationality-based discrimination but was part of a larger structural problem. They reported that new adjunct teachers and other fixed-term public sector staff, the 'precari', also faced poor conditions of employment, and that the university system as a whole was at breaking point.

Further structural issues identified in the above accounts, and above all the repeated claims of arbitrariness, call into question the application of European norms in the Italian university context. Most respondents linked their dissatisfaction at work to a failure of the European Union institutions to uphold their rights in Italy.

Other accounts of budget difficulties and institutional protectionism offer a partial explanation for the increasing casualization of teaching provided by the lettori (Blitz 1999), as does the devolution of funding to university institutions that have been left to address shortfalls in the national budget for higher education. The current challenge to protect the pensions of lettori is indeed one consequence of the increasing fragmentation of the university system with its varied contracts and different sets of entitlements based on one's legal status. The recent decision by the University of Siena to rescind the rights of lettori to supplemental contributions (trattamento integrativo) that had made up a large proportion of their salaries was the result of extreme financial pressures within that institution.

It is also important to highlight the role of competition over status and non-material goods, including titles and teaching privileges. The fact that much of the antagonism towards the lettori has been expressed in the context of the introduction of specific terminology to distinguish them from university lecturers and the professoriate demonstrates the import-ance of status and titles in this protracted dispute. Occupational status has long been a valuable resource in the Italian university context (Clark 1977); hence the introduction of new terminology and the attempt at reclassification must be understood as an attack on the standing of the lettori. We further record that changes in occupational status have also given rise to material consequences as a result of the casualization of employment, the proliferation of new types of contracts and adjustments to the pension plans of lettori.

The lettori problem also raises important questions regarding institu-tional management, governance and oversight. Many respondents described arbitrary procedures that interfered with their ability to do their jobs, noting that there were few effective means of redress. Several argued that the national union, the CGIL, no longer represented their interests, since there was now a number of lettori with a range of administrative or technical contracts. Others noted the presence of a lettore among the members of the national secretariat of the CGIL and emphasized that only the CGIL had consistently represented all the different categories – lettori, ex-lettori and CELs.

Some maintained that there could be no national solution to the lettori problem since the situation of the lettori differed markedly from one institution to another. One activist within the CGIL, however, concluded that in spite of its deficiencies, the 1996 national contract had at the very least provided financial and normative parameters that had protected the lettori and ensured that they had certain basic rights (such as a right to maternity leave, rights to leave of absence, employment protection, etc.) that those hired at a later time did not have. He nonetheless recognized that lettori were constantly forced to seek redress before the courts to receive salary payments and entitlements in order to protect their pensions. Such processes have since been jeopardized by the introduction of the Gelmini law and, as recorded in the above account by an anonymous respondent (Anon. 6), even those gains can be reversed and future pension payments are now uncertain.

CONCLUSION

The central argument presented in this chapter is that discriminatory decisions to exclude staff on the basis of nationality were followed by attempts to separate and segregate non-Italian teaching staff, whose occupational roles and entitlements were determined by both the state and superiors on an arbitrary basis. Such treatment not only violated their EU rights to free movement and settlement but also brought about lasting personal harm. The lettori struggle is therefore illustrative of some of the obstacles that a particular group of migrants faced as they sought to exercise their rights to free movement and settlement in the European Union. Italy is a core member of the European Union. The fact that the lettori have had to rely on administrative courts and international institutions to adjudicate over employment matters for almost 20 years exposes the lack of effective mechanisms to resolve labour disputes in Italy. The Gelmini Reform does not resolve this matter but rather draws yet another arbitrary line that seeks to prevent the resolution of substantive grievances. This epic story calls into question the promise of free movement and respect for other EU norms, including the prohibition against discrimination on the basis of nationality and the right to equal treatment for EU citizens.

NOTES

1. For example, Eurofound (2011) acknowledged that, 'Nonetheless, the extent to which a general principle of non-discrimination applies in the EU remains unclear.'
2. Relevant European Court rulings include: Case C-33/88, *Pilar Allué and Carmel Mary Coonan v Università degli studi di Venezia* [1989] ECR 1591; Joined Cases C-259/91, C-331/91 and C-332/91, *Pilar Allué and Carmel Mary Coonan and Others v Università degli studi di Venezia and Università degli studi di Parma* [1993] ECR I-4309; Case C-90/96, *David Petrie and Others v Università degli studi di Verona and Camilla Bettoni* [1997] ECR I-6527; Case C-119/04, *Commission of the European Communities v Italian Republic* [2006] ECR I-6885; and Case C-276/07, *Nancy Delay v Università degli studi di Firenze, Istituto nazionale per la previdenza sociale (INPS) and Repubblica italiana* [2008] ECR I-3635.
3. See Decreto Presidente Repubblica 11 luglio 1980, n. 382, *Riordinamento della docenza universitaria, relativa fascia di formazione nonché sperimentazione organizzativa e didattica* (also known as *La Riforma Universitaria*), http://w3.uniroma1.it/studiorientali/leggiru/dpr_382_1980.htm (last accessed 14 May 2010).
4. 'L'article 48, paragraphe 2, du traité CEE s'oppose à ce que la legislation d'un Etat membre limite en toute hypothèse à un an, avec possibilité de renouvellement, la durée des contracts de travail des lectuers de langue etrangère, alors qu'une telle limite n'existe pas, en principe en ce qui concerne les autres enseignants', *European Court Reports* (Luxembourg: Court of Justice of the European Communities, 1989), p. 1592.
5. Interview with C.S., 18 March 1996.

6. Letter sent to the European Parliament's Committee on Petitions by Martin Reynolds and others, 3 March 1995.
7. One petitioner stated that, 'Our employer still refuses to recognise these decisions and to comply with and apply in full EU law. ... As a result, we are still compelled to remain under court protection and continue to be discriminated against, with respect to our Italian colleagues, in regard to: (1) social security and medical benefits; (2) pension benefits; (3) security of tenure; (4) salary scales.'

6.   Displaced Serbs in Croatia

> I sit doing nothing, waiting for good luck to arrive. It is like waiting for rain in the middle of summer. They are always saying on TV it will be done but for seven years they have just been saying the same and people are dying in the meantime.
>
> (B.C., interview, Stirmca, 24 April 2004)

INTRODUCTION

Returning refugees and internally displaced people in post-conflict situations often find that their mobility rights have been compromised as a result of the trajectory of war and the political and economic structures left in place. This chapter examines the mobility options of returning refugees in Croatia, the newest EU member state, and describes the contrasting reintegration experiences of ethnic Serbs and Croats in post-war Croatia over the past 20 years. It describes a situation where migrants enjoy vastly different access to housing, employment and social services on the basis of their ethnic identity, property ownership and time spent in exile, while noting how societal discrimination has negatively impacted their personal well-being and created further intra-group divisions. It concludes with an assessment of the impact of long-standing societal discrimination on the free movement of former refugees and displaced people.

RESEARCH CONTEXT

On 1 July 2013 Croatia joined the European Union. Its admission had been a long time coming. Since the European Commission first recommended that the European Council open membership negotiations with Croatia in April 2004 (Commission of the European Communities 2004), the prospect of Croatia's membership hung to a large extent on its resolution of the Serbian problem. One important pre-condition to EU accession was the integration of the Serbian community into Croatia and the return of approximately 200,000 Serbs who had been displaced by the Yugoslav war of 1991–5 (Commission of the European Communities

2004, p. 26). This demand put the then Croatian government at odds with a significant section of the Croatian public that had been reluctant to see the Serbs return. Public opinion research at the time found that 63 per cent of respondents opposed the return of Serbs and identified them with the former occupation of Croatia by the Yugoslav National Army (JNA) (Vuković and Bagić 2004). Structural factors, including lack of economic opportunity, made return an unattractive proposition and many Serbs complained that persistent discrimination in public life, especially in the judiciary, further weakened the potential for long-term sustainable returns (Blitz 2003; Human Rights Watch 2003; Ivanisevic and Trahan 2004; Norwegian Refugee Council 2002; US Department of State, Bureau of Democracy, Human Rights, and Labor (hereafter 'US State Department') 2004).

In spite of an unsympathetic public, displaced Serbs did return to Croatia. Figures from the Organization for Security and Cooperation in Europe (OSCE) put the number of registered Croatian Serb returns at 110,000 (OSCE 2004). This raised the question: which migrants should be able to return and under what conditions? This question has broader significance because, while there is a growing literature on refugee return, there has been little discussion of the different typologies of return and the options available to returnees. Most studies tend to amalgamate the experiences of refugees and concentrate on return as an end-point in the refugee cycle (Toft 2000). This approach has a number of deficiencies. It only tells part of the story and ignores the challenges of adaptation and social integration facing the returnee. In reality all returnees do not share the same experiences and do not enjoy equal access to resources in their home state. The emphasis on return downplays sources of conflict that may persist in the form of ethnic, national and social cleavages even after the war has ended (Schmitter and Karl 1991).

This chapter begins with an overview of the historical and legal barriers to return in Croatia. The second section introduces the empirical findings and prepares the way for a discussion of the main determinants of successful reintegration. The data are based on material gathered during three research visits in June 2001, April 2004 and August 2006, when semi-structured interviews were conducted (n = 48) with displaced persons, Croatian government officials, international relief agencies, human rights monitoring organizations, non-governmental organizations (NGOs) and legal authorities in Zagreb, Split, Sisak, Knin, Vukovar and Beli Monastir. Further desk research was conducted in 2012 and 2013.

THE END OF YUGOSLAVIA AND THE WAR IN CROATIA, 1991–5

The drive to separatism and eventual secession of Croatia was activated not by disgruntled minorities in the periphery but from the political elites at the very centre in Belgrade and to a lesser extent in Zagreb (Conversi 2000; Magaš 1993). The response to Slobodan Milošević's programme of increasing centralization of power was the revival of the Croatian national project that polarized Croatia's two main ethnic groups. The election of the charismatic Franjo Tudjman in 1989 as leader of the newly formed Croatian National Union (HDZ) further exacerbated inter-ethnic tensions. This was quickly followed by their victory in the 1990 multi-party elections. These elections set the stage for Croatia's bid for independence from the Serb-dominated Socialist Federal Republic of Yugoslavia and, while Tudjman focused on reviving national symbols and chronicled Croatia's past glories, Croatia's Serbian minority, concentrated in the Danube region on the Eastern border with Vojvodina and in the Krajina region, became nervous and transferred its allegiance to the newly formed Serbian Democratic Party (SDS). Serbian fears were escalated by the state-controlled media based in Belgrade that likened the emergence of the new Croatian state to the independent state created by the pro-Axis Croatian Ustašhe that had been responsible for killing hundreds of thousands of Serbs 50 years earlier (Thompson 1999). Attacks on minority rights and the formation of paramilitary groups further antagonized the rebels, and in 1991 the Serbian minority boycotted the referendum on Croatian independence (Tanner 2001).

Rather than participate in the new state, the local Serb population sought to secede from Croatia and formed the self-proclaimed Serbian Autonomous Territory of the Krajina, which was endorsed by Belgrade but which received no other international recognition. The JNA and leadership of the SDS developed a strategy for redistributing weapons collected from territorial defence units in Croatia, giving them to Serbs in and around Knin. Conflict between the Serbian rebels and the Croatian military took place shortly after the country's declaration of independence on 25 June 1991. The separatists were assisted by the Serb-dominated JNA, which occupied one-third of Croatia and enabled them to create the 'Serbian Republic of Krajina' (RSK) with its capital in Knin. The rebel Serbs were led by Milan Martić, a figure who was indicted by the International Criminal Tribunal in the Former Yugoslavia

(ICTY) for Crimes against Humanity and Violations of the Laws of War in 1995. These indictments were amended in 2000 and again in September 2003.

During the war Croatia saw two major refugee flows. The first in 1991 followed the initial attack and occupation of Eastern Slavonia and Krajina that expelled the majority of the ethnic Croat population. Large numbers of Serbs were also expelled from Croatia proper and sought refuge in Serbia and the Krajina region. The second refugee flow occurred four years later when the Croatian government reclaimed three-quarters of the territory under Serb control during two rapid military operations, Flash and Storm, in May and August 1995, respectively. Eastern Slavonia, the final pocket of Croatia controlled by Serbian forces, was transferred to the United Nations by means of the Erdut Peace Agreement of 1995 and was formally returned to Croatian control on 15 January 1998.

Official sources estimate that during the first refugee flow, approximately 84,000 Croats fled from areas under Serbian control and another 70,000 ethnic Serbs who had been displaced settled in the Danube region. According to the Croatian government's former Office of Displaced Persons and Refugees (ODPR),[1] approximately 300,000 Serbs had fled by the end of the war and needed shelter (Ellis and Barakat 1996). Others left after territory around the Danube was transferred to the United Nations to administer in 1995 and then again when this region reverted to Croatian government control in 1998 (OSCE 2001).

International human rights authorities have recorded extensive evidence of war crimes committed against civilians in areas under Serbian control, especially in the Danube region in and around the city of Vukovar that was flattened by the JNA assault. The severity of these crimes, including the murder of hundreds of elderly Croat civilians who were removed from a hospital in Vukovar, still resonates with the Croatian public, and in spite of peace agreements there remains widespread hatred of the Serbian minority that is blamed collectively for the crimes carried out by the JNA and RSK forces.

It is important to record that crimes, including killings and the destruction of civilian property, were also committed against ethnic Serbs both during and after the war, perpetuating cycles of conflict. The most intense period of violence which affected the Serbian minority took place during 'Operation Storm' (4–7 August 1995), when local Serb civilians were put at risk by the shelling of Knin and forced to flee as part of an organized military campaign.

Some characterized the exodus of the Serbian population of Krajina as the result of 'ethnic cleansing', since the migration of the local population was accompanied by attacks on civilians and the introduction of other means of terror (Croatian Helsinki Committee for Human Rights 2001). Human rights authorities challenged the Croatian government's claim that Operation Storm was an internal police operation that violated principles of international humanitarian law (Rakate 2000). The Croatian government was, however, vindicated when the ICTY overturned its previous judgment and acquitted Ante Gotovina and Mladen Markač, the Croatian generals who directed Operation Storm (see International Criminal Tribunal for the Former Yugoslavia 2012).

In the immediate aftermath of Operation Storm, revenge attacks were exacted against the Serb civilians and hundreds of elderly Serbs were reported murdered (Amnesty International 1998). There was also at least one instance of Croat-on-Croat crime that continued for years as some key witnesses of war crimes were killed. The indictment of the Croatian generals, including the commander of Operation Storm, Ante Gotovina, served to exacerbate inter-ethnic tensions. During the start of the Mesić Presidency in 2000 and as a result of a backlash by provincial nationalists (Blitz 2003), increasing numbers of ethnic Croats were charged with war crimes for atrocities committed during the war in Croatia and also Bosnia (Peskin and Boduszynski 2003). Although an amnesty was put in place in 1996 and was intended to cover those who engaged in 'armed rebellion' (i.e. participated in the RSK Army), thousands of indictments were re-issued against ethnic Serbs from 2000–2002, often with little evidence. Few of these indictments resulted in convictions but indictees were nonetheless subject to arrest and denied compensation upon their release. The aim of the mass indictment policy was both to block return and redistribute blame (Blitz 2003, 2005).

DISCRIMINATION DURING THE EARLY YEARS OF INDEPENDENCE

The ethnic nature of the conflict from 1991–5 was reflected in many of the policies introduced by the Croatian government (see Blitz 2003). In 1991 the government of Franjo Tudjman introduced a law that sought to deny returning refugees citizenship in the new state and barred habitual residents from returning to their homes on the grounds that they needed to show five years' continuous residence prior to application, thus deterring those who had been displaced from returning. Those most affected were Serbs, Roma and Bosniaks (European Commission Against Racism and Intolerance (ECRI) 1999).

The first mechanism for the organized return of displaced persons was established in 1997. This facilitated two-way returns from and to the Danube region and limited the right of return to a fraction of the population. Before they could return to their homes, all displaced persons were permitted to remain in the houses they temporarily occupied or else were provided with alternative accommodation. This return mechanism broke down with the departure of the UN administration when thousands of Croats returned spontaneously to reclaim their homes. Of the 90,000 people who had been displaced from the Danube region prior to 1995, only a handful of Serbs were facilitated by the two-way return mechanism. The majority of Serbs displaced to the Danube region left for third countries as a consequence of harassment and psychological pressure (OSCE 2001, p. 5).

After restricting returns to residents of the Danube region, further regulations were introduced limiting the right of return to ethnic Croat citizens and residents married to Croat nationals. It was only international criticism that forced the government to adopt new revisions to these restrictive laws. Yet the new legislation, known as the Mandatory Instructions and the more extensive Programme for Return and Housing Care of Expelled Persons, Refugees and Displaced Persons, continued in the same vein by describing Serbs as persons who had 'voluntarily abandoned the Republic of Croatia', even though many fled during periods of intense human rights abuses (Rakate 2000). Under the threat of international sanctions new laws were introduced, but they did not supersede the old discriminatory laws. Critics within the humanitarian sector claimed that Croatia 'ended up with a confusing mix of contradictory laws that continued to stymie refugee and displaced person return' (US Committee for Refugees and Immigrants 1999, p. 2).

After introducing laws that denied minorities their basic right to return, the Tudjman government adopted a housing policy that left minorities further disadvantaged. The war had destroyed approximately 195,000 homes, and it was therefore imperative that a solution be found to ease the burden on the transitional state. The former Tudjman government passed many laws regarding the government's take-over of private property, while denying others the right to formerly state-owned property. The most notable of these was the Law on Temporary Take-Over and Administration of Specified Property (LTTP) of 1995 (Official Gazette NN 73/95, NN 7/96 and NN 100/97). Legal owners of property saw their rights curtailed by the 1996 Law on Areas of Special State Concern that created the term 'settlers' and gave ethnic Croats private or state-owned property for their own use. Many Serbs were further dispossessed by the application of the pre-war Law on Housing Relations that gave the original owners an exceptionally short window of 90 days to return and reclaim their property. The vast majority of those dispossessed were tenancy rights holders, residents of socially owned property who lived in apartments leased by the state or state enterprises. Court hearings conducted in absentia enabled the administration to dispossess tens of thousands of Serbs in this way. According to Human Rights Watch more than 23,700 tenancy rights holders saw their rights to residency terminated through corrupt court proceedings during this time (Human Rights Watch 2003, p. 34).

In 1998 a Return Programme was established for the repossession of property that had been allocated to temporary users (Official Gazette NN 92/98). Municipal housing commissions were created to administer the procedures, but their decisions could only be enforced on the basis of prior court decisions. More than 21,000 properties, mostly Serb owned, were handed over to housing commissions that frequently presided over corrupt practices (OSCE 2001). Forms of abuse included: (1) backdating housing commission decisions; (2) paying for evictions of illegal occupants by the rightful owners at a cost of 5000 DM, while the police sometimes protected the illegal owner; (3) using the police to forcibly remove occupants, sometimes including Bosnian Croat settlers; (4) occupying multiple homes; and (5) occupying productive property (e.g. barns), denying the legitimate owners the right to re-start their livelihood (A.B., F.C., interview with the author, Osijek, 16 June 2001; G.S., interview with the author, Zagreb, 19 April 2004).

CONTINUITY AND REFORM

Following the 'Knin Conclusions' in March 2001 the new government committed itself to addressing key problems, including the issues of return and integration. Important reforms were instigated between 2001 and 2003, including a new Constitutional Law on National Minorities (CLNM). These reforms introduced clauses regarding the representation of minority groups in the Parliament as well as new educational provisions and a Law on Areas of Special State Concern (LASSC) that altered the way in which returnee issues were to be administrated. The housing commissions that had frustrated the return of property to former refugees and displaced persons were abolished. Claims were now to be heard instead by the ODPR (that was instructed to prioritize owners' claims of repossession above tenants' rights). On paper at least, the

LASSC appeared to break with the traditions established during the Tudjman era that had discriminated in favour of ethnic Croats from both Croatia and Bosnia over the Serbian population.

Former Croatian President Mesić and former Prime Minister Račan went on record, urging Serbs to return and insisting that conditions were ripe for the reintegration of Serbs into Croatian society. For Mesić their return was a pre-condition for Croatia to become a serious state (Agence France Press 2003). Evictions of Bosnian Croats who had occupied Serbian homes in the Krajina region started to take place in spring 2002 (RFE/RL NewsLine, 6 September 2002). In practice, however, the most positive reforms of this period were limited to the establishment of a legal framework while the pace of refugee returns slowed (OSCE 2003). As for judicial matters, the Račan government was exceptionally slow to react (e.g. by refusing to arrest Ante Gotovina for crimes committed during Operation Storm). Human rights authorities noted that during the leadership of Ivica Račan (2000–2003), the government adopted an ambivalent position due to the fragility of the coalition and public opposition to minority rights and property restitution (see Norwegian Refugee Council 2001, 2002). For fear of upsetting the nationalist parties neither Mesić nor Račan seemed prepared to tackle the issue of returns head on (Ivanisevic 2009).

The return of the nationalist HDZ party in December 2003 and the election of Ivo Sanader as Prime Minister raised a number of suspicions concerning inter-ethnic relations in Croatia. These fears were in part placated by the government's repeated statements on refugee returns and the expansion of the housing and social care schemes in early 2004. In the meantime high profile indictees were not handed over to the ICTY. Human rights monitors, including the US State Department and Human Rights Watch, noted a persistent bias in favour of Croats throughout the justice system (Ivanisevic and Trahan 2004; Minority Rights Group International 2003; US State Department 2004).

DEMOGRAPHIC REALITIES

Official policies of discrimination and corrupt institutional practices presented a number of challenges to the idea of minority returns (see Ivanisevic 2009).

The demographic effects of the war had a profound impact on the ethnic composition of Croatia that the amnesty had only partially addressed (Norwegian Refugee Council 2002). The Serbian minority in Croatia had been dramatically reduced from 12.6 per cent of the overall population (approximately 4,334,142) to just 4.5 per cent (Republic of Croatia – Bureau of Statistics 2001). The local economy of Knin was considerably worse off than other parts of the country, and this fact deterred many Serbs from attempting to return. The majority of returnees were elderly Serbs whose only prospect was a state pension (US State Department 2004). By April 2003 approximately 240,000 Croatian Serbs remained in exile, mostly in Serbia and Montenegro, and had seemingly decided against return (SETimes.com 2003). By 2005 a minority of ethnic Serbs, including returnees, were reported living in collective centres within Croatia. According to the ODPR there were 46 collective centres still operating in Croatia in January 2005. Ten of these had been categorized as internally displaced people – refugee accommodation facilities (Nebojša Paunović, email to Jeroen Jansen, 4 May 2005), and the number of occupants was estimated to be fewer than 1700.

The repossession of housing presented a most significant barrier to the sustainable return of refugees and displaced minorities (Human Rights Watch 2003; US State Department 2004). The problems associated with housing turned on the resolution of lost tenancy rights and to a lesser extent the reconstruction of destroyed property and the repossession of occupied property (Ivanisevic 2009).

In the mid 2000s the government began a construction programme, building houses for Serbian residents. Under the terms of the government arrangement returnees had to confirm that they were prepared to live in the reconstructed property for at least ten years and must have arranged a lien on the property to establish its value (even if it was badly destroyed) before they could receive any assistance. The value of the property was then converted into an interest-free loan that would have to be repaid or else the state would repossess the house. Elderly Serbs living on pensions feared they would never be able to repay the government and thus pass on their homes to their children (A.J., phone interview with the author, 13 October 2003). The same applied to those without regular income, whose property rights were conditioned upon their staying in a depressed region for at least ten years, irrespective of local economic offerings.

Some Bosnian Croats were evicted after 2002, but the process of repossession was painfully slow and marred with political influence in terms of judicial hearings, threats of violence against returnees, and the looting and destruction of private property upon the departure of the illegal occupant (Human Rights Watch 2003; Ivanisevic and Trahan 2004; US State Department 2004). Returnees had been attacked in some instances and even murdered (US State Department 2004). Many of the settlers who occupied Serb homes were not prepared to leave until conditions improved in Bosnia and most never returned. The loss of tenancy rights enjoyed by occupants of former socially owned property was by all accounts without an easy solution.

For individuals forcibly repatriated from third countries, there was no obvious resettlement path. Failed asylum seekers were not entitled to returnee status and would not be entitled to temporary accommodation under the government return programme (Lunzhof, letter to Nick Swift, 13 June 2003). A person who failed to apply for reconstruction assistance before the deadline, or who had been denied reconstruction assistance, thus had no further options to explore.

ECONOMIC AND SOCIAL WELFARE

Those who returned voluntarily were entitled to a welfare grant of 350 Kuna per person per month (approximately 50 Euro), even though in practice few citizens could be supported by social welfare. According to the 2001 census, of all 15,000 inhabitants of Knin, only 1463 persons were listed as receiving social welfare (Republic of Croatia – Bureau of Statistics 2001b). Two additional concerns included access to state pensions and the issue of convalidation – the recognition of periods of time spent in employment. The government had introduced a number of schemes that made it difficult for ethnic Serbs to claim past years of work that should have contributed to their pension. The issue of convalidation was particularly important because it related to final pay pension schemes. To secure a convalidation of one's working papers, it was necessary to produce two witnesses who qualified by having worked with the applicant and whose own employment status had itself been certified by means of convalidation. Given the social distance between ethnic groups, this was especially difficult to achieve (A.J. and M.A., interview with the author, 19 April 2004). Returnees tended to rely on members of their own ethnic group for support, and most were in the same situation. There were also obvious practical difficulties, since many refugees did not have complete files nor did they have copies of their employment log, stored in their employer's office and left behind when they were forced to flee.

ACCESS TO EMPLOYMENT

Limited private sector activity in areas with the highest concentration of returnees (Republic of Croatia – Bureau of Statistics 2001) and above average unemployment further weakened the economic prospects of returnees. It was noted that ethnic minorities enjoyed access to the grey economy that by its nature was structured around personal ties. While many returnees lost connections as a result of war and displacement, there was also widespread labour market discrimination so that ethnic Croats enjoyed an absolute monopoly on public sector jobs (Human Rights Watch 2003).

DISCRIMINATION AND THE JUDICIARY

One major source of discrimination against Serbs was the inconsistent application of the 1996 law on amnesty and the conduct of domestic war crimes (see Blitz 2003; Ivanisevic and Trahan 2004; US State Department 2004). In 2004 the US State Department noted that 'questions remain regarding the criminal justice system's ability to conduct fair and transparent trials in these complex and emotionally charged cases' (US State Department 2004, p. 3). Trials operated on ethnic lines in terms of the appointment of judges, manner of prosecution and the nature of judgments brought to bear against the accused (Ivanisevic and Trahan 2004; US State Department 2004).

This point is underscored by the findings of Human Rights Watch in 2004 that found continuing ethnic bias in war crimes prosecutions. During 2002 the OSCE determined that 28 of the 35 persons arrested for war crimes for comparable offences in Croatia were Serbs. Serbs also comprised 114 of 131 of those under judicial investigation (19 of 32 persons indicted and 90 of 115 persons put on trial). According to the OSCE, this trend appeared to continue in 2003. By way of comparison, the Office of the Prosecutor for the ICTY issued just over twice as many indictments against ethnic Serbs as against ethnic Croats (a ratio of 11:5) for crimes committed in the Croatian war (Ivanisevic and Trahan 2004).

Some argued that the judiciary was indeed reforming and noted that relatively few Serbs had been sentenced for war crimes by a court of law and that some incorrect decisions had now been overturned (Hedl 2005). Extensive irregularities at the pre-trial stage (Human Rights Watch 2003; Ivanisevic and Trahan 2004; US State Department 2004), in addition to procedural irregularities at the point of prosecution and political scandals (Pilić 1999), suggested otherwise. Witnesses called to present evidence in high profile cases refused to make the journey from Serbia for fear of physical attack. Death threats, as reported in the high profile *Lora*[2] and *Gospic* cases (OSCE 2002), created a sense of fear such that one commentator claimed 'chronic witness intimidation' and an 'often hostile local public' hampered the war crimes process (US State Department 2004).

MEDIA REPORTING ON RETURN

The media stirred up ethnic tensions that only enhanced the Serbian community's vulnerability, especially during the *Norac* case and the 2001 demonstrations in support of the generals. Hrvatsko Slovo and Slobodna Dalmacija were identified as 'the main inciters of the extremist writings whose main purpose is dissemination of hatred and intolerance' (Croatian Helsinki Committee for Human Rights 2001). International monitors also noted the expansion of hate speech that fuelled public disturbances (OSCE 2004). The Helsinki Committee further claimed that the 'most extreme standpoints are being promoted with the goal of cleansing Croatian space from others who think differently and spread their culture in these regions' (Croatian Helsinki Committee for Human Rights 2001). Zadar local weeklies also continued to publish articles attacking Serbs planning to return, accusing them of armed rebellion; such reports 'not only threaten the security of Serb returnees in the area but also dissuade others from returning' (Dokoza 2003).

RETURN, INTEGRATION AND DIFFERENTIATION

In order to assess the barriers to return and the challenges to freedom of movement, questions were asked regarding property ownership; dates of departure, circumstances of exit and dates of return; actions taken to repossess homes; problems encountered and explanations for such problems. The participants' responses were then analysed and sorted into the following themes: (1) migratory paths and patterns of settlement; (2) relocation and personal identity; (3) acceptance and integration; (4) faith in government; (5) community; and (6) motivation and passivity.

Migratory Paths and Patterns of Settlement

Most of the Serbian participants interviewed had moved from Croatia to Bosnia, and then to Western or Eastern Slavonia before returning home. The experience of the Croatian participants was more varied and included settlers who had arrived from Bosnia. In almost all cases the participants who identified as returnees had participated in some form of convoy and group exit during the war. The living conditions that greeted returning migrants were markedly different from one ethnic group to another and from one set of migrants to another. For example, one Serbian couple, Rado and Mile, had been living in a one-room wooden cabin in a collective centre outside Sisak. The cabin was dark and the only décor consisted of plastic soft drink bottles filled with earth and turned into hanging planters. By contrast most of the ethnic Croat participants interviewed had been able to return to permanent housing, often at the invitation of the Croatian government.

Some participants returned to formerly occupied but otherwise functional accommodation; others waited in collective centres while damaged housing was reconstructed; and former tenancy rights holders lived in collective centres without a clear plan for the future. The Bosnian Croats were fortunate to be housed at the very least in semi-permanent structures with heating and double glazing that the OSCE mockingly described as being like 'Club Med'. They and their neighbours owned cars and thus were able to move more freely. Others were even more fortunate, having received a formal invitation to settle. In Josip's case, the state authorities offered him the possibility of securing temporary property, which he immediately followed up by requesting a temporary permit for housing from the municipal authority.

Relocation and Personal Identity

Some participants challenged the use of the term 'returnee', feeling that it had been imposed on them by external parties: 'We have been classified as returnees but I didn't return anywhere. When I return to my apartment, then I will see it as a return to normal life' (Mile, interview with the author, Sisak area, 20 April 2004).

The absence of 'normal life' was reflected in other contradictions, including confusion over the participants' self-described identity and the new occupations that they had discovered since their exit during the war. One middle-aged couple (he an accountant and she a metalsmith before the war) found themselves tending cattle in Eastern Slavonia to survive. Like other older participants, they were able to accept the challenge of rural life and subsistence farming more easily than younger returnees.

For others it was not relocation but the change in local demographics that affected the way participants identified. One man in his 60s claimed that his status as an ethnic Serb had confined him to being a minority, which had a negative effect on his self-esteem. His decision to remain in Croatia during the war and not take up arms was of little consolation in a post-war society, where his own individual claim to be a 'remainee' was subsumed by his membership in a group whose collective identity was defined by the majority population. As he explained:

There is another problem for Serbs. For the first time in 200 years, they have become a national minority. So I who remained here ... I have a mortgage on my back that I am discriminated against in general life. I don't want to consider myself less valid because I am considered a minority. (D.C., interview with the author, Knin, 21 April 2004)

Acceptance and Integration

While the research participants fell into two main camps defined by their ethnic attachments, one participant in Vukovar noted that there was an important distinction to be made between returnees, who had experienced the pains of exile and loss, and those who remained during the war (L.M., interview with author, Vukovar, 15 June 2001). Within the minority Serb population returnees were generally in a better position than those who were described by one participant as 'civil victims of the war' (NGO group interview, Vukovar, 15 June 2001). Of all the minority groups, the Roma remain the most vulnerable and least well integrated in the post-war era.[3]

Ethnic Croat returnees and settlers quickly found social acceptance and opportunities for integration in post-war Croatia, while ethnic Serbs did not. The lack of opportunities for non-Croats was made evident by the following account by a senior Serbian local in Knin:

> After Operation Storm, the political structures told me I couldn't get a job because I am Serb. Nobody here was choosing to which nation I was to belong. Now if you are looking for a job, they are still looking at what type of blood is flowing through your veins. (D.C., interview with the author, Knin, 21 April 2004)

He claimed that since the war ended there had been some obvious changes in policies towards minorities but suggested that covert discrimination was now the rule. Contrary to the Croatian Constitution, he argued:

> Patterns of discrimination are not as direct as after Operation Storm but are more 'hidden' ... Still, there is obstruction that we feel in every aspect of life ... property and unemployment, rights of national minorities. (D.C., interview with the author, Knin, 21 April 2004)

His colleague described the local employment policy in Knin, where migrant workers were bussed to low-level jobs. This account sustained the common view that the use of migrant labour was closely linked to the settlement programme of the Tudjman and subsequent governments, and that these policies only served to reinforce the divide between Serbs and Croats of working age:

People are not employing Serbs. Here's one example, a lady got a job in [a] hospital. She had 20 years of experience. But the very same day, the doctors signed a petition to say they wouldn't work with her. Another bad example ... we have 16 teachers in secondary school. Perhaps eight are from Knin ... the rest are from other parts of Croatia. While we have others registered, there are ten buses coming in on a daily basis with workers from outside the city. (interview with the author, Knin, 21 April 2004)

Faith in Government

All of the research participants questioned the government's ability to carry out the ambitious reforms regarding housing. For those living in collective centres, the confusion and disbelief over the proposed housing reforms added to their own sense of powerlessness. As one elderly man noted, 'our word goes into the wind – we are common people' (B.C., interview with the author, Stirmca, 24 April 2004). After more than a decade, some of the participants felt that too much time had passed and that the government could no longer provide a meaningful solution to the problems of return, reintegration and housing.

The reality of death and the banality of their displaced lives was a constant source of frustration and undermined the participants' belief in the state:

> There's always hope for better but now these hopes are nearing the end. Some people die here like Iva Seselj. People need to have strong nerves not to think about what they went through and not to think about why they cannot lead a normal life. I used to cry a lot before but saw it wasn't good for my health. This is survival basically, nothing more. (Radojka, interview with the author, Sisak area, 20 April 2004)

Some Serbian returnees noted the irony of the new housing and recon- struction plans that treated death as a likely precursor to the resolution of their housing problems: 'They are saying come work on the roads with us because this will be a road to your graveyard' (B.C., interview with the author, Stirmca, 24 April 2004).

Participants living in collective centres were especially dubious of the government's willingness and capacity to relocate them. Some focused on practical problems, including the many groups that needed to be satisfied in advance of their own needs:

> first they will deal with private property, then property will be for war veterans and who knows when ... people say you have to wait for the law to change, then they say there is no money. (Mile, interview with the author, Sisak area, 20 April 2004)

> It's a promise but we need something concrete. The new house is being built but it is for people who have money to purchase it. For me it is a vicious circle, but we are a bit tired of this now. There are no steps forward. What is the benefit of talks with no outcome? (Radojka, interview with the author, Sisak area, 20 April 2004)

Others claimed that the root cause of the problems they were facing was political and had yet to be addressed:

> It's not easy to build a house or a state. The Croatian state is still a baby. It's not democratic, not legal. It is still growing. When it is 18 years old, I don't know how serious it will be. Croatia is the first champion in signing agreements then not following through with actual implementation. (D.C., interview with the author, Knin, 21 April 2004)

Community

For both ethnic Serbs and Croats the concept of community provided essential support to returnees and helped them to cope with the daily challenges of unemployment and exclusion. For two elderly sisters, having a small group of neighbours was a major factor in their decision to return to their village (Marta and Doma, interview with the author, Sisak area, 20 April 2004). In the major towns community institutions have been set up in response to international donor activity that continues to provide assistance in the form of grants and training. In the city of Knin the Unemployed Association, with more than 4000 registered members, was assisted by the Swiss Development Agency, CARE and the Austrian government. The organization experimented with income-generating activities that sought to engage returnees. According to the Director, one glass recycling project in the wealthier city of Osijek was able to employ 200 people (M.J., interview with the author, Knin, 21 April 2004).

For the ethnic Serbian population, cultural organizations, such as the Joint Municipality Council in Vukovar and the Serbian Society of Knin, that promoted identity and provided educational support and access to books and music, were especially valued. According to the Director of the Serbian Society, the organization was re-established in 1997 when the city recognized that it could 'nourish the national identity and contribute to the restoration of a multicultural society' (D.M., interview with the author, Knin, 21 April 2004). The staff interviewed claimed that while the organization is operating out of only one room, the provision of books and information on Serbian culture provides great comfort to a minority community that has seen its numbers decline by more than 80 per cent.

By contrast those living in collective centres enjoyed no support from the broader community; this had a marked effect on the quality of their existence. Most of the inhabitants of collective centres had no family support and since aid agencies began withdrawing from Croatia, there have been no obvious economic opportunities or community-based activities to occupy them. An elderly woman now living in a collective centre that houses mostly Roma and Serbs described the level of outside support she received:

> We don't have a group. There's no support group. The only thing that happens in the collective centre is an Italian NGO that comes – teenagers, bring gifts ... they decorate the centre. They come for Easter, Christmas, summer time. (Radojka, interview with the author, Sisak area, 20 April 2004)

Motivation and Passivity

Both ethnic Croats and minority Serbs who actively searched out economic opportunities, developed networks of support and lobbied the state institutions saw their fortunes improve faster than those returnees who waited for the state to provide for them. For Croats, while there was massive unemployment there were also functioning institutions that provided opportunities to work in low-level positions. After many years unemployed, Velijko, an ethnic Croat from Bosnia, was able to resume work as an electrician. He identified three pre-conditions for his success: support from his brother, who provided housing, receipt of Croatian citizenship and having a trade which ultimately led to his employment. Among the Serbian returnees the most successful were young, well-educated, English-speaking locals who were able to find jobs in international agencies or NGOs.

Being proactive also seemed to benefit those who sought to repossess their homes and, in spite of persistent discrimination, some ethnic Serb respondents were able to secure permanent accommodation. The key to their success was a clear understanding of the legalities regarding housing repossession, unrelenting use of court instructions and procedures, and persistent lobbying of municipal authorities:

> First when I arrived in 1997 I submitted an application in the municipal authority office. When I arrived in Belgrade I immediately wrote to the Helsinki Committee and authorities in Knin (police, Ministry of Justice) so that I could be registered. I had heard on Croatian TV that those who don't

claim property in time will lose [it] so I decided to take action. I received
application forms but as new laws were adopted, I always needed additional
documents. There was no organized system for submitting applications. For
some reason, ours was treated as the last application even though we had
applied on so many occasions. The number we were given was 192. Since
1999, when we returned to the area around Knin, at least once a week I
visited the housing commission. (Natasha and family, interview with the
author, Knin, 21 April 2004)

A change in housing policy ultimately enabled Natasha's mother to press
for repossession of the house through the courts, and in 1997 she
received a letter from the municipal authorities announcing that, because
of the abolition of the Temporary Housing Permit system, the illegal
occupant's permit had been cancelled. It was at this point she saw a copy
of the permit that gave the occupant the right to one apartment, not the
whole duplex. In 2003 Natasha's mother started a lawsuit against the
illegal occupant. She sued on behalf of the family on the grounds that
according to his Temporary Housing Permit, the occupant had only been
entitled to an apartment, not the whole duplex nor the garage and cellar,
which the occupant and his family were using illegally. The case was
finally resolved when the illegal occupant received alternative accommodation that he agreed to accept. In March 2004 Natasha's mother sued
for compensation from both the occupant and Croatian state for damages
incurred from 1997 to 2004.

Those who did not actively attempt to repossess their homes or press
the state to provide alternative housing saw little improvement in the
quality of their existence. While Serbs were considerably worse off than
ethnic Croats from Bosnia, individuals and families from both ethnic
groups could be found living in collective centres for the best part of a
decade. The most disadvantaged included ethnic Serb tenancy rights
holders such as Rado and Mile. With the cancellation of their tenancy
rights through the courts, there was little opportunity to appeal as
Natasha's mother had done. One couple, who had appealed to the
European Court of Human Rights, had been ill-advised by a local NGO,
filing their case before Croatia had ratified the European Convention.
They consequently received a negative decision and now felt completely
dependent on the state to resolve their housing situation. In the meantime
their existence in the collective centre was characterized by monotony
and loneliness. The mother described how she spends an average day:

We watch TV. Maybe we do some knitting. We play cards. It's monotonous. We
can go out but we're not interested in it. We go to Sisak, then return. It's maybe
two hours. (Radojka, interview with the author, Sisak area, 20 April 2004)

THE PROSPECT OF RETURN

The above findings raise two important themes for consideration: in the first instance, the issue of agency and the prospect of return and integration; in the second, the nature of the return options available.

The returning refugees, displaced persons and settlers all exercised little control over their migratory paths. Regional policies, as well as programmes on repatriation from third countries, substantially influenced a pattern of forced returns to Croatia. As illustrated by their migratory histories, mass evictions of Croatian Serbs and Bosnian Croats from parts of Bosnia have fuelled the migration to Croatia and created two distinct patterns of settlement, structured according to ethno-centric policies and governmental programmes which favoured ethnic Croats.

The effects of the war on refugee flows and the political course of the conflicts in the former Yugoslavia also conditioned the experience of refugees and their current options regarding return and reintegration. Those who settled inside Croatia generally experienced more dislocation than those who settled in Serbia. Those who fled their homes in 1991, for example, were able to settle in Eastern Slavonia (where they enjoyed greater protection during the Serbian occupation), but like Rado and Mile, given the course of the war, the liberation campaigns waged by the Croatian Army and the return of occupied land to the Croatian government following the withdrawal of the United Nations, these migrants were ultimately unable to put down extensive roots and develop networks of support. Moreover, since they were not refugees they were among the last to receive assistance from refugee organizations and international agencies. Refugees who settled at least temporarily in Serbia still enjoyed the opportunity to go back and forth, thus preserving the option of integrating into Serbia or returning to Croatia. Given the structural constraints described above, the notion of being proactive in order to improve one's lot is of limited value. As illustrated in the case of Natasha's mother, those who owned property were able to exercise their rights, albeit through lengthy and complicated legal processes. Those whose homes were destroyed as well as former tenancy rights holders did not have these options.

The degree to which migrants can exercise control over their lives, make important choices and address problems such as securing permanent housing turns on a number of factors, most important of which are ethnic identity, property ownership, and time spent in exile and away from home. Property ownership and the lack of options abroad are identified as important factors in the decision to return and the extent to

which migrants are prepared to do battle with official bodies. Other
factors, including the extent to which migrants enjoy family support and
have access to social networks as well as the degree to which they have
been able to participate in community structures, events and programmes,
also play a critical role in the degree to which returning migrants can
exercise personal autonomy and improve their living conditions. These
factors, however, were often inter-connected with the primary determinants discussed above. The most vulnerable tended to be minorities who
neither owned property, had family support nor had much involvement in
community-based associations.

These findings present a variety of return and reintegration experiences
and suggest a range of return scenarios.

Bosnian Croats who fled conflict in Herzegovina and Central Bosnia,
such as Marinko, Vesna and Zelijko, enjoyed an altogether privileged
status in Croatia. The settlers, with their Croatian citizenship, had the
right to work and vote, were fully integrated into Croatia and now form
the majority in some cities such as Knin. The settlers' dependence on the
Croatian state, their employment as migrant labour in place of local Serbs
and the fact that they had been settled in defensive positions such as
along the border with Herzegovina, strengthened Croatia's historic claim
to certain regions and may be considered a policy of settlement as ethnic
colonization.

Displaced persons who remained inside Croatia and refugees who
settled in Bosnia had altogether different experiences from refugees who
fled to Serbia. Internally displaced Serbs, especially those who self-
identified as 'remained', were generally worse off than refugees who
settled in Serbia. Internally displaced Serbs had generally been evicted or
threatened with eviction from parts of Croatia or from inside Bosnia and
had to rely on the Croatian state while their final housing status was
being determined.

The above findings serve to illustrate that the majority of Serbian
returnees were elderly and no longer in the workforce. These returns
were motivated by a mix of factors: the promise of a pension, lack of
economic opportunities in Serbia, housing ownership in Croatia, senti-
mental attachments and regional return policies (including compulsory
evictions and restrictive laws prohibiting the ownership of secondary
homes). Thus we can address another category – the return of retirement.

As in the case of Natasha, we discern a category of younger returnees
who settled as a result of housing repossession. Most retirees also
returned as a result of home repossession and have few options other than
to return. The case of Natasha and her family highlights a particular
sub-group of former refugees who were able to return only as a result of

judicial intervention and personal advocacy. It is important to note that cases where the returnee was able to repossess his home without the need for further investment were rare (see also Ivanisevic 2009).

There is a final category of migrants who were unable to return to permanent homes and remained on the margins of Croatian society. These former holders of tenancy rights mostly lacked support structures and were especially vulnerable (e.g. Rado and Mile).

CONCLUSION

This chapter documents the situation during and after the war in Croatia when attempts to marginalize the minority Serb population effectively created a multi-layered society where different groups of citizens enjoyed varying degrees of access to essential resources, including housing and employment. The effects of war and the nature of the discriminatory post-conflict environment gave rise to three categories of migrant seeking integration in Croatian society: refugee-settlers (Bosnian Croats), cross-border returnees (former refugees); and internal returnees (Serb IDPs who settled inside Croatia). While ethnic Croats from Bosnia were fully incorporated into the Croatian state and were able to make the transition from refugee to citizen, their situation stood in marked contrast to the Serbian minority. Governmental support to Bosnian Croats in the form of invitations, grants and aid facilitated their transition and integration that could be characterized as resettlement through ethnic colonization. This process of differentiating between the Croatian majority and the Serbian minority, however, also created further polarization within the Serbian minority. The Serbs became divided on the basis of property ownership, time spent abroad, family support and access to social networks, as well as the degree to which they were able to participate in community structures. The process of differentiation is most marked from 1998 onwards, when there was an increase in international pressure and when the UNTAES region was returned to Croatia. The migration of Serbs from the Danube region back to Krajina and Western Slavonia, coupled with increasingly vocal criticism from international donors, opened the door to a variety of return options and created new categories of returnee which enjoyed vastly different opportunities to exercise their rights to mobility.

NOTES

1. This agency has been renamed several times. It was first renamed the Ministry of Public Works, Reconstruction, and Construction Office for Expelled Persons, Refugees and Returnees. It is now part of the Ministry of Tourism, Sea and Development.
2. The *Lora* case involved eight former members of the 72nd Military Police Company – Tomislav Duić, Tonči Vrkić, Miljenko Bajić, Josip Bikić, Davor Banić, Emilio Bungur, Ante Gudić and Andjelko Botić – indicted for war crimes against civilians between March and September 1992. The prosecution said the men humiliated, abused and tortured their mainly Serb prisoners, causing the deaths of two, Nenad Knežević and Gojko Bulović, and leaving two, Milosav Katalina and Djordje Katić, seriously injured.
3. According to the OSCE office in Vukovar, in 2001 there was only one Roma business in Vukovar and more than 500 people of Roma origin had left in that year.

7. Internal migrants in Russia

Authorities continued to require intercity travelers to show their domestic
passports when buying tickets to travel via air, railroad, water, or road.
(Quoted in US Department of State, Bureau of Democracy,
Human Rights and Labor 2014)

INTRODUCTION

This chapter explores the effects of residency policies on the rights to
freedom of movement in Russia. The setting for this study is Moscow, a
city that has enjoyed a particular status as an exclusive centre that
historically restricted the admission of residents from other regions. Since
the collapse of the Soviet Union, Moscow's economy has ballooned,
attracting migrants from across the country. Many migrants arrive
spontaneously in search of jobs. Even more come as a result of targeted
managed migration programmes (Blitz 2007; Migration Policy Centre
2013; Russian Life 2006; Yablokova 2014). In addition to being a key
economic driver of modern Russia, Moscow has established itself as a
recognized powerbase that, under the leadership of former Mayor Yuri
Luzhkov, has confronted the federal administration over economic policies and has consequently been a target for Putin's recentralizing agenda.
One key aspect of the new assertiveness of the municipal government has
been the use of registration controls to manage the flow of migrants into
the city.

While there is a long history of residential and territorial stratification
in Russia (Blitz 2007; Höjdestrand 2003; Matthews 1993; Shearer 2004),
the reorganization of Russia since the collapse of Communism has seen
the extension of greater individual rights to free movement and settlement (Codagnone 1998a, b; Light 1995). With the introduction of a new
Constitution in 2001, Russians were formally granted freedom of movement. Article 27, paragraph 1 of the Russian Constitution states, 'Everyone who is lawfully staying on the territory of the Russian Federation
shall have the right to freedom of movement and to choose the place to
stay and reside.' This provision is conditioned on the requirement that
individuals register their place of residence within the Russian Federation

for periods of longer than 90 days as set out in Article 3 of the Law on the Right of Russian Citizens to Freedom of Movement, the Choice of a Place of Stay and Residence (1993, amended 2004). The Federal Law No. 127-FZ of 2 November 2004, which amended the above Article, stipulates that registration does not affect the constitutional rights of Russian citizens:

> Registration or non-registration may not serve as a ground or condition for the implementation of the rights and freedoms of citizens, provided for by the Constitution of the Russian Federation, the laws of the Russian Federation, the Constitutions and laws of the Republics within the Russian Federation.

In practice registration has been used to undermine the right to freedom of movement and has made it especially hard for some migrants to settle in cities such as Moscow.

This chapter investigates the conditions of skilled migrants living without proof of residency (registration) in Moscow. It also explores how the use of municipal laws has instituted new inequalities, based on differentiated options for mobility as described in terms of three new categories of citizenship. It begins with a brief history of residency controls in the Soviet Union and their revision during the Russian Federation's first 15 years of democratic rule, and goes on to describe the everyday obstacles that limit new migrants' access and participation in Moscow. The empirical basis for this study draws upon data gathered during field visits to Moscow in January 2005, when interviews ($n^1 = 30$) and focus groups (4) were conducted with migrants from other regions, and again in winter 2006 when further interviews were conducted with employers ($n^2 = 6$). Participants included a mix of 3:2 men to women; 80 per cent were ethnic Russian; all had access to the internet and were educated beyond degree level. Additional research and telephone interviews were conducted in spring 2011 and 2013.

THE PROPISKA IN THE SOVIET REGIME

'Propiska' literally means record and was used to designate place of residence in the internal passports required by Soviet law from 1932 onwards. While the propiska stamp had its antecedents in Tsarist Russia, when residency permits were used to tie serfs to the land (Matthews 1993; Rubins 1988; Schaible 2001), the propiska system came into effect during the height of Stalin's programmes of industrialization and collectivization. By restricting access to scarce resources, including food and housing (Shearer 2004), registration under the propiska quickly served to record the movement of people within the Soviet Union, demarcating those fit for inclusion or exclusion in the greater Socialist project. Living space was also allocated (zhilploshad) on the basis of nine square metres per adult (Höjdestrand 2003). Even though it had no constitutional foundation, the propiska epitomized the extension of the state into the lives of everyday Soviets. By the 1950s it had expanded across the former Soviet Union (Schaible 2001). It remained unchallenged until 1991, after which it was abolished and replaced by a system of registration controls with many similar characteristics that continued to regulate the right to residency. This section examines why the tradition of restricting mobility was carried over from the Soviet era into the contemporary period.

During phases of intensive economic development and agricultural collectivization, the propiska was used to curb the flight of migrants from rural areas to the growing industrial centres, above all the regime-zones of Moscow and Leningrad (Matthews 1993). Since only those who were able to secure the official stamp enjoyed access to civil, social and political rights such as employment and voting in key regions, the propiska acted as a pre-condition to settlement and also controlled social relations. It enabled the authorities to track the whereabouts of residents (Human Rights Watch 1998) and also served as a part of a broader campaign of internal security and terror.

The propiska became central to the state's obsession with socially engineering Soviet citizens. According to David Shearer its surveillance function reflected Stalin's preoccupation with borders and territorial security and was a vital part of the state apparatus that enabled the Soviet leadership to redistribute resources, colonize land, and identify, control and exterminate specific populations (Shearer 2004, pp. 880–81). 'The dual aim of the passport and residency laws – to count (*uchet*) and to cleanse (*ochistit*) – was clearly stated in the preamble to the December 27 decree that initiated the system' (Shearer 2004, p. 840). This was evidenced by official discrimination against designated ethnic and national populations,[1] including deportation and executions. Rather than incorporate certain groups, the state introduced a limit system (limitchiki) that addressed the gaps in the labour force by establishing quotas of those guest workers engaged on time-limited contracts, providing them with temporary registration and collective housing.

Just before the Soviet Union collapsed, the propiska system was starting to show visible cracks (Schaible 2001). In 1991 the USSR Constitutional Supervision Committee ruled that the propiska laws violated freedom of movement and outlawed the practice. Rather than impose strict controls on movement, the committee determined that the state was only permitted to ask migrants to inform authorities of their place of residence (Katanian 1998). This ruling, however, came to no avail since the Soviet Union collapsed before the law came into effect in January 1992. Fearing a rush of migrants and motivated by security fears and racist claims principally against Caucasians and other non-Russians (Pilkington 2002; Vitkovskaya 2002), regional authorities in Moscow, St Petersburg, Krasnodar and Stavropol quickly reinstated the propiska through regional laws in defiance of earlier constitutional rulings (Cherepova 1999; Human Rights Watch 1997; Rubins 1988; Schaible 2001).

RESIDENCY RESTRICTIONS IN CONTEMPORARY MOSCOW

In 1993 the federal government formally abolished the propiska system and replaced it with a system of registration. Both the terms 'propiska' and 'registration' are currently in use and, in spite of the fact that the Russian Constitutional Court ruled in 1996, 1997 and 1998 against the use of restrictions to the right to free movement (see Parliamentary Assembly, Council of Europe 2001), the new system is remarkably similar to the instruments used in Soviet times (Blitz 2007; Rubins 1988). According to the Russian Federal Migration Service, registration is administered by 'territorial bodies of federal executive authority, authorized to exercise the functions of control and supervision in the field of migration, in other areas – local government' (Federal Migration Service 2013). All Russian nationals seeking to stay longer than 90 days in a city other than their own are required to register by providing their identity documents, a statement of residence and a document which provides evidence of tenancy or a letter of invitation. In principle the use of registration assumes the citizen has the right to free movement as opposed to the former system that was based on gaining permission prior to settlement (Katanian 1998). In 2001 approximately three million people were estimated to be 'effectively non-persons in the eyes of the law' (Schaible 2001, p. 344) and were recorded as encountering significant barriers that prevented them from enjoying the right to free movement as well as many other civil and political rights.[2] This figure does not include the estimated five to six million illegal workers in Russia (Russian Life 2006).

The Constitutional Court has attempted to uphold the right to free movement but has been constrained by both the extent of its rulings and weaknesses in the judicial system to ensure implementation (Blitz 2007;

Rubins 1988). Over the past 15 years, the Court's rulings have addressed elements of the propiska system but have yet to break the back of authorities that insist on controlling migration and settlement. In the case of Lyudmila Sitalova, who in April 1995 had claimed that the housing code violated Article 40.1 of the Constitution (that provided everyone with the right to a home and freedom from being arbitrarily deprived of a home), the Court's ruling simply upheld the right of a tenant to host guests in a rented space. In 1996 the Constitutional Court issued a more declarative ruling on the payment of registration fees that it found unconstitutional. This ruling enabled the Court to reproach regional governments which were charging excessively high fees, above all Moscow city government, that had been requiring new residents to pay a fee of approximately US$7000 in order to receive a residence permit. In an important ruling the Constitutional Court struck down the Moscow region law on 2 July 1997, claiming that it acted as a regional tax that discriminated against residents' rights to live anywhere in the Russian Federation (NUPI 1997).

In spite of the above decisions and the provision that registration should be free, city authorities have been condemned for extracting fees from migrants and refusing to register others. The 2013 Human Rights Report on Country Practices produced by the US State Department notes that:

> Authorities often refused to provide government services to individuals without internal passports or proper registration, and many regional governments continued to restrict this right through residential registration rules that closely resembled Soviet-era regulations. Darker-skinned persons from the Caucasus or of African or Asian origin were often singled out for document checks. There were credible reports that police arbitrarily imposed fines on unregistered persons in excess of legal requirements or demanded bribes. (US Department of State, Bureau of Democracy, Human Rights, and Labor 2014)

What is most striking is that the wording of the 2013 report on freedom of movement in Russia has hardly changed over the past decade. The 2003 State Department report on the situation in 2002 records that 'despite constitutional protections for citizens' freedom of movement, local governments restricted this right, in particular by denying local residency permits to new settlers from other areas of the country' (US Department of State, Bureau of Democracy, Human Rights, and Labor 2003).

The continued refusal to implement the law on registration warrants further consideration.

First, it should be noted that even though power over registration policy was entrusted to regional bodies, and in the case of Moscow the city government, all the regions of the Russian Federation with the exception of Chechnya had strong incentives not to undermine the central state, treating migration as a matter of internal security rather than civil rights. The accusation that migrants (undesirable elements) are often refugees and internally displaced persons from other parts of the former Soviet Union who pose a security threat (Pilkington 2002) was made by governments composed of like-minded apparatchiks (professional members of the Communist party) (Loiberg 1998). Thus the Putin government, which successfully reprimanded regional governments for their abuse of power over taxation and natural resources, has been particularly tolerant of sub-national efforts to restrict in-migration in spite of Constitutional Court rulings and condemnations by human rights groups (Human Rights Watch 2011; Light 1995, p. 15).

Secondly, over the past 25 years the pattern of internal migration did not provide an immediate cause for a radical change in policy. During the last phases of Communism and throughout Russia's first decade as a democratic state, both inter-regional and intra-regional migration were remarkably consistent. In numerical terms the level of inter-regional and intra-regional migration in Russia appears profoundly important – between 1990 and 1996 about 23 million people changed their residence, either within the same region (12.5 million) or from one region to another (10.6 million) (Codagnone 1998b). Recent empirical studies, however, suggest that Russia's transition from state Socialism had little impact on overall internal migration rates (Gerber 2005), a finding confirmed by the International Organization for Migration (IOM 2012). This finding stands in contrast to the level of immigration of ethnic Russians from former Soviet Republics and the increasing number of migrants from neighbouring states (Migration Policy Centre 2013; Pilkington 2002). Thus there was little attention given to the revised laws on registration and the residency rights of migrants.

Thirdly, the prevalence of clientelism provides a potent explanation for the continued use of unconstitutional and economically disadvantageous practices that prevent skilled migrants from settling in Moscow and leaves them vulnerable to abuse (White 2003). As one former journalist explained, 'Everyone working in state institutions doesn't have problems [like other citizens] because the laws were designed for them' (Galina, Moscow, 25 January 2005). One argument for former Mayor Luzhkov's defiance centred on the need to support his large bureaucracy. As a local analyst put it, 'new laws ensure the flow of new bribes' (Khrushcheva 1999). For this reason, Human Rights Watch claimed that 'there is not only no incentive to remove the regulations, there is indeed an active incentive to continue to invoke them' (Human Rights Watch 1998, p. 2). Matthew Light shares this view and notes that sub-national governments have been reluctant to pay the social costs of migration, and above all the added burden on the housing market, especially while they reap the rewards of fee-based systems, fines and controls on migration (Light 1995).

Finally, it is important to note that the current challenges to citizens' rights to free movement often involve third parties, including employers and landlords who must approve documents and engage with bureaucracies. For both employers and landlords the lack of registration not only adds to their administrative burden but also leaves them vulnerable to exploitation (Blitz 2007; Höjdestrand 2003, p. 5).

FREEDOM OF MOVEMENT AND CITIZENSHIP

The central theme that this case study explores is the effect of registration policies on inequality. Interviews with new migrants to Moscow explored the effects of registration on several aspects of their lives. One key objective was to examine how their situation now differed from native Muscovites. Questions asked focused on the ways in which participants interpreted their claims to citizenship and considered: (a) type of residency status; (b) definitions of being unregistered; (c) sense of self and personal identity regarding residency status; (d) legal barriers; (e) moral and social issues associated with registration; (f) challenges of dealing with state authorities; (g) access to civic services; (h) democratic challenges; and (i) effects of residency on personal life.

While the participants represented an elite section of Russian society, it is worth recording that more than 3 million Russians have been denied rights to residency and free movement. The participants' experiences were typical of new migrants to Moscow and other cities and regions within Russia. Many regional governments have continued to restrict residency, the most egregious violators being the Stavropol Krai, the North Caucasus and Voronezh, near the border with Ukraine (see Human Rights Watch 1998; Katanian 1998; Rubins 1988). In spite of their educational status the participants were representative of new migrants to Moscow in that they were young, did not have family or long-standing roots in the city and relied on alternative sources of information to manage their lives – primarily the internet.

Interview and focus group data highlighted how the process of registration both continued Soviet practices and diverged from the former system of propiska and internal passports, creating new modes of exclusion. The findings also recorded the arbitrariness of the system and regional discrepancies in its application that polarized relations between newcomers and established Muscovites. Economic discrimination against new migrants led to political marginalization, separation and alienation for most, but some participants used role-playing and problem-solving tactics to get past the restrictions. A small number of participants engaged in dissent and opted out of the system altogether.

ARBITRARINESS AND REGIONALIZATION

While all participants were now able to travel internally within Russia, their ability to settle in Moscow was still compromised by numerous restrictions that appeared quite arbitrary. One participant from Lermontov explained that the process of registration was in some respects even more arduous than previous practices and now seemed quite ridiculous, given the relative openness of Russian society and knowledge of other national systems. He explained how the use of registration now created increased social distance between Russian citizens:

> Imagine this. You go from London to Glasgow and someone asks you why did you come? And if you go to a hospital they tell you to come back to London. You'll go on the streets of Glasgow and the local police will check your status. In Russia this is normal procedure. (Yuri, Moscow, 21 January 2005)

Many individuals complained that they were arbitrarily stopped, searched and even arrested:

> You're just waiting for a bus and didn't touch anybody. I've been picked out of a crowd of people. I was stopped at the metro by militia, so I asked them to show me their documents. The militia took my documents without even looking. 'You seem to be the cleverest here – no one asks for documents. Let's go to the station.' (Karen, Moscow, 23 January 2005)

Several argued that the arbitrary way in which the police and public agencies targeted migrants reflected broader problems with law enforcement and the rule of law in Russia, undermining their civil rights on a daily basis:

> There is a Constitutional Court decision that says we just need to inform the authorities where we live. But it hasn't been realized in practice because the militia interferes with our registration. We have the right to be here and to be

registered and must always prove we have the right to live here ... Our officials just don't believe us. (Karen, Moscow, 23 January 2005)

One advocate explained that the mid 1990s saw the mass exit of professionals from the law enforcement sector. He charged that the militia worked to conceal their lawless actions and were assisted by the prosecution service and court systems that refused to take on cases of abuse. When such cases did reach court, they resulted in acquittals. There was evidence of a compact between the police, public prosecution service and judiciary: 'Instead of taking correct measures they [law enforcement bodies] just took short-term measures for show – in order to calm down people in society and minimize damage' (Mikhail A., Moscow, 24 January 2005).

Many hours of conversation focused on the prevalence of arbitrary arrest by police and militia and the continued practice of discrimination against non-Muscovites by state-owned enterprises. A central theme of these interviews exposed a widely held belief that a level of arbitrariness and lawlessness undermined the development of a culture of individual rights that applied equally to all Russians:

> Of course registration demolished our human rights. There is a law on Russian territory that everyone has freedom of movement according to the Constitution. For instance to walk to work, to clinic and you are stopped by militiamen. Why are you here? They say return to your hometown. I tell them I'm Russian and they say prove it. I show them my documents and they say these can all be bought on the Arbat. (Karen, Moscow, 23 January 2005)

The director of an advocacy group stated that the lack of public accountability was at the root of the arbitrariness and lawlessness described by the interview participants: 'This is Putin's style of governing. Everything explodes, submarines sink but no one takes responsibility. People are just replaced' (Mikhail A., Moscow, 24 January 2005). Others complained that the arbitrariness of the current system was built into the design of the registration laws. One former student from Grozny described the contemporary practice of registration as a 'vicious circle', noting that residency was often a pre-requisite for registration (Ivanov, Moscow, 22 January 2005). His friend elaborated on what he described as an unresolved problem: 'Even if you buy a flat, you need to register ownership. But for that you need at least temporary registration. If you have no registration, all your documents won't be accepted' (Aleksey I., Moscow, 23 January 2005). He then explained that registration rested on multiple factors, including the goodwill of public officials who, if they did not like the look of someone, could determine both the outcome and length of the registration process by refusing to provide the necessary forms (Aleksey I., Moscow, 23 January 2005).

Interviews with employers recorded that the inconsistent reading and application of the law on registration also applied to the corporate sector, making employment conditional upon registration with the city and regional governments, even though it was beyond the employer's remit. Several reasons were given for this practice, including ignorance of the current laws and the potential intrusion of state authorities in a company's affairs:

> Some employees demand a permanent registration in the Moscow region as a condition for employment, which is of course an essential violation of the constitutional human rights. But we can do nothing about it because a labour commission may come to a company and start checking. Even though the registration issue is not the labour commissioner's business, he may ask: this employee has a permanent contract in your company, so why isn't he/she registered in Moscow? A person may live in Moscow or change his/her address every three months and whether a person is registered or not concerns only him/her and the local authorities. A company isn't liable for the registration issue at all. (Human Resource Manager, Moscow, 24 February 2006)

While Russian policies on registration continued Soviet practices, they also introduced distinctly new features (above all the regionalization of service provision) that negatively affected the way in which citizenship was experienced. The devolution of authority to the sub-national governments, coupled with the growth of the private sector and the increase in regulations and intervention by state bodies, reportedly undermined the quality of life available to non-registered migrants. Participants insisted that, even though the registration process was now the legal responsibility of the regional and city authorities, the application and acceptance of the registration procedure varied widely from one locality to another, giving rise to further claims of arbitrary enforcement of the registration policy and the creation of second-class citizens.

One Ukrainian national described how the increase in regulations added a new layer of complication and precariousness, affecting even the most mundane activities. While she was free to move from one city to another, she was forced to shop around for particular services, including bank accounts and SIM cards (Alesiya, Moscow, 23 January 2005). Her Russian associate, Aleksey, illustrated the absurd geographical discrepancies in the application of registration policy. He related the tale of a young woman registered in Moscow who was denied the right to purchase a SIM card for her mobile phone in Volgograd but did so successfully in St Petersburg (Aleksey I., Moscow, 23 January 2005). It was simply a matter of chance as to where and when one's registration status would crop up and complicate the course of everyday life.

Yet beyond the mundane examples of purchasing SIM cards, decentralization of policy over registration also introduced far-reaching effects on the degree to which unregistered migrants were able to access social and educational services in Moscow. One woman noted that in order to have a baby she would be forced either to seek out private treatment or travel to her city of origin. David, a Russian citizen originally from Georgia, spoke about how he needed to wait until the very beginning of the school year in order to learn if a place was available for his child to attend a local Moscow school (David, Moscow, 29 January 2005). Others less fortunate complained that they were subject to costly penalties, as illustrated in the case of Sergei, a former officer in the Soviet Army. Sergei had been registered in the Soviet Republic of Latvia (where he enjoyed a different legal status) and was now forced to pay between US$8000 and US$10,000 to regulate his papers so he could receive medical care in Moscow (Sergei, Moscow, 29 January 2005).

ECONOMIC DISCRIMINATION AND NEW OPPORTUNITIES

New migrants to Moscow encountered several types of discrimination that undermined their quality of life by adding to their financial burden. Unlike native Muscovites, non-registered individuals and even those with temporary registration were denied credit and loans from banks but were still required to pay for rental utilities in advance. Others noted that the growth of the private sector had created new possibilities for circumventing the system – for example, by paying for services such as health insurance and schooling. The fact that they still required some form of documentation to get around the system demonstrated their reliance on political authority, and for this reason they may be categorized as 'conditional subjects'. Ironically, new market opportunities now enabled Russian citizens – both registered Moscow landlords and unregistered residents, such as conditional subjects – to profit from the system of registration and even to expose some of its more ridiculous tenets. For example, consider 'zhilploshad', the proposed allocation of living space:

> If you are the owner of one square metre of an apartment, the law allows you to register one square metre of a flat. So you can register 100 people in one flat. Of course you [the tenant] need to go to court and pay for communal

services, about 1100 Roubles for six months, if the owner of the flat agrees. (Aleksey I., Moscow, 23 January 2005)

Most participants identified as conditional subjects reported that the growth of private sector activity had helped to improve the economic prospects of new migrants. Rather than relying exclusively on the state, the fate of new migrants was now bound up with the policies of their employers.

> Sometimes it is impossible to get a job in state-run ministries without registration. It is quite difficult to find a job even in banks. In Nikoil and Rolisip investment companies there is an unwritten rule to take people without residency. (Aleksey I., Moscow, 23 January 2005)

> I am now working in a staff agency and 70 per cent of the people there have no registration. Employers now accept people without registration. They say if you can work, we'll help you. When I started working, at first they said they only need Muscovites, they only understand the mentality. Now it's changing. (Yelena, Moscow, 23 January 2005)

> Five years ago it [registration] was the first question I was asked. Now skills are more important. (Yarloslav, Moscow, 23 January 2005)

These views were confirmed in interviews with employers in medium to large sized private firms. The Human Resources Manager of a metal-works company with offices in Moscow, St Petersburg, Yekaterinburg and Samara explained that her firm was bound by law to disregard registration in the selection of staff:

> As to Russian citizens ... we have a labour code which says that to be employed a person has to provide a passport, a [degree certificate], a pension certificate and a military card, if applicable. If a person does not have any of these documents I as an employer may reject employment. All other documents are not mandatory. In case a candidate does not have a registration or a tax number certificate, I as an employer do not have [the] right to refuse employment to him/her because of these reasons. (Human Resources Manager, Moscow company, 24 February 2006)

While the offer of employment ensured that participants could enjoy an easier life, it is important to record that those without registration did not enjoy the same level of protection as local-born Muscovites or the same economic trajectories as registered professionals in similar positions. Even with a job offer, the most fortunate of participants were denied important civil and economic rights that could substantially affect their long-term security – for example, the right to license businesses and inherit property – which reinforced their claims of being second-class citizens:

I am practically a Muscovite. I have a circle of friends from anti-Soviet times. I have no problems to get a job because I work within this circle. Now I have mandatory medical insurance because I got it at a time when I could. If I lose it, I can't renew it. I am now waiting for documents for permanent residency. I can't inherit a flat because my documents are not valid. (Vadim, Moscow, 23 January 2005)

Another distinction between Muscovites and unregistered migrants that hindered their economic opportunities was convincing even friendly employers of their intentions to remain in Moscow. One employer reported that, in spite of the legal mandates, non-residents did not have the same attachments as local Muscovites, and this could prove detrimental to both their retention and the quality of their work. The co-owner of a stained glass window company explained why he no longer employed unregistered staff:

Earlier I didn't care about whether my employee has a registration in Moscow or not. But later I just stopped hiring people from other cities. Nothing holds these people here. They can steal something, borrow money and slip away. For me is important not the fact of the registration itself, but that a person feels home, comfortable in Moscow, that this person is a settled person, not a nomad.

Muscovites have normally nothing or little to worry about, that's why they can concentrate on work. Non-Muscovites have many things to worry about, a lot of problems to solve. It affects [the] quality of their work adversely. (Igor, Moscow, 8 March 2006)

POLITICAL MARGINALIZATION, SEPARATION AND ALIENATION

An essential difference in the quality of citizenship experienced by native Muscovites and unregistered Russian citizens concerns voting provisions. Research participants were unable to vote in local Moscow elections and also experienced difficulty voting in federal elections, even though they met the formal citizenship criteria. Explanations for political exclusion included the extraordinarily complex system of public administration regulations and, most importantly, the supremacy of residency as the right that granted access to other civil rights. One man stated that: 'If you have legal registration you can vote in federal elections but it takes a huge amount of effort' (Aleks, Moscow, 22 January 2006). Another assumed that voting would require a return journey to his city of birth:

I have never voted. First everything was legal, then I didn't have the possibility of course. I am living quite close – only five hours by train – but still I don't want to make a special action [journey] for voting. (Anton, Moscow, 22 January 2005)

In response to the question 'How do people feel about not being able to vote?', participants expressed varying degrees of dissatisfaction. One admitted that he had 'got used to it', and while it was not 'nice', elections were not important for him since he did not consider himself a 'patriot'. His colleague was less complacent:

People are angry about the fact they can't vote in local elections. Of course we can go to court but the Russian system doesn't work on the basis of precedent ... so one win doesn't lead to change of practice. (Konstantin, Moscow, 25 January 2005)

Fellow migrant Alexei added that he felt a sense of injustice and asked, 'How can registered Muscovites have more rights than other Russian citizens?' (Alexei I., Moscow, 23 January 2005).

In addition to their political disenfranchisement, one irrefutable similarity between Soviet and contemporary Russian regional practices includes the use of registration as a means of social separation. A professional from Archangelsk explained that since Moscow was always the most desirable city where many social benefits were concentrated, 'people in power had to limit those benefits' (Aleks, Moscow, 22 January 2005). The net losers of this policy were the unregistered newcomers who lacked long-term personal security. One migrant described the effect of separation as being 'on an island with no inhabitants' (Sergei, Moscow, 23 January 2005).

The participants interviewed argued that since 1991 the use of registration controls and their implementation by state and regional agencies have left open the possibility for continued discrimination on the basis of residency, which was substantially similar to former Soviet practices. Both ethnic Russians and nationals from parts of the former Soviet Union reported having experienced discrimination in the form of police harassment, denial of access to essential services and poor treatment in Moscow hospitals. Some women spoke about living in fear of the authorities. Kristina, who admitted 'hating the state and all state institutions', described how she would seal herself off in order not to come into contact with the police: 'I didn't open the door. I warned friends that they should call by mobile or intercom. I also warned neighbours but we still have a problem because we can't complain to local militia' (Kristina, Moscow, 22 January 2005).

The effects of the discriminatory treatment described above fostered a profound sense of alienation; interviewees self-identified as 'marginal'. In the words of a Human Resources Manager originally from Siberia, they have been 'thrown out of society' (Yelena, Moscow, 23 January 2005). Her Ukrainian colleague shared similar sentiments, explaining that her status as both non-registered and non-Russian affected the way in which she was treated in social circles as well: 'We feel like second-class citizens. I feel like I have a big load on me. The majority of my friends are Russians. Sometimes this is an embarrassment' (Alysia, Moscow, 22 January 2005).

Male research participants also described how their status as newcomers left them embarrassed and excluded. Sergei reported that when he was denied the right to marry in Moscow, his fiancée declined his marriage proposal for fear of exposing his non-registered status to her family and friends. Several others spoke of a hostile environment that permeated both their social and personal lives. As second-class citizens non-registered individuals lacked protection and were exposed to blackmail and abuse by the authorities as well as by greedy employers and landlords. Their vulnerability was compounded by the fact that many were unable to retaliate through legal channels, again for lack of registration. Recognizing that he would face similar discrimination, Alysia's fellow Ukrainian associate, Ruslan, decided it was preferable to remain a non-national and use Moscow as an economic base: 'We wanted to become Russian citizens but felt if I became Ukrainian it would be better because Ukraine treats its citizens better' (Ruslan, Moscow, 22 January 2005). Others stated that they too chose to live as foreign nationals rather than validate the Russian system that had victimized them.

ROLE OF CIVIC ACTORS, PROBLEM SOLVING AND ROLE PLAYING

While there were many similarities between Soviet procedures and the practices employed by Moscow city and regional governments regarding the application of registration policy, one particularly interesting development concerned the way in which individuals responded to the restrictions placed upon them by the establishment. Participants described in interviews how they employed sophisticated diversionary tactics and engaged in role playing and problem solving to escape from the scrutiny and interference of state authorities. Specifically, participants explained how they would resist the police, which was invariably cited as the principal authority most likely to infringe upon citizens' rights on the grounds of verifying registration documents.

In response to frequent police harassment, a number of members of the advocacy group, Nelegal, produced information guides and explained how new migrants could minimize the chances of abuse by the authorities. There was a shared belief that the police used profiling techniques to identify targets for extortion and were, in the words of one human rights activist, 'good psychologists' who could 'pick out from a crowd those who can be exploited' (Mikhail A., Moscow, 24 January 2005). A bright IT consultant offered a general rubric that was based on prevention of harassment and the understanding of the police profiling techniques:

> First you must avoid the police. It's quite easy. You can divide migrants into several groups: poor, rich, smart, stupid. All these controls in the streets ... documents are only checked so money can be taken. First of all you must be well dressed ... Moscow tries to protect the highest level of living. Poor people are embarrassed by the militia, and it is easiest to exploit them and people who can't protect themselves – those who have never read laws or Constitution. Second, don't be in a hurry or too drunk. Third, don't call attention by carrying big bags. There is a rule that if a person wears glasses he will never be stopped – or if he is carrying a newspaper. (Aleksey I., Moscow, 23 January 2005)

Aleksey's colleague, Mikhail, explained how he too used evasive tactics in the knowledge that the police used narrowly defined profiling techniques:

> If I have registration I just show it. I don't talk. I try not to look at them. I try to look like an ordinary person who is just carrying on. Often I travel with a book. But reading a book is not [a] guarantee even though the probability is a bit lower. (Mikhail B., Moscow, 23 January 2005)

Others told how they would directly confront the police by threatening legal action when stopped, or they would use sarcasm and ridicule to challenge their interrogators. One young professional reported how he would tease police who attempted to arrest him:

> Police approach you without any reason. According to law, militiamen must have reasons. I always say I am a vagabond. Then they say we'll imprison you. They don't even know the law was cancelled ten years ago. (Yuri, Moscow, 22 January 2005)

His associate, Kristina, admitted that she felt she was now reduced to playing a character, a Muscovite with crazed eyes who has a lot of problems. When stopped she would threaten the police with legal consequences, which she now considered to be more effective. She added that this was a strategic ploy: 'It's not that people trust the judiciary, it's just that they threaten the police because they are scared of laws' (Kristina, Moscow, 22 January 2005).

Arguably the costs of avoidance described above have added to the stress and anxiety of many respondents:

> We always must be pro-active and think several steps forward. I also feel constant concern and anxiety. (Galina, Moscow, 25 January 2005)

> I have to think every minute to bring registration or I can be dismissed or my employers can stop me from working officially. It is something I always have to think about. I can't say it is so stressful but it is always in the background. (Yelena, Moscow, 23 January 2005)

> It's very frustrating and irritating. It is almost constantly stressful. When I see a policeman, I feel disgust. It is terrible to think about it. (Mikhail B., Moscow, 23 January 2005)

AVOIDANCE AND CIVIC PROTEST

In interviews participants expressed how they addressed the challenges of the registration policy. Two principal routes of dissent were identified: first, avoidance by purchasing services and deliberately opting out; secondly, civic protest. Both responses reflected widespread dissatisfaction in the level of democratic entitlement they experienced, the growing degree of arbitrariness and lawlessness in Moscow, and the absence of a state they could call upon. As Mikhail retorted, 'Where is the state? We pay taxes' (Mikhail B., Moscow, 23 January 2005). In response to this question, his associates answered:

> The state is in the TV set and the state sets rules. Mostly stupid rules. (Kristina, Moscow, 22 January 2005)

> Democracy is expressed in the details. I can be stopped and arrested. (Anton, Moscow, 22 January 2005)

Others added that the state not only had a moral obligation to uphold their rights but a contractual one as well (Mikhail B., Moscow, 23 January 2005). In recognition of the state's failure to protect and provide, several participants explained that they had chosen to opt out as much as possible. One man from Nizny blatantly stated: 'The less you touch the shit the better. I prefer to pay someone to do it' (Anton, Moscow, 22 January 2005). His mode of action was affirmed by Kristina from

Krasnoyarsk, who explained why she resorted to purchasing forged documents to get the authorities off her back. She had been living in Moscow for three years and, after having registered two or three times, decided not to register any further, claiming that she simply had neither the time nor the nerves to communicate with legal bodies. She resented the process of registration that she described as a disgusting procedure 'like being interrogated'. She bought registration for US$60 and subsequently found life much simpler (Kristina, Moscow, 23 January 2005). Others commented on how they avoided local and regional state authorities by buying services, including private medical insurance, education and health care. For a number of those interviewed, highly skilled migrants working in the growing private sector, this was possible and was indeed the only way to create the sort of lives that they wanted. One woman interjected that 'the only way one can have a baby in Moscow is to pay' (Yelena, Moscow, 23 January 2005), thus illustrating the relevance of the category of conditional subjects.[3]

Another group of participants had chosen to confront the state directly through organizations such as 'My Right' that focuses on police brutality and offers legal support and a 24-hour helpline. My Right also issues complaints to the Human Rights Ombudsman and takes cases to court on behalf of victims of police brutality. As mentioned above, Nelegal provides both information and advocacy on registration issues and abuse of civil liberties. Galina Nowopaschina, one of the founders, explained how she became involved in civic protest. In 1999 a website had been set up by a concerned citizen, Sergei Biryukov, in response to restrictions imposed by the former Moscow Mayor's Office following the 1999 bombings.[4] For her part Galina was working as a Sales Manager for a subsidiary of Siemens. When she learned that she was subject to register in order to continue her work, she wrote to the head office in Germany, informing them that Siemens was violating the Russian Constitution. In response to her letter, the demand for registration was removed from Siemens' website. This action provoked considerable press interest, including articles in *Izevstia*. Galina's action was also acknowledged by fellow activist, Boris, author of a guide on how to avoid the police. He invited Galina to join a fledgling organization. With one more activist, they pioneered the creation of Nelegal, the first citizens' organization dedicated to promoting free movement in Russia.

Having served as a witness six times before the Moscow city court, Galina concluded that the organization should issue court actions against authorities that tried to prevent individuals from registering and enjoying their rights to free movement. They opposed the state of lawlessness and supported the need to protect the social rights of individuals. Galina recounted how she received a letter from one couple who were renting a room in Moscow and had been approached by the militia in search of bribes:

> I advised them to say, 'I will go to court if you continue to diminish [harass] me … I will write to the court.' Then, the militiamen stopped bothering them. People should believe they are landlords before the authorities and not slaves anymore. (Galina, Moscow, 25 January 2005)

According to Galina, the organization's greatest success was raising consciousness and changing the perception of civic protest that in turn helped to reduce the sense of fear from public authorities, including the police: 'We always say the authorities are guilty – we are not guilty. We are not anarchists. We are ready to register' (Galina, Moscow, 25 January 2005). Such actions illustrate a remarkable degree of civic participation, and thus individuals such as Galina might be better described as resident participants – their identity being determined by both their formal status and preference for political engagement.

DECENTRALIZATION, RESIDENCY AND CITIZENSHIP

The restructuring caused by the devolution of authority over migration and the state's refusal to insist on the application of Constitutional Court decisions have created a new spectrum of rights and rules that apply to distinct groups of citizens on the basis of residency, place of birth, possession of documents, ethnic attachment and appearance, as judged by the local police. Such qualifications determine access to social services as well as the enjoyment of basic rights, including the right to education and to inherit property, and thus give rise to claims of new and differentiated forms of citizenship such as Muscovite, conditional subject and resident participant, as outlined below:

1. Muscovites – residents of Moscow who as a result of birth can live in the city without the aggravation of registration; are eligible and able to vote in both federal and local elections; are able to buy, sell and inherit property; and enjoy regular access to state social services and educational establishments.
2. Conditional subjects – migrants who need to register with the authorities in order to live and work in Moscow but are often prevented from doing so and have difficulty in voting and accessing social and educational services; are barred from public employment and therefore drop out of the state sector, preferring instead to use

the private sector to achieve access to services; their actions are, however, conditional upon documents and payments.

3. Resident participants – a minority of migrants who currently live outside the law in Moscow but nonetheless insist on the implementation of constitutional and legal provisions regarding free movement and other essential civil rights; their lives are constrained by the arbitrariness and lawlessness of the regional and state systems of governance, which prevents them, like conditional subjects, from accessing state social services, educational establishments and government sector employers; while they can only operate as full citizens in their home cities, they assert their claims to national citizenship through protest.

The introduction of restrictive laws and practices regarding residency have effectively institutionalized new social identities of migrants in Moscow; for example, those identified with the organization Nelegal, the Nelegalni. These exclusive laws have by default redefined the category of Muscovites as citizens who enjoy political and economic freedoms on the basis of their residency status. One particularly distinct feature of this class of citizenship is their privileged access to the Moscow housing market. Of the three categories of citizenship there are effectively two classes consisting of Muscovites and others, namely conditional subjects and resident participants. These two categories are distinguished from each other primarily on the basis of resistance: the conditional subject finds some way (usually in the private sector) to get around the regulations, while the resident participant actively struggles against them. While many Russians seek to avoid the obstacles in their path without engaging in overt opposition, and in this sense the category of conditional subject applies to a vast majority of the population, there is an important theoretical distinction to be made in terms of the way in which these two groups experience and interpret their claims to citizenship. In the case of conditional subjects, citizenship is understood as a concept imposed by the state, as defined by laws and regulations. For resident participants, however, the concept of citizenship is more fluid and challenges the current design of civil–state relations, which defers to the state.

The deconcentration of power over residency policy has primarily empowered sub-national authorities which have gained greater access to soft money in the form of fees, fines and bribes. However, this study also documents some important developments in centre–periphery and civil–state relations. The regionalization of registration policy has, for example, indirectly undermined the state's legitimacy by casting doubt over its ability and willingness to punish unconstitutional actions and reign in recalcitrant actors, including former Moscow Mayor Luzhkov. Similarly the re-evaluation of the need for registration by the private sector and the criticism voiced by individual protestors such as Galina and groups like Nelegal have furthered weakened the state's authority over migration policy, even if it has not been accompanied by friendlier policies on registration and settlement.

There are several reasons why the deconcentration of power over migration has failed to create more liberal policies on free movement. As recorded in interview, the increasing authoritarianism of the bureaucracy (Blitz 2007; Human Rights Watch 2006; Shevtsova 2010; White 2003) and the lack of respect for civil rights and the rule of law, coupled with an unprofessional police force, traditions of racism and xenophobia, and a culture of harassment, extortion and bribe taking help to explain the lack of policy reform and the prevalence of abuse against unregistered migrants. Moreover, the relative weakness of Russian civil society in the face of an increasingly authoritarian regime also works against the prospect of effective reform.

Finally, when reviewing the perpetuation of residency restrictions and controls on mobility, the particular status of Moscow city needs to be taken into account. Moscow has historically been a catalyst for Russia's political development as both the ancient capital and seat of the Soviet empire, and many Russians accept that Muscovites have superior rights and advantages. Within Moscow, residency policies enjoy substantial local support from those who consider migration a security issue and want to see tight controls against newcomers to the city. This support may further account for the relative lack of resistance and preference of avoidance by groups such as conditional subjects to illegal policies on registration.

CONCLUSION

The history of residency and registration policy in Russia, and particularly in Moscow, records how the right to freedom of movement is constrained in practice. As this study shows, the transfer of authority over residency to Moscow city and regional governments has left many migrants subject to discriminatory regulations on mobility and denied them access to essential services, including housing, health care, education and the labour market. It also exposed potential abuse by the police and corrupt public officials who demanded registration fees and extracted bribes.

The discrimination shown to migrants from cities outside Moscow region by official bodies suggests that we may speak of new categories of citizenship based on residency status, as illustrated by the examples of Muscovites, conditional subjects and resident participants. While people born in Moscow, Russia's wealthiest city, enjoy full access to the state, including social and educational services, medical insurance and government sector employment, they also benefit by being able to buy and inherit property, one of the most significant indicators of long-term economic and personal financial health. By contrast, non-Muscovites face a different trajectory and must struggle to assert their rights to function or opt out of the state by purchasing services available through the private sector.

The application of unconstitutional laws regarding residency controls and the prevalence of arbitrary enforcement mechanisms have also created intra-group divisions. This is most apparent in the case of conditional subjects and resident participants. Although some Russians have reported feeling powerless and unable to influence the course of political decisions (White 2003), we can, by distinguishing between these two categories of non-Muscovite, better appreciate how citizenship is experienced and interpreted. The emergence of these new categories of citizenship calls into question the right to free movement and illustrates how Soviet legacies of mobility control continue to affect everyday Russians.

Finally, we note that this study has further relevance beyond Russia. Freedom of movement remains highly problematic across the former Soviet Union. In Belarus, Abkhazia and South Ossetia in Georgia and Kazakhstan, Turkmenistan, Uzbekistan and Central Asia, the propiska, entry and exit visas and similar controls remain in use.[5] Arguably, the application of these residency controls is not far removed either from China's Hukou system, which has undergone a parallel process of reform and partial relaxation but nonetheless continues to undermine the right to free movement.

NOTES

1. The Soviet state also discriminated against political dissidents, social misfits, former criminals and others who were not allowed within a 100 km range of key cities. This restriction was applied to people accused of 'parasitism' – those who could not find work and housing through the authorities – and consequently, the propiska system often led directly to the creation of homelessness (Höjdestrand 2003, p. 4).
2. According to Human Rights Watch, this includes the 1993 Russian Federation Law of Freedom of Movement and Choice of Place of Residence within the Boundaries of the

Russian Federation (FZ 5242-1), Article 12 of the International Covenant on Civil and Political Rights and, since one cannot work legally, nor receive medical treatment, nor attend state schooling without the propiska, it also includes the International Covenant on Economic, Social and Cultural Rights (Article 6) and the UN Convention on the Rights of the Child (Articles 24 and 28).

3. See Levine, Rudnitsky and Ames (2006) for an account of the costs and processes of paying for births in state hospitals.

4. In September 1999, there was a series of attacks on four apartment blocks in the Russian cities of Buynaksk, Moscow and Volgodonsk which killed 293 people and injured 651. The explosions occurred in Buynaksk on 4 September, Moscow on 9 and 13 September and Volgodonsk on 16 September. This was a period of considerable insecurity since there were several other bomb alerts at the time and a number of bombs were defused in Moscow.

5. See the High Commissioner on National Minorities report in Organisation for Security and Cooperation in Europe (2011a).

8. Discrimination and immobility in Slovenia

> They erased us from the register of permanent residents. They put us in the
> central register – in this register you can find the people who are dead.
> This data goes to the archives. This is the end.
> (D.R., interview with the author, Maribor, 15 June 2004)

INTRODUCTION

This chapter investigates the ways in which restrictive citizenship laws deprived tens of thousands of residents of the right to freedom of movement through the cancellation of their residency status. It describes the processes by which more than 25,000 former Yugoslav citizens were deleted from the Slovenian State Register in 1992, were stripped of their acquired rights and subsequently became known as 'erased persons'. Beginning with a brief review of Slovenia's political transition from the late 1980s to the present day, it describes how political elites and the national media channelled public opinion against 'Southerners' from the former Yugoslavia in order to reposition Slovenia as a European state outside the Balkans. This in turn created new social categories of citizen and non-citizen.

The following section examines the facts of the erasure before introducing the empirical findings that explore the processes of forced alienation, the loss of residency and mobility rights, and the way in which the concept of erased person has been constructed. Perceptions of erased persons are examined through personal testimony and official discourse. The empirical basis for this study draws on interview data gathered during two field visits to Slovenia in June 2004 and January 2005, when interviews (n = 46) and focus groups (n = 4) were conducted in Ljubljana, Maribor, Ptuj, Velenje and Celje with members of the Erased and their families. Further interviews were conducted by phone and additional research was carried out in 2010, 2011 and 2012.

CONSTRUCTING THE SLOVENIAN STATE

The current state of Slovenia emerged as an ethno-political construct during a period of intense ethnic competition that defined both the first (Royalist 1918–41) and second (Communist 1945–91) Yugoslavia. Before 1918 foreign powers and the Italian territories (most importantly Vienna) governed Slovenia. The Slovene population existed as a minority in the multi-ethnic meeting ground between the Adriatic and the Alps. The creation of the first Yugoslavia elevated the province as a defined political unit alongside Serbia and Croatia. By emphasizing ethnic incompatibility between its constituent parts, the first Yugoslavia enabled the Slovene nation to take advantage of its newly found majority status that provided the first formal structure for national unification (Gow and Carmichael 2010). There were, however, limitations to this model, and ethnic tensions between Slovenians and their Austrian, Hungarian, Italian and Croatian competitors were not resolved by the first Yugoslav formula.

Attempts to assimilate Slovenes living in Italian- and Austrian-controlled areas further antagonized Slovenian national sentiment that had been sustained during the interwar period and during both the Fascist occupation and Communist rule. Under the first Austrian Republic the Slovenian Carinthian minority was subject to extensive attempts at Germanization. This was continued by the Austro-Fascist regime and included the absurd attempt to divorce the Slovenian language from its historical base and create a 'special nation' that could be assimilated into the Nazi framework. In coastal areas the rise of Italian Fascism in the 1920s and 1930s was similarly accompanied by a brutal policy of forced assimilation and territorial expansion. This repression led to massive refugee movements that were legitimized by the Treaty of Rapallo in 1920, transferring large amounts of Slovenian territory to Italy. This move was finalized by ratification of the Italian–Yugoslav Treaty of Osimo in 1977.

The expulsion of ethnic Germans, Austrians and some Hungarians after the Second World War further altered the multi-ethnic demographic in favour of the Slovene majority. They responded with an active pro-gramme of 'ethnic homogenization' during the second Yugoslavia (Komac 2001, p. 267). Even though the population of Slovenes living within the borders of the tiny republic had been sharply reduced, these outward migrations precipitated an ethnic compromise where the remaining Italian and Hungarian minorities in the South Western and

North Eastern regions were consolidated into the state, receiving formal recognition as protected minorities in the 1974 Constitution.

It was the second Yugoslavia that eventually gave birth to the independent state of Slovenia in 1991. Modernist accounts note the essential role that Communism played as both a facilitating and ultimately galvanizing force for Slovenia's aspirations to statehood (Gow and Carmichael 2010; Ramet 1996; Schöpflin 2000). Initially Slovenia had been among the most fortunate of the former Yugoslav republics in that its citizens were formally defined as belonging to a constituent nation (aroid) that guaranteed their status as nationals rather than members of ethnic groups (narodnosti) who could not lay claim to a territorial unit within the former Socialist Federal Republic of Yugoslavia (SFRY) (e.g. Muslims, Roma, Albanians and Jews). This status preserved Slovenia's cultural heritage by protecting the Slovene language in the school curriculum. At the same time the official recognition given to Slovenia empowered intellectuals to develop the Slovenian cultural identity beyond its peasant roots as newspapers, books, art and films were tolerated even during the most repressive years of Communism (Gow and Carmichael 2010; Komac 2001; Velikonja 2002).

In the late 1980s the decision by Serbian political elites to reorganize power within Yugoslavia provoked further ethnic tension as Slovene nationalists publicly contested the growing asymmetries within the Federation. Their dissent focused primarily on cultural issues, but the nationalists also mobilized around claims that Slovenia was paying too much to subsidize underdeveloped regions such as Kosovo. By 1988 Belgrade's tolerance of Slovenia's cultural distinctness was put in question by the introduction of educational reforms that challenged the supremacy of the Slovenian language in schools and gave rise to the belief that the republic's 'literary history' was at risk (Boris Novak, interview with the author, Ljubljana, 10 June 2004). In response to Serbia's re-centralizing policies Slovenian intellectuals publicized the risk to the Slovenian language in a series of articles in leading magazines and newspapers – *Nova Revija*, *Mladina* and *Delo*. The starting point was the declaration by Professor Jože Toporišič that Slovenes would 'either continue to assimilate linguistically and become a minority within Slovenia or change their relationship with their Southern neighbours' (Gow and Carmichael 2010, p. 94). This view was endorsed by the Foreign Minister, Dimrij Rupel, whose article in *Nova Revija*, 'Contributions to a Slovenian National Program', alleged that Slovene was now a second-class language in the SFRY. Rupel's argument would receive greater acclaim by an angry Slovenian public following the high profile trial of Janez Janša and three of his colleagues, including the editor of the influential *Mladina*, for publishing an exposé, claiming that Belgrade was planning a military crackdown on Slovenian liberalism. It was not just the substance of the trial that inflamed the Slovenian public but also its form; the trial was conducted in Serbo-Croatian even though it was on Slovenian soil.

The question of the Slovenian language thus galvanized the Slovenian public that was mobilized into new fora for political activism following the Janša trial. Nationalist outpourings were quickly channelled into the creation of a Committee for the Protection of Human Rights and a mix of political parties that included the Social Democratic Alliance, Slovenian Democratic Union, Slovenian Christian Socialist Movement, Green Party and a revitalized Slovenian Peasant Union. Although opinion polls published as late as March 1990 suggested that Slovenia was unprepared for independence (Ramet 1996), continuous protests over Belgrade's reassertion of hegemony encouraged Slovenian political parties to unite over a nationalist position, the logical conclusion of which was statehood. The DEMOS coalition of left-wing opposition parties emerged in 1990 and would eventually lead Slovenia to independence.

The first step towards independence came in September 1989, when the General Assembly of the Yugoslav Republic of Slovenia adopted an amendment to its Constitution asserting Slovenia's right to secede from the Socialist Federal Republic of Yugoslavia. This paved the way for a referendum on 23 December 1990 in which 88 per cent of Slovenia's population opted for independence. On the back of this referendum the Republic of Slovenia declared its independence on 25 June 1991, the same day as Croatia. Two days later Slovenia came under attack by the Yugoslav People's Army (JNA). Unlike in Croatia, however, the JNA retreated after only ten days, and, while its neighbour spent much of the 1990s recovering from the Serb-led occupation, subsequent population displacements and the divisive policies of the Tudjman regime, Slovenia was free to define its alternative to Communism; it was also free to develop the ethno-centric base which had propelled it towards statehood.

UNCERTAINTY AND XENOPHOBIA AFTER INDEPENDENCE

The reorganization of Slovenian politics into a multi-party system gave the immediate impression that the embryonic state was founded on universal principles of human rights and pluralistic democracy. At first glance Slovenia's efforts to build state and nation seemed highly positive as the young state offered declarations of tolerance. It quickly adopted a new Constitution, introduced laws aimed at reforming its Parliament, banking and public administration systems and prepared for eventual accession to the European Union. For this reason Slovenia was heralded as among the most democratic states in the new Europe and a post-Communist success story (Bebler 2002; Ramet 1998; Schöpflin 2000; Vučetić 2004).

In reality, however, Slovenia's route from independence to eventual membership in the European Union was marked by 'uncertainty and confusion' over its political identity (Ramet 1996, p. 226). Igor Lukšič maintains that during this period pre-existing corporatist traditions that stressed collective ideals were repackaged under the banner of pluralism as illustrated by the emergence of new political parties (Lukšič 2003). He notes that the 1991 Constitution made little mention of the role of parties and contends that in the early 1990s non-elective bodies were prioritized, above all the Catholic Church, which was able to 'fortify its position as the moral, legal, and political hegemony in Slovenia' at the expense of the new democratic institutions (Lukšič 2003, p. 521). The prevalence of corporatist traditions, as opposed to an open and competitive democratic system, was similarly expressed by one human rights expert who claimed, 'We don't have parties but political clubs in Slovenia' (A., interview with author, Ljubljana, 5 January 2005).

The most important challenge to Slovenia's glowing reputation was the rise of xenophobia. Although xenophobia existed in Slovenia during the Communist period, in the 1970s it was marked primarily by negative attitudes towards economic migrants from the other republics rather than by the expressions of cultural nationalism and collective blame that surfaced in the 1980s and continue to this day. As the decade progressed, opinion polls and survey data on inter-ethnic relations post-independence recorded a pattern of specifically anti-Southern (anti-Balkan) sentiment among the Slovenian public, state officials and media (Komac 2001; Komac and Medvešek 2004; Lobnikar et al. 2002; Volčič 2005; Zorn 2005). The police were especially problematic and reportedly abused non-Slovenes as well as homosexuals (Lobnikar and Pagon 2002). In the arts Southerners were regularly portrayed as 'cleaners, porters, gangsters' and associated with undesirability, backwardness and low socio-economic status (Velikonja 2002, p. 6). Critics of the growing xenophobia were met with accusations of 'traitor' and even received death threats (Boris Novak, interview with the author, Ljubljana, 10 June 2004). Not surprisingly in this context, non-ethnic Slovenes reported high levels of discrimination in both their public and private lives, expressed in two-tiered employment practices that favoured Slovenes, as well as by difficult relations with state authorities, limited opportunities for political participation and unequal treatment by the police (Komac and Medvešek 2004).[1]

One important characteristic of the increased nationalist and xenophobic sentiment was its variation in intensity (according to ethnic groups). For example, Slovene perceptions of its German-speaking and Hungarian minorities were generally good. Relations with the community in Istria, however, were reportedly more tense as Italian groups admitted a sense of alienation in the face of Slovenia's growing ethno-centricity and exclusive interest in Slovenians abroad (Komac 2001, p. 277). Croatians who were fellow Catholics were generally better received than Orthodox Serbs, Bosniaks, Albanians and Roma communities (who were at the bottom of the social order). The range of hostility shown towards the former Yugoslavs was replicated among the new minorities who expressed their own inter-ethnic conflicts and prejudices against each other along hierarchical lines as well (Komac and Medvešek 2004, p. 289).

Structural explanations for the rise of ethno-centrism and intolerance in Slovenia combine political culture and geo-political and institutional factors. Explanations of political culture focus on the institutionalization of the Slovene nation, defined by its distinct language, rural traditions and Catholic heritage (Gow and Carmichael 2010). These characteristics were emphasized both prior to and after Slovenia achieved independence. Although there was consensus over the specificities of the Slovene nation, the programme of identity definition required some reinvention. In spite of the presence of large numbers of non-ethnic Slovenes from the former Yugoslavia, political and cultural elites sought to reposition Slovenia as sometimes a former and other times a non-Balkan state (Velikonja 2002). The confirmation of Slovenia's ethno-centric path was established as public protests against Belgrade encouraged political and cultural elites to take their lead from a public that had unequivocally expressed its distaste for Yugoslav traditions and the peoples living within its borders in the aftermath of independence (Komac and Medvešek 2004; Velikonja 2002; Zorn 2005).

Geo-political influences that contributed to the rise of xenophobia ranged from bizarre, xenophilic statements in favour of political unions with the former colonial powers, Italy and Austria (Ramet 1996), to high-level conflicts over territory and state capacity. Although relations soured between the ethnic majority and Italian minority in Istria in the first few years of independence, this conflict that was the result of low-level tensions between Italy and Slovenia paled in significance to the disputes that occurred between Slovenes and former Yugoslav groups (Komac

2001). In contrast Slovenia's Yugoslav neighbours posed three important challenges to its sovereignty: the Serb-led attack on Slovenian soil contested its very legitimacy and put the Slovenian military at risk; the territorial contest between Croatia and Slovenia threatened its access to the Adriatic and its important trading partners in Western Europe; and the arrival of tens of thousands of refugees, mostly from Bosnia and Croatia between 1991 and 1996 (Slovenia was a small state and completely unprepared, without an asylum policy). These three crises served to further increase the social distance among Slovenia's ethnic communities.

Institutional arguments for the rise of xenophobia and intolerance relate to tensions between communities over constitutional provisions that record the state's ethnic preferences. These replicated the Communist tradition of organizing ethnic privilege according to majoritarian principles that prioritize specific collective historical identities. After the Slovene majority, the Italian and Hungarian populations were at the top of the pyramid as 'autochthonous minorities' who received specific protection under the Slovenian Constitution, including collective rights to representation in the Parliament. According to the Constitution the Roma communities that might arguably be considered autochthonous were also to receive collective rights but these have yet to be defined by law. By contrast, the situation of new minorities, especially those from the neighbouring states of the former Yugoslavia, has yet to be resolved; hence, Croat, Serb, Bosniak, Macedonian and other minorities receive no special collective rights. The Constitution simply guarantees the right of individuals to use their own language and practise their culture and religion – but as individuals, not as communities. This provision has been challenged by constitutional experts who argue that communities transmit culture, not individuals (Matevž Krivic, interview with the author, Ljubljana, 5 January 2005). Moreover, in spite of its claim to protect certain communities and individual cultures, state funding is overwhelmingly concentrated on the Slovene majority: in 2003 approximately 150–200,000 people who belonged to the recognized Italian, Hungarian and Roma communities, as well as those from the former Yugoslavia, received a total of 80,000 Euro for cultural activities (Baltic 2005). For the above reasons Miran Komac claims there is a 'deep gap between legal and societal citizenship' in Slovenia (Komac 2001, p. 276).

One unifying theme in the above vindications for Slovenian ethnocentrism is the tradition of privileging ethnos over demos. This applies with respect to ethnic Slovenes now living in Austria, Italy and Hungary who are seen as co-nationals and also in the context of non-ethnic Slovenes residing in Slovenia. Diasporic communities are treated like a fifth column or rather as 'extensions' of the parent nation, which negatively influences the chances of assimilation or integration into Slovenian society (Komac 2001, p. 275). This tendency to reduce ethnic communities to extensions of neighbouring states was exposed in the citizenship laws that were introduced in the 1990s and the scandals over the erasure (Zorn 2005).

CITIZENSHIP AND ERASURE

With the creation of the independent state in 1991 the Slovenian government was faced with the task of defining formal citizenship policies. Ethnic Slovenes were to receive citizenship on the basis of jus sanguinis, effectively transferring Slovenian nationality under the former Yugoslav system. Under the principle of jus soli, non-ethnic Slovenes who were considered autochthonous minorities were allowed to natural-ize if they were born on the territory. The remaining issue to be resolved concerned the 221,321 foreigners who could not be classified as either ethnic Slovenes or recognized minorities. All those who were not ethnic Slovenes were given six months to apply for permanent residency in Slovenia. Table 8.1 provides a breakdown of the current demographics of Slovenia and the number of new minorities registered in the 2002 Census.

Prior to independence, there were many indications that Slovenia's secession from the Federal Republic of Yugoslavia would be met with protection arrangements for non-ethnic Slovenes who were not covered by the existing constitutional provisions given to the autochthonous minorities from the Hungarian and Italian communities.[2] One means of protection was the offer of citizenship to all foreigners who had resided permanently on Slovenian soil at the time of the Plebiscite. To this end the Act Governing Citizenship was introduced in June 1991, providing the non-autochthonous minorities with the opportunity of naturalization. According to Article 40, former Yugoslav nationals, resident on the territory of Slovenia, could apply but were restricted to a six-month period. More than 170,000 were granted citizenship in this way, but thousands of others who either did not know about the law or who simply failed to apply were denied status.

After the six-month period ended on 26 December 1991, conditions both for former incorporation in the Slovenian nation and participation in Slovenian society became considerably harder. It is argued that the 1991 Citizenship Act should be seen as a societal deal made to appease international and especially neighbourly concerns over the fate of non-ethnic Slovenes living in Slovenia (Andreev 2003; Matevž Krivic,

Table 8.1   Ethnic composition of Slovenia

Albanians	6186	0.3%
Bosniaks/Muslims/Bosnians[1]	40,072	2.0%
Croats	35,642	1.8%
Macedonians	3972	0.2%
Montenegrins	2667	0.1%
Serbs	38,964	1.9%
Roma[2]	3246	0.2%
For orientation: Slovenes	1,631,363	83.1%
The total population of Slovenia	1,964,036	100%

Notes:

[1] The term 'Bosniaks' was formally introduced in 1993 in Bosnia and Herzegovina with the intention to replace the term 'Muslims', which by that time was used to denominate the Bosnian Muslims in the sense of ethnicity. However, on the Census, held in Slovenia in 2002, both terms were used – Bosniaks and Muslims. In addition to this, a significant number of the Bosnian Muslims living in Slovenia declared themselves as Bosnians. The latter name is not recognized as an ethnic denomination, but it was recorded in the Census due to the great frequency. This name confusion can be understood as a consequence of the relatively recent name change (from Muslims to Bosniaks); however, these three different categories that appeared in the 2002 Census can in a great majority of the cases justifiably be seen as one ethnic group (Danilo Dolenc in Miran Komac and Mojca Medvešek 2004, pp. 44–5). On the Census there were 21,542 declared Bosniaks, 10,467 declared Muslims and 8062 declared Bosnians.

[2] A significant portion of Roma in Slovenia had immigrated to Slovenia from other republics of Yugoslavia.

Source: Sircelj (2003), p. 141.

interview with the author, Ljubljana, 9 June 2004). If this is true, the deal expired with the formal deadline at the end of 1991, after which there was a subsequent return to illiberal and ethno-centric practices that sought to limit the potential integration of unrecognized minorities in the young state. It was at this point when large numbers of Slovenian residents were disenfranchised and when the act known as the erasure began.

In February 1992 Article 81 of the Aliens Act came into force and designated new categories of non-citizens. In effect all those who had been registered by means of the Aliens Act were deregistered and lost their residency rights as well as the social and economic privileges that came with residency status. The Erased included a wide range of individuals who did not have common ties to each other. There were approximately 500 officers from the JNA, many of whom did not see active service and had intermarried with Slovenes; Bosniaks, Croats, Serbs and Roma who had migrated to Slovenia for work (especially in the mines); and civilians born in Slovenia whose birth had been registered in one of the other republics. The only unifying factor was that these individuals were perceived as 'Southerners' and thus exogenous to the Slovene nation.

Jelka Zorn argues that 'the erasure was enabled by an opportunistic interpretation of the Aliens Act of 1991, which came into force at the independence of Slovenia and did not contain any specific provisions that would ensure that the legal status of these people would remain regulated' (Zorn 2011, p. 69). The manner in which the erasure took place, however, was both highly organized and secretive. Residents were asked to present their documents to state agencies and appear before the town hall or local administrative unit. According to Dedić et al. (2003), there was considerable uniformity of practice: residents were notified by official authorities to appear in person, at which point their documents were often confiscated or destroyed – punched, defaced, cut up – in front of them. Those who lost their residency status became official foreigners, effectively stateless persons who automatically lost access to the social and political privileges they had enjoyed for decades, including their free movement rights (see Amnesty International 2005). The cancellation of their status left them especially vulnerable, as evidenced in a tragic case taken up by the Helsinki Monitor of Slovenia (HMS):

> Franjo Herman, a 62-year-old construction worker, died on 13 July of untreated cancer. He had lived in Slovenia since 1955 and was erased from the register of permanent residents and citizens because of his Croat ethnic origin. As a consequence, he lost his right to social health and security. In August 2000 he was diagnosed with cancer but was refused the necessary operation free of charge because Mr. Herman was not a Slovene citizen or permanent resident. In November 2000 he had been admitted to a medical check up on the intervention of HMS but further treatment was refused, including a prescription for free pain killers which he needed urgently. After a court had decided that he should receive medical treatment, he was hospitalized for a week and was dismissed twice. Slovene citizenship was restored to him a week before his death in order to secure the right to inhumation (foreigners may only be cremated). (International Helsinki Federation for Human Rights 2002, p. 278)

Several of the Erased were subject to arbitrary removal and were deported from Slovenia (ECRI 2002). One estimate is that approximately 20 people were expelled (Matevž Krivic, interview with the author,

Ljubljana, 9 June 2004). HMS, an independent human rights organization, contends that the number is far greater and was carried out by transporting handcuffed individuals (without the knowledge of destination states) by bus, plane and ferry to Croatia, Macedonia and Montenegro, respectively (Miklavic Predan 1998).

Jelka Zorn has created a list of abuses that the Erased suffered following this administrative act (Dedić et al. 2003). Based on extensive interviews with members of the Erased, she noted that those who lost their residency rights also suffered the violations shown in Table 8.2. While human rights activists agree on the nature of the violations, there is considerable debate over the numbers of those affected by the erasure. According to HMS, more than 180,000 people were affected. This number has been challenged by both the Association for the Erased and Slovenian Constitutional Court that estimated the number affected at 25,671 (Zorn 2011).

The issue of the erasure was brought before the Constitutional Court, which decided on 4 February 1999 that it was unlawful and ruled that the 1991 Foreign Citizens Act violated the Constitution for failing to determine the conditions for the acquisition of permanent residence permits by citizens of other former Yugoslav republics who did not apply for Slovenian citizenship or whose applications had been turned down (see Constitutional Court Decision U-I-284/94). The Constitutional Court specifically ruled that the Foreign Citizens Act violated Articles 2 and 14 of the Constitution regarding the principles of the rule of law and equality, respectively. The Court also charged that the expulsion of individuals violated human rights and freedoms protected in the Constitution under international legal agreements to which the state was a signatory. The Court therefore ordered that corrective legislative measures be introduced to regulate the status of the Erased.

In response to the Court the government proposed legislation that attempted to extend the franchise in some key areas. In 1999 it introduced the Regulation of the Status of Citizens of Other Successor States to the Former SFRY in the Republic of Slovenia, establishing a three-month period within which persons with unregulated status could apply for Slovenian citizenship. While approximately 7000 people were able to regulate their status by means of this new law, the legislation did not restore permanent residency retroactively but only granted residency rights from 1999 onwards. The way in which this law was designed therefore excluded those who had been expelled and had been unable to return as a result of the erasure.

In 2002 the government introduced amendments to the Act on Citizenship. These did not give permanent residency status retrospectively but

Table 8.2   Examples of violations against the Erased

TYPE	DESCRIPTION
CIVIL AND POLITICAL	Denial of right to legal and judicial protection
	Fracturing of the family unit, violation of the child's right to live with its parents
	Violation of the right of the family to form associations and of the formal recognition of fatherhood
	Violation of right to choose place of residence (Erased forced to obtain a permanent residence address in a foreign country)
	Prevention of free movement across borders
	Violation of right to privacy of post
	Exclusion from political participation and public activity
	Creation of Slovenian refugees (Erased expelled to other ex-Yugoslav republics as refugees)
ECONOMIC AND SOCIAL	Prevention of legal employment or loss of job
	Denial of right to pension
	Violation of right to apply for social aid
	Causing material damage (termination of employment records, payment of administrative and court fees, lawyers fees)
	Denial of rights to property ownership, founding a company, opening bank accounts, mobile telephone subscriptions, car registration in own name
PERSONAL HARASSMENT	Exposure to arbitrary behaviour by the police on a daily basis
	Third-party harassment over phone and in letters and lack of police sanction for such conduct
	Exposure to brutal treatment by clerks (i.e. humiliation and withdrawal of information, therefore prolonging procedures)

recognized long-standing residency and allowed those who had a registered permanent address in Slovenia on 23 December 1990 and had lived there since to apply for Slovenian citizenship. The 2002 Act gave applicants the longest period of time to date to apply by granting them a one-year window of opportunity, but it contained one important deficiency. It failed to regulate the status of those who had not lived continuously in Slovenia after 1990, once more excluding those who were forced to leave or were expelled as a result of the erasure.

The shortcomings of the 2002 legislation were recognized by the Constitutional Court, which ruled in April 2003 that the Act on the Regulation of the Status of Citizens of Other Successor States to the Former SFRY in the Republic of Slovenia was unlawful on two grounds. First, it noted that the Act did not grant permanent residency retroactively to those citizens of other SFRY republics who were removed from the registry of permanent residents from 26 February 1992 onwards, but simply gave them an opportunity to apply for it. Secondly, it failed to address the problem regarding those who had been forcibly removed under the Aliens legislation and who were unable to apply for permanent residency status. The Constitutional Court therefore called upon the government to issue permanent residency permits retroactive from the date of the erasure (see Constitutional Court Decision 2003 U-I-246/02).

In response to the Constitutional Court the Parliament adopted the Technicalities Bill in October 2003 that only covered 3800 people who could prove that they had lived permanently in Slovenia since the erasure in February 1992 – a fraction of the Erased. The government then adopted a second instrument known as the Systemic Bill that was intended to cover those who could claim permanent residency status, but who had not lived in the country for the entire period.

The parliamentary debates over these bills raised new concerns about the stability of the centre left government and exposed the rising trend in xenophobia that the nationalists had carefully engineered. Press reports at the time claimed that the debates prior to the adoption of these bills demonstrated that the coalition and opposition were 'completely divided' over the issue of restoring the status of the Erased (Slovenia News 2003). They also chronicled how the issue of the Erased developed from a point of constitutionality to test Slovenia's internal ethno-national principles of organization.

In protest to the government's attempts to regulate the issue of the Erased, the main opposition, the Slovenian Democrats (SDS), initiated a campaign to collect MPs' signatures with the aim of calling a referendum on the bills. In November 2003, for fear that the proposed bills could pave the way for multi-million Tolar compensation claims, the National Council (upper chamber) voted 26 to five against the first Technicalities Bill that aimed to implement the Constitutional Court decision and establish the necessary legal framework for restoring residency rights to some of the citizens erased in 1992. The dispute between the government and the opposition quickly degenerated into an inter-parliamentary struggle, arousing nationalist passions and simultaneously preventing further attempts to implement the Constitutional Court rulings. On the heels of a veto in the National Council the SDS filed a demand to hold a referendum on the bill just as the Interior Minister Rado Bohinc announced that the ministry would start issuing decrees to reinstate the permanent residency rights of the Erased. Bohinc's declaration angered the opposition, which pledged that it would try to censure the minister. As the crisis heated up, the Slovenian President, Janez Drnovšek, stepped in and urged all parties to abandon the idea of a referendum that, while it could not overturn a Constitutional Court decision, would nonetheless create further division and encourage nationalist passions during an election year.

Throughout 2004 the crisis over the Erased deepened as the Parliament failed to set a date for the referendum and the nationalist bloc, consisting of the SDS and New Slovenia, issued further threats to oust Bohinc, who had started issuing corrective decrees that reinstated the residency rights of the Erased. As of mid May approximately 3100 such decrees had been issued (Amnesty International 2004). When the Constitutional Court ruled that any referendum would be unconstitutional, the leader of the SDS, Janez Janša, took this as an opportunity to strengthen his populist platform and seek alternative measures to block the bill, including inciting xenophobia. Janša and the nationalist bloc achieved a referendum in April 2004 that produced alarming results. Although the voter turn-out was just over 30 per cent, approximately 95 per cent of those who voted rejected the bill. The level of public animosity towards the Erased astonished international observers who had not understood the potency of this issue.

CURRENT SITUATION

Since 1991 many former Slovenian residents have left Slovenia; some were readmitted following the introduction of the 1999 Act regulating the Status of Citizens of the Former SFRY, but others have since been expelled. A particularly disturbing trend is the expulsion to Bosnia of children of the Erased once they reach majority. In spite of pressure from the European Union and the decisions by the Slovenian Constitutional Court in 1999 (U-I-284/94) and 2003 (U-I-246/02), governmental attempts to settle the problem have so far failed to account for those who did not meet the original criteria as established in 1991. In July 2004, under pressure from the nationalists, the Slovenian Ministry of the Interior stopped issuing corrective decisions, and no new steps have been taken to implement the 2003 Constitutional Court ruling to restore the rights of the Erased. The Association of the Erased and some human rights authorities consequently appealed for political action and have secured the support of Amnesty International that brought the issue to the attention of the UN Committee on Economic, Social and Cultural Rights in November 2005. In 2012 the EctHR ruled in *Korić and Others v Slovenia* that the State had failed to resolve the problem of the erasure and had violated the Erased's rights to family and private life (see European Court of Human Rights 2012).

FINDINGS

This section seeks to understand how the political restructuring that took place during the transition from Communism to the creation of an ethnically defined state fostered greater social distance between ethnic communities as well as how the act of erasure was institutionalized. To this end it explores the way in which the Erased perceived the process of erasure and interprets their impressions of their Slovenian neighbours and reclassification as non-citizens.

The findings presented below are the result of semi-structured interviews with members of the Erased (n = 40) and human rights authorities, journalists and political leaders (n = 6). Those interviewed consisted of men and women and included Serbs, Bosniaks, Croats, Roma and other nationals from the former Yugoslavia. The interviewees were asked to explore their sense of deterioration in job status, housing, relations with other family members and standard of living. Questions were also asked about how the erasure affected their sense of belonging, self-esteem and perceptions of the hostility of the general public.

The above-mentioned themes were explored in greater depth during four focus groups with: (1) former JNA officers; (2) Roma; (3) families; and (4) Bosniaks in June 2004 and January 2005. These four categories were selected for their relevance to the story of the Erased: the former JNA officers were most commonly scapegoated in the media and by nationalist politicians; the Roma have been among the most vulnerable people in Slovenia and are the subject of specific constitutional provisions that are aimed to provide greater opportunities for civic and political participation; families bore the burden of the erasure and many family units were divided as a result (Zorn 2005); Bosniaks were not only among the least popular ethnic minority in Slovenia but the fact that Bosniak teenagers have been deported from Slovenia also identifies them as targets. Interviews and focus groups were held in cities across the country (Ljubljana, Maribor, Ptuj, Velenje, Celje) in order to arrive at a general picture of state policy and allow for possible variations in the degree of alienation expressed by members of the Erased. In order to protect the identity of vulnerable individuals, initials have been used rather than full attributions.

INTERPRETING THE ACT OF ERASURE

Responses to the question, 'What does it mean to be erased?' produced three types of answer. First, some participants offered legal definitions of this controversial term. One view was: 'Erasure is the wrong term. The files were simply transferred from one file [residency] to another file [former statuses]. They were erased from the area of legal residence' (M.Z., interview with the author, Ljubljana, 9 June 2004).

A second category of response focused on practical explanations for the meaning of being erased. Many participants claimed that the erasure was best illustrated by the restrictions it placed on them that contrasted with the 'state of normality' they associated with Western European countries and that entailed having money, freedom to buy simple goods and social protection in the form of medical insurance:

> You are not entitled to work. There's no health insurance. You can't drive a car. Can't go to the employment office. If the police ask questions, they have the right to expel you. There are other things like buying and selling … You are not entitled to go to university. Maybe you can but only as a foreigner. But you are not even a foreigner here. You are complete[ly] paralysed. (A.T., interview with the author, Ptuj, 15 June 2004)

More than one participant commented that the erasure had reduced them to being undocumented workers who could only secure low-level jobs (B.P., interview with the author, Ljubljana, 10 June 2004). Further discussion with the Erased exposed themes of powerlessness, exclusion and victimization, as evidenced by statements made regarding their sense of self-worth and the physical barriers placed upon them. As one Roma man noted, 'I can't leave Slovenia because I can't come back' (A.M., interview with the author, Ljubljana, 11 June 2004). The intractability of the change of status dominated many interviews in which participants described situations of powerlessness in terms of being 'ruined', 'para-lysed', 'worthless, helpless and deserted' and 'humiliated'. One articulate participant claimed that he had been 'killed by the pen not by the gun' and insisted that one needs to understand the erasure in terms of the destruction of one's civic status (D.L., interview with the author, Celje, 10 June 2004). His associate in Ptuj advised that Orwell offered a better understanding of the erasure than he could provide in a few words, while another simply described the erasure as 'one of the greatest catastrophes' and that his past was now 'invalidated': 'For me personally it means to have 20 years of my life and work thrown into the water by a country which I perceive as my homeland' (B.P., interview with the author, Ljubljana, 10 June 2004).

The importance of having a state identity for one's own personal validation was emphasized by participants who stressed the psychological effects of the cancellation of their status. Developing the notion of wasted years in discussion, several participants commented on how their loss of formal identity affected their sense of self-worth and mental health:

> Being erased means that you are worthless. I didn't know who I was. I wasn't a Serb, Croat or Slovenian. According to myself, I am Slovenian. For two years I was nobody. Today I am also illegal here. (M.U., interview with the author, Ptuj, 15 June 2004)

By contrast those who had been able to acquire citizenship through the legal amendments introduced following the first Constitutional Court ruling spoke of receiving status as a great prize. One woman commented that it was 'almost like winning the lottery – you can work, visit the doctor and don't need to be afraid of the police' (G., interview with the author, Velenje, 14 June 2004).

Others focused on the practical hardships and, above all, the way in which official discrimination following the erasure acted as licence to other forms of abuse by the state authorities. The police were the primary antagonists, and respondents spoke of how they had been subjected to repeated searches, fines and verbal harassment in their dealings with them. One participant reported how the police had entered the family apartment in the middle of the night and abducted her husband, who was put in the boot of a police car alongside eight other Bosnian construction workers and taken to the station for questioning (D.L., interview with the author, Celje, 10 June 2004). A man who identified as a Bosnian Serb claimed that the police and courts engaged in discrimination against minorities. He reported that following an accident with a motorcycle, the person responsible not only damaged his car but also attacked him in a rage with a helmet, breaking his arm and his wife's finger:

> The police spent more time going through my papers than with handling the attacker because they saw I was a foreigner. The court failed to prosecute the attacker properly and he later walked free. I felt disrespected by the court. (M.P., interview with the author, Celje, 10 June 2004)

One woman spoke of how she had developed alternative coping mechanisms, including running from the police on sight (D.L., interview with the author, Celje, 10 June 2004).

Claims of powerlessness were illustrated by further commentary on the daily life of erased individuals and suggested that the symbolic destruction of the person (erasure) might lead to physical removal. The fear of removal was highlighted in interviews with the former JNA officers, some of whom had been expelled in 1991, even before the erasure had been instituted. In interviews and focus groups, former JNA officers recorded how the administrative courts removed those who were considered a threat to state security. Throughout the 1990s there were lists of individuals circulated to border police who, in collusion with Hungarian police across the border, actively prevented those on the lists from re-entering the country (S., interview with the author, Celje, 14 June 2004). One officer recounted in detail how he had been expelled under police guard and had to rely on the Ministry of the Interior and Office of the Ombudsman to secure his re-entry. His friend was less fortunate and had to spend six and a half years in exile following the cancellation of his passport and denial of his application for citizenship.

A third category of response raised issues of civic participation and the loss of social rights that should have been derived from the right of residency. One father described the erasure as having made him invisible even before his children:

> It's like you don't exist. I could go to the school prom but couldn't legally be a father to my own children. On my first child's birth certificate it says father unknown. On the second, I was asked to leave the space blank. (Sel, interview with the author, Velenje, 14 June 2004)

Family issues were common, especially among the Bosnian participants whose children reached their majority in the period following the erasure and with some of the older interviewees who were now economically dependent on their children. The Bosniak group felt doubly trapped by the war in their country of origin and the growing racist sentiment in Slovenia that was expressed in expulsions and denial of the right to schooling (A.B., interview with the author, Celje, 10 June 2004). At the other end of the spectrum, older participants recorded how the erasure had reduced their pension payments and left them economically vulnerable. This was especially important to the expelled JNA officers, who had lost years from their pensions and were denied payments. One officer even waited for more than 12 years to receive his pension (M., interview with the author, Ljubljana, 11 June 2004).

IDENTITY AND STATE LEGITIMACY

The act of erasure was conducted through subterfuge and through the physical destruction of documents (see Dedić et al., 2003; Zorn 2005). However, it is important to point out that the administrative procedures associated with the erasure were not immediately understood by most victims and, for the vast majority of the Erased, their loss of formal identity was only revealed as they became excluded from official Slovenian society or encountered immediate problems. Although one woman claimed to have felt 'shocked, threatened, humiliated' and considered suicide upon leaving the public administration office (D.L., interview with the author, Celje, 10 June 2004), most of those interviewed stated that it was only as they tried to regulate aspects of their personal lives that they learned of their status and the extent to which they were resented by public authorities. One Roma man from Bosnia reported:

> When I told them I couldn't go to the place of my birth [to regulate my status] because of the war in Bosnia and the broken communications, the official answered, 'you can make yourself a pair of wings and fly to your hometown'. (A.P., interview with the author, Ljubljana, 10 June 2004)

The erasure was delivered as a form of political punishment for the former JNA officers and was accompanied by verbal abuse and the physical closure of borders. One man who was expelled and was only able to re-enter the country illegally reported, 'I was told from the Army that people from Bangladesh will get citizenship before you' (N.V., interview with the author, Celje, 11 June 2004).

The loss of one's formal status took place at a time when there was a marked shift between state and society. Although Slovenia, like most former Communist countries, had enjoyed little legitimacy, the timing of the erasure coincided with Slovenia's promotion as a legitimate, democratic state. Many participants connected the erasure to Slovenia's successful political transition, including its declaration of independence, shift from the former Yugoslavia and, more recently, its membership of the European Union, which they claimed gave the state even greater licence to discriminate against them:

> There are people here who are drunk because of independence. Now they are drunk because they joined the EU. If they claim that they have a legal state, then they should behave like it and provide compensation. (S.T., interview with the author, Celje, 14 June 2000)

While some participants sought to explain the act of erasure as a result of ethno-centric traditions (one claiming that it was the product of 'genetic chauvinism'; S.T., interview with the author, Celje, 14 June 2004), most of the Erased saw themselves as scapegoats. One journalist developed this point:

> Politicians were trying to excuse themselves because there were officers from the JNA. That was the main excuse. But kids who were born here when this whole thing [the erasure] started ... Some people didn't ask [questions] because they didn't have any reason to ask. The JNA was seen as occupiers. This was an issue of scapegoating. What was most important were all the talks about the money. The Parliament, Janusz Dvoršek and Milan Kučan both knew. They didn't say a word. (N.D., interview with the author, Ptuj, 16 June 2004)

As time passed, the Erased lost even more access to a state that in their eyes grew stronger as they became increasingly marginalized. One man in Ptuj described the sense of powerlessness he felt after 14 years, lamenting:

> They have all the papers that say they are right because you don't exist. It's like you come from Korea without a passport and you can't see an end – there's no way out. No documents. No driver's licence. You can't buy anything; can't sell anything. (A.T., interview with the author, Ptuj, 15 June 2004)

CREATING SOCIAL DISTANCE

As the Erased lost their formal status and saw Slovenia emerge as a legitimate international actor, participants claimed that they were ostracized by former friends, co-workers and neighbours. Many commented that friends associated the act of erasure with a form of punishment and suggested that they must be guilty of an offence for the state to behave as it did. Several added that they had been turned into public enemies on the grounds that the state would one day be required to pay large sums of compensation if the issue of the erasure was resolved. Having been censored by the state, members of the Erased recorded that their neighbours eventually bought into the practice of indiscriminate and collective blame. One response has been, 'you are one of the Erased ... that's not possible because you are a good guy' (Z., interview with the author, Velenje, 14 June 2004). His colleague provided the following personal testimony:

> When this happened in 1992, I couldn't believe it happened. My colleagues, friends, didn't want to know me anymore. I was very social and built my house near the border. All the people would come to visit, including police and friends. Then they stopped coming. (V., interview with the author, Maribor, 15 June 2004)

Participants recorded in interview that the formal cancellation of their status as residents precipitated a process of alienation that they claimed was the by-product of former Communist practices – above all, the uncritical acceptance of political authority and the reliance on a media that with few exceptions refused to probe deeper into the controversy. One brave journalist who had published the initial stories on the Erased in *Mladina* claimed that there was a tendency to engage in self-censorship and that he too had problems publishing serious articles because his former editors claimed 'it didn't raise the numbers of readers' (Igor Mekina, interview with the author, Ljubljana, 13 June 2004). The net result was an increase in hostility towards the Erased as both individuals and as members of a perceived collective group. This hostility applied at all levels – from the Parliament, where nationalist politicians attacked the Erased, right down to family units, as explained by one woman in Ptuj:

> My husband was on my side but his family wasn't. But when this started, they blamed me. I said nothing. I have my opinion. We haven't any contact. It was awful for my husband. I also lost all my friends. Slowly we argued, then relations were cold. Then we drifted apart. Now when we meet, we say hello and nothing else. (M.U., interview with the author, Ptuj, 15 June 2004)

Others cited a broader trend in xenophobia against former Yugoslav nationals and specifically 'Southerners' that was marked by racist rhetoric and formal discriminatory practices. One noted that the Erased were routinely called 'chefurs', an offensive term defined to the author as 'yugo-niggers' (V.P., interview with the author, Ljubljana, 10 June 2004). Another added that a child with a non-Slovene surname would need to perform in school much better to receive the same grade as a Slovenian child, and that this ethnic bias was evident in all types of public interaction (D.L., interview with the author, Celje, 10 June 2004).

There were three important components to the xenophobic reaction. First, there was general resentment of Yugoslavia that was most clearly directed at the former JNA officers. Secondly, there was a fear that Slovenia would be embarrassed by the international community and that taxpayers would be forced to carry the burden of compensation claims. Thirdly, with the influx of thousands of Bosnian refugees in 1992 and 1993, there was a rise in anti-immigrant and, specifically, racist rhetoric:

They only wanted professionals. There was this atmosphere; they wanted Southerners out of Slovenia. This was an evident political wish to have clean people here – not people the government doesn't want, people they need to spend money on. (M.B., interview with the author, Ljubljana, 9 June 2004)

The media were to blame, alongside opportunist nationalists who seized upon the crises over asylum seekers and the Erased. One commentator described how scapegoating took place during this period: 'The television spent the entire week showing where one asylum seeker was accused of stealing' (B.B., interview with the author, Ljubljana, 10 June 2004).

LIVING OUTSIDE A STATE OF LAW

The erasure produced several long-standing effects. Participants commented on how the erasure had denied them the opportunity even to resolve their status both formally and through personal networks. A frequent accusation raised was that 'after the erasure, all the doors were closed to us' (R.M., interview with the author, Ljubljana, 10 June 2004). One important consequence was that almost all aspects of their public lives had become casualized. Forced to exist outside a state of law and thus without official protection, participants reported acts of exploitation from employers who did not pay wages, and sometimes from the state that still exacted fees and fines. One man, for example, whose employer was prepared to retain him in spite of his status, described the absurdity of having to apply for, and pay for, a temporary visa every six months so that he could keep his job (M.P., interview with the author, Celje, 10 June 2004). Another, who secured status after the second Constitutional Court ruling, commented that he has only been able to earn a minimum wage, and this required him to work endless hours and take up irregular employment away from the family home. This also prevented him from having a secure relationship with his children. He had been distressed by the fact that he could not discuss his status or hardships with others for fear of being removed from his job:

> During the time of the erasure, you were not allowed to be ill. I would have to work and could only see my child once in two weeks. They made mental invalids of us. We couldn't read newspapers or listen to the radio. We had to work every possible hour. I worked for 350 hours a month driving a taxi and I had to keep quiet. (Z., interview with the author, Velenje, 14 June 2004)

DEPORTATION AND THE BREAK-UP OF FAMILIES

One family of Bosnian origin explained how their children had been removed from Slovenia at the insistence of the state, in spite of their refugee status and long-standing connection to Slovenia. The daughter was born in Doboj, Bosnia in 1980, and the father began working in mines in Slovenia in 1981. When the wife came to Slovenia in 1992 with their three children (age twelve, ten and two-and-a-half) as refugees, the father had temporary residency, and the wife and children received a residence permit. In 1995 the father filed papers for permanent residency but was turned down by the ministry because it was found that he had been outside the country for 13 days. Officially the five family members were refugees from 1992 to 1996, when the father received permanent residency. He received Slovene citizenship in 2002. From 1992 to 1998 his daughter lived with the family in Valenje, Slovenia on the basis of temporary residency. In January 1998 her father sought to extend her residency but was told that this would not be possible because she would turn 18 in two months (March 1998) and would have to leave the country at that time. A few days before her birthday he took her back to Bosnia, as instructed, where she stayed with a family in Gračanica. Since 1998 the daughter has only been able to visit her family in Slovenia on one-month tourist visas. Even though the family became Slovene citizens in 2004, the daughter had been repeatedly refused a temporary residence permit in Slovenia.

In another case a woman who was erased with her daughter explained how the erasure and the abuse she suffered at the hands of the state affected her family life and children. In 1992 she placed her older daughter, who was mentally ill, in a special day care unit. The costs were enormous, so her Bosnian father offered to take the child with him to Bosnia and then send her to a relative in Germany. However, the war in Bosnia interrupted the family's plans, making it impossible to leave Bosnia until 1995. After the war ended in 1995, the woman brought her daughter back to Slovenia, where she unsuccessfully tried to obtain documents to enrol her in school. Slovenian officials told her that if she herself had no documents, then the child could not obtain any either. Since 1996 the daughter has been living in Bosnia, unable to rejoin her mother.

ERASURE AND MOBILITY

The above findings raise a number of points for consideration. The formal revocation of citizenship took place in this instance during a period of political restructuring and without the occurrence of forced migration or conflict. Rather, the acts that rendered so many stateless continued during a period that was recognized as both peaceful and formally democratic. The above findings demonstrate a direct and negative relationship between the cancellation of formal status, economic and civil rights, and mobility rights, including the right to freedom of movement. As evidenced by the deportations described above, the slippery slope from the denial of one's political rights to civic and social ostracism ended with violence against the Erased in the form of deportations and deaths (Zorn 2005). Seven individuals committed suicide as a result of their persecution (Matevž Krivic, interview with the author, Ljubljana, 9 June 2004). Although the Constitutional Court recognized the illegality of the erasure and the need to protect non-citizens, the refusal of the Parliament to introduce implementing instruments and the overwhelming public perception of 'Southerners' as undeserving suggest that in practice a distinction was drawn between insiders and outsiders in Slovenia. Miran Komac contends that, for this reason, Slovenian society is best described as 'pre-multicultural' (Miran Komac, interview with the author, Ljubljana, 5 January 2005).

This account introduces analytical challenges to the way in which the Slovenian state has been described. Although there was also evidence of democratic activity, as illustrated in the inter-parliamentary struggles between political parties, the Constitutional Court, the executive and the government, the evidence of the political and public support for the erasure suggests that it may be too premature to describe Slovenia as a truly consolidated democracy. Rather, the emerging picture is of an ethno-national state with corporatist traditions that have in part been protected by the legacy of Communism and the refusal of citizens to question the actions of the state. There is considerable evidence of statism. Even after the erasure, state interference could be detected in the application of fines, the imposition of temporary permits in some cases, the use of the police to expel family members and the grudging acceptance that the situation needed to be corrected as a result of constitutional court rulings. The state played a central role but was nonetheless assisted by civic interests, above all the nationalist bloc and populist media. For this reason the allegation that Slovenia is characterized by corporatist as opposed to pluralistic values carries considerable weight (Lukšič 2003).

The above findings recall the usefulness of constructivist approaches to understanding how identity formation and state creation interact and bear on the conferral of citizenship and associated rights. The distinctiveness of the Slovene majority was a constant factor that united state interests during the transition from Yugoslavia, the struggles of post-independence and Slovenia's outreach to the European Union. The constructivist account also helps to explain how some communities once excluded (e.g. Hungarians and Italians) were eventually incorporated into the Slovenian state and how the creation of the new category of erased person drew upon ethnic antagonisms. Ethnic contest was institutionalized in the new state through different constitutional provisions for citizenship and occurred at all levels, even among the new minorities who expressed racist views of those outside their ethnic group (Komac and Medvešek 2004), thus affirming the artificiality of this social category of erased person. The Hungarian and Italian minorities nonetheless enjoyed a full range of rights, including rights to freedom of movement, unlike the Erased.

CONCLUSION

The case of Slovenia illustrates the fragility of rights and how protection frameworks can quickly unfold. As this research records, the slippery slope from formal exclusion through the cancellation of status precipitated furthered attacks by both the state and third parties on the rights of former residents. Once Slovenian elites embraced the ethno-nationalist position, a new category was created, and the Erased were further vulnerable to abuse. Mobility rights, including the right to remain, which the Erased had enjoyed, were shown to be contingent on civic rights and the security of citizenship. With the revocation of residency rights, other acquired rights, including mobility rights, were lost. We also note that the reconfiguration of Slovene citizenship took place during a period of political restructuring and was not produced by forced migration or inter-state conflict. Lines were simply drawn around people. As one of the Erased put it, 'We didn't come from anywhere. We were here. They put us in that category' (A.T., interview with the author, Ptuj, 15 June 2004).

NOTES

1. In a study of 4000 participants, Miran Komac and Mojca Medvešek noted that not only did intolerance towards non-ethnic Slovenes grow but was differentiated according to ethnic origin. In this social hierarchy, Bosniaks and sometimes Roma were at the bottom, followed by Serbs (Komac and Medvešek 2004).
2. Most notably, the Plebiscite on Sovereignty and Independence of 23 December 1990 and the Statement of Good Intentions presented by the National Assembly following the announcement of the Plebiscite affirmed Slovenia's commitment to international human rights agreements and guaranteed the right of citizenship to all minorities.

9. Analysis

The most important issue we have to deal with is freedom of movement.
(Anna Lindh, Swedish Social Democrat and former Foreign Minister,
murdered in 2003)

In Chapter 2 we suggest that there are five central themes that may be
drawn from the literature, informing our understanding of the ways in
which freedom of movement and mobility rights more broadly affect
access to other substantive rights. The case studies provide a window for
investigation.

FREEDOM OF MOVEMENT AS A CONDITION FOR ACTION

The idea that freedom of movement is a condition of action suggests that
the right to move is fundamental and may be seen as a gateway right. The
writings of Arendt, Sen and others point to the transformative power
associated with the right to freedom of movement that they claim should
be understood in expansive terms – not simply in terms of the ability to
move but also in the right to settle and remain. This understanding aligns
with the interpretation of European law provided in Chapter 3, where we
note the relationship between citizenship rights and the practical enjoyment of one's mobility. In addition the European Convention on Human
Rights, which applies beyond the European Union, interprets the right to
freedom of movement to include the rights of liberty of movement,
freedom to choose one's residence and the right to leave one's country.
The European Convention also protects the rights of individuals from
expulsion.

Spanish Doctors

In the case study of the Spanish and other European medical doctors
employed in the UK, we note that the opportunity to migrate opens the
door to personal and professional activity. Whereas in Spain and other
parts of Europe, structural impediments prevent home-trained doctors

from obtaining secure employment, the UK may offer a secure alternative. In this context the migration of medical personnel has its roots in a series of EC directives that grant mobility rights expressly to that category of professional. The mobility rights protected under the EU Treaties further allow foreign-trained doctors to take advantage of specific recruitment campaigns. Without question the EU's commitment to promote freedom of movement is essential to the story of successful migration and relocation.

The idea of freedom of movement as a gateway right is affirmed by the statements made by the Spanish doctors regarding the expression of their personal autonomy through the exercise of their profession, through their own personal development as a result of training and working in a second language, and as a result of their increase in social status. In this context the right to economic activity, not guaranteed in Spain, is a condition for both action and identity.

The experiences of the Spanish doctors should not only be read in the light of their rights to move and settle in the UK, as protected under EU law, but also in the context of their relocation to a specific part of the UK where their skills have been easily absorbed. Local economic and geographical considerations played an important role in the successful relocation of the Spanish doctors who settled in poor, urban parts of Northern England. The experiences of Spanish doctors also highlight that occupational type and job specialization are factors influencing the prospect of successful free movement.

Foreign Language Teachers in Italy

The case study of the foreign language teachers working in Italy provides an insight into the relationship between the right to freedom of movement and the idea of action. In this setting, however, it is not simply the right to migration that determines access to work and protection but rather the associated substantive rights that are protected by the European Union Treaties under the banner of freedom of movement. The prohibition against discrimination on the basis of nationality (Article 18 TFEU) is above all central to the expression of freedom of movement and influences the degree to which intra-European migrations may result in establishment and settlement in another EU member state.

We note how in this setting official discrimination undermined the occupational, social and economic status of the lettori and how over time this deteriorated even more as a result of new laws. Further changes in the occupational status of the lettori, many of whom were compelled to take on new contracts as part-time workers, reduced their pensions and their options to engage in meaningful economic activity.

Croatian Serbs

The case of displaced Serbs in Croatia further illustrates the relationship between freedom of movement and the potential for action and meaningful work. For many years displaced Serbs were unable to claim their rights unless they were present on Croatian soil. In the early 1990s their citizenship rights were restricted as a result of absence during the war, and this had an enduring effect on their ability to recover their status, property and economic entitlements.

For those Serbs who had either returned or remained in Croatia only to be placed in collective centres, the realization of the right to free movement had little meaning, especially considering the absence of property ownership and opportunities for work. Arguably it was not the lack of mobility rights that attributed to their sad lives in collective centres and dire cabins but rather the absence of the associated rights that give meaning to the idea of establishment and settlement. The effects of displacement and the loss of rights during and immediately after the war had a particularly long-lasting outcome on their sense of identity and self-esteem. Having a 'mortgage on one's back' further reduced the possibility of their engagement in the newly independent state. As noted above, those who managed to recover their rights were especially proactive and were prepared to challenge the state.

Opportunities to return or, in the case of ethnic Croats, to settle may have been provided by law but successful settlement was determined by ethnic affiliation and social networks. Local community support was vital in the case of ethnic Serbs. By contrast ethnic Croats were able to integrate into the state with ease, as illustrated in the case of interviewee Velijko, an ethnic Croat from Bosnia who resumed work as an electrician.

Internal Migrants in Russia

The case study of internal migrants in Russia records how patterns of population control from the Soviet era continue to influence the way in which internal migration is regulated in practice and how that undermines the potential for action, as Arendt describes. Although freedom of movement is a formal right, this study shows it is routinely violated. Internal migrants enjoy little freedom of movement. The use of registration controls to manage the flow of migrants into Moscow (and application of similar systems into other cities) undermines their access to

Moscow, along with its amenities and state services. As the US Department of State, Bureau of Democracy, Human Rights, and Labor (2014) records, the Russian authorities often refused to provide government services to individuals without proper registration, and many regional governments continue to restrict the mobility rights of Russians relocating from one city to another.

The relationship between residency and registration as described above illustrates how rights to free movement, however protected in law, may be violated in practice. While registered Russians are entitled to travel freely between cities, participants described a vicious circle where residency was often a pre-requisite for registration. Thus in order to establish oneself legally, one already needed to be established. Moreover, in the absence of formal registration, migrants were denied access to job and housing markets, education and social services.

In this case study the right to establishment that is associated with the right to free movement is held out as a gateway right. We also note the many inequalities that result from lack of registration, with expectant women describing how they would be forced to either pay for private hospital care or be forced to return to their city of origin for the baby's birth. Some parents spoke of the uncertainty of enrolling their children in local schools; others mentioned the barriers they experienced in marrying partners and described problems they faced opening bank accounts and purchasing SIM cards as well as the denial of credit and loans from banks. Participants described how they were unlikely to improve their situation and noted that they were denied the right to set up businesses or inherit property, a restriction that they believed would carry over to their children who were born outside Moscow.

We note that the denial of the rights to freedom of movement and establishment also affects the migrants in this study indirectly. Many interviewees claimed that their lack of status placed them under great strain as they needed to devote time and energy to circumventing the system, which they reported affected both their health and quality of work. Others identified anxiety, fearing that they could be dismissed for lack of registration.

The Erased in Slovenia

The case study of the Erased in Slovenia demonstrates most clearly how freedom of movement is linked to action and other essential rights. It describes how the erasure became a slippery slope where the formal exclusion of more than 25,000 former Yugoslav citizens (non-Slovenes) precipitated further attacks by both the state and third parties on a wide range of civil, political, economic and social rights as a result of the cancellation of their status. The Erased existed outside a 'state of normality'.

The cancellation of status left the Erased without the right to vote and without state protection. They were denied the right to own property, set up companies or open bank accounts. The Erased were also subject to harassment by the state, and above all by the police. In some of the most tragic cases the loss of this right ultimately undermined the family unit and some children were deported. Other parents were denied the right to marry and record their name on their children's birth certificates. The Erased lost mobility rights, including the right to residency, and were forced to obtain a permanent residence address in a foreign country. They lost the right to freedom of movement and were denied the opportunity to travel abroad. The loss of economic and social rights was equally traumatic. The Erased lost the right to legal employment and had no right to protection in the workplace, no pensions and no right to social assistance. This in turn cost individuals who needed to engage lawyers and take cases to court.

The testimonies of Erased interviewees record a wide range of ways in which the loss of their acquired rights undermined their potential for action. They speak of being 'completely paralysed', 'ruined', 'worthless', 'helpless', 'deserted' and 'humiliated', losing not only years of their lives but also their homeland. As a result they were ultimately powerless. Some described how the loss of their status left them vulnerable to deportation – which did occur, as recorded in the accounts of Bosnian parents. Many focused on the loss of economic status, of having been reduced to low paying jobs and of being undocumented workers in precarious states of employment. By contrast those who were able to regularize their status described a situation of normality where one could work, visit the doctor and live without fear of the police.

MOTIVATIONS FOR MIGRATION

The right to freedom of movement is an individual right that, as noted above, protects the rights to enter and leave states and establish residency; it is intrinsically connected to other rights. In this context the degree to which individuals have autonomy over their mobility is of critical importance to understanding how the right to freedom of movement and associated rights are experienced in practice. We note in the previous sections that motivations for migration, both inter-state and intra-state, include both personal and structural factors. These are explored in the review of the case studies below.

Spanish Doctors

The Spanish doctors record that while professional reasons were among the most central for their migration, personal factors also played a part in their decisions to relocate to the UK. We note in particular some of the post-materialist explanations for relocation, including the pursuit of personal satisfaction, greater autonomy at work, the opportunities to travel, to seek adventure and to employ a second language. Geography was also an important factor and in this context the doctors interviewed took their mobility rights for granted. Several spoke of the possibility of going back and forth to Spain. The issue of social status, now improving as a result of their establishment in the North of England, is also a factor that, while it may not influence their desire to relocate, may affect their decision to settle and remain. The fact that the NHS fosters a diverse and cosmopolitan work environment, where doctors maintain a relationship with their patients, was also cited as a positive reason for remaining in County Durham.

The above individualistic explanations for migration should, however, be considered alongside the structural push–pull factors, notably the scarcity of medical jobs in Spain, the availability of jobs in the UK as a result of staff shortages in highly specialized areas, and the potential to earn greater salaries in the UK. The lower density of doctors in the UK as compared with Spain illustrates the relevance of neo-classical accounts for migration in terms of the planning and promotion of international recruitment and also provides the rationale for post-materialist explanations that centre on improved status as a result of being part of an exclusive group of professionals. Related to the above regarding the nature of the work environment, we note that recent trends in public spending in the health sector made the British medical system a more attractive prospect for the Spanish doctors. Again this shows how structural considerations, namely state spending, may give rise to post-materialist preferences for greater job satisfaction. The fact that the UK shifted its traditional recruitment preferences from Asia to attract larger numbers of doctors from the EEA (with a specific target of increasing the number of foreign doctors by 10,000) further informs the context in which Spanish doctors were attracted to the UK.

The case study of the Spanish doctors also draws attention to the role of individuals as sources of influence in the migration and relocation processes. In this setting we note that one Spanish doctor who had settled in the UK many years previously had directed the UK Department of Health to County Durham and later led a local professional organization, namely the Workforce Development Confederation, to establish direct links with medical institutions in Aragon and Catalonia.

Foreign Language Teachers in Italy

Among the lettori interviewed, the main motivation for their establishment in Italy was personal. Many had partners and families in Italy; others sought out the adventure of teaching abroad. Those interviewed described how their migratory decisions and paths were in effect a test of the right to freedom of movement as protected in the European Union Treaties, though they recognized that their decision to move and settle in Italy was determined by individual choices.

Croatian Serbs

The return of ethnic Serbs to Croatia was motivated by both personal and structural factors. Some ethnic Serbs spoke of their desire to return to Croatia, where they felt an ancestral attachment. Many simply spoke of their desire to return to their physical homes. Few returnees spoke of return as an expression of justice, and none identified return with the idea of reconciliation. Their motivation to migrate was mostly determined by their limited opportunities elsewhere, the poor economic situation in Serbia and their removal from host countries. Although some mentioned that they received small welfare grants, financial assistance was not central to their decision to return (in contrast to some of the Bosnian Croat settlers interviewed).

Internal Migrants in Russia

Most of the participants interviewed had relocated to Moscow for work. They noted that Moscow was always the most desirable city in Russia because jobs and social benefits were concentrated there. Their motivations for migration were overwhelmingly personal and expressed in terms of the lure of Moscow, though for some entrepreneurial migrants, lack of opportunity in their home city also served to push them towards Russia's capital city.

The Erased in Slovenia

The Erased interviewed had settled in Slovenia and were not recent migrants. Some were the descendants of migrants, their parents having moved for work decades earlier from other Yugoslav republics. As noted above there was no opportunity for voluntary migration. Some individuals were removed by the Slovenian police and effectively became refugees in neighbouring states.

OPEN BORDERS AND FREEDOM OF MOVEMENT

In the literature review, we noted that the discussion of open borders is often confused with the right of freedom of movement. In practice, however, the relaxation of immigration controls, while a necessary condition for international migration, is not synonymous with the rights to freedom of movement as enumerated in the European Union Treaties and the European Convention on Human Rights. In the case studies presented, the primary interest is in intra-state mobility and the degree to which individuals are able to access their rights in their country of settlement. The focus on open borders is therefore of greatest relevance in the context of immigrants who have tried to settle in the host state or return to their country of origin, or where internal migration controls remain in place.

Spanish Doctors

In the case study of the Spanish doctors what is particularly striking is the potential problem with their return to Spain. Although they are able to move back and forth between the two countries, the suggestion that by working abroad one may lose contacts and be locked out of protected systems such as the Spanish medical profession introduces further challenges to the idea of freedom of movement. While mobility rights may open the door to economic activity, they do not guarantee employment, and local contextual explanations may provide greater insight into the reasons why people have managed to settle.

Related to the above, we note that successful relocation from Spain to the UK resulted from the cooperative efforts of many individuals, organizations and state bodies, and above all the Department of Health and local NHS partnerships. The relocation of foreign doctors to County Durham took place against a backdrop of considerable administration and planning, including tailor-made induction programmes, contracted accommodation services and weekly support group meetings, not to mention the active involvement of individuals such as Dr. José Miralles Garcia. The evidence from the study of Spanish doctors calls attention to the dangers of relying on human capital and push–pull explanations for migration and highlights a complex and collaborative process of recruitment.

Foreign Language Teachers in Italy

While non-Italians were able to settle in Italy, discrimination undermined their substantive rights to freedom of movement. This case study exposes the gulf between opportunities for migration assumed under the open borders camp and the challenges of settlement required for the full expression of freedom of movement.

Croatian Serbs

The relative ease with which returnees were able to move between Bosnia, Serbia and Croatia introduces an interesting dimension to the discussion of freedom of movement. In the absence of visa controls, displaced people were able to move between states, to participate in 'come and see' visits and in many cases to maintain two homes, often before deciding to sell off their original home. This fluid situation presented a distorted picture of the degree to which people had in fact returned to Croatia and indeed of the process of post-conflict stabilization. It did, however, give formerly displaced people greater autonomy over their lives.

For those who did choose to return and settle, the lack of economic opportunity and the endemic discrimination of ethnic Serbs undermined their ability to access other rights associated with free movement, and above all economic entitlements. Many of the problems that resulted from the above discriminatory practices were mediated by the international community and indirectly also by Croatia's neighbours that took in displaced persons.

Internal Migrants in Russia

This case study illustrates that while the internal borders of the Russian Federation are open, there are multiple barriers to freedom of movement. The use of registration controls deters many from exercising their rights and, for those who make the journey to Moscow, their opportunities to settle are again restricted by the need for documentation. While ethnic

Russians may attempt to circumvent the system by seeking employment in the private sector, the above account records the many barriers that discourage them from establishing themselves in Moscow. We also note the recent reports from human rights monitoring bodies that record that, although Caucasians and others may enter Russia, they are denied opportunities to settle. Vast numbers of migrants, often undocumented, are forced to live 'underground'.

The Erased in Slovenia

The case study of Slovenia focuses on an event which took place before Slovenia joined the European Union and during a period when Slovenia had closed its borders to its neighbours as a result of the wars in Croatia and Bosnia. The Erased were unable to migrate easily, though some obtained false papers through back channels. The Erased therefore enjoyed neither open borders nor freedom of movement for the reasons described above.

FREEDOM OF MOVEMENT AND DEMOCRACY

Cosmopolitan and liberal theorists of international relations emphasize the positive aspects that international migration may bring, including greater openness and opportunity irrespective of nationality. This line of argument is evident in Hosein's writing in addition to the work of early theorists of European integration who hold that the socialization of different European nationalities has a peace-building effect. The right to freedom of movement is provided in international human rights instruments, including the European Convention on Human Rights, accession to which is central to membership in the European Union and other international organizations. Thus access to instruments that provide the right to freedom of movement has been equated with a shift towards democratic reform. In the sections below we review the relationship between freedom of movement and substantive democratic practices that protect rights to equality of opportunity, political participation, human rights, access to justice, education and health services, and personal security.

Spanish Doctors

The case study of the Spanish doctors provides little evidence of the relationship between freedom of movement and democracy. While participants spoke of the nature of the work that offered them considerable autonomy, and similarly spoke of the ease with which they integrated into life in Northern England, there was no discussion of political engagement, access to justice or human rights concerns. The right to education was affirmed in their accounts of their children's schooling in England.

Foreign Language Teachers in Italy

The case study of the lettori exposes the failures of intra-European socialization. The discriminatory practices and claims of structural corruption challenge Haas's functionalist account that European integration, as evidenced by the intra-European migration of EU nationals, seeks to 'break down the clustering of affections' (Haas 1968, p. 157). In this study national ideologies and local identities have not been weakened by the forces of economic integration and the physical assimilation of non-Italians in a traditionally Italian workplace. Patterns of exclusion and peer selection kept non-Italians as outsiders. We note that from the beginning the lettori, unlike Italian academics, did not need to be successful in a competitive entrance examination (concorso) to work in the university system and that their very presence challenged the hierarchical structures within the university sector.

The separation of the lettori into three groups, following the introduction of DPR 382 and their reclassification, deepened the division between the non-Italian and Italian staff. While this did not affect their political rights of participation, it did produce considerable inequalities that undermined both the spirit and letter of European Union law. We note that the lettori, who by definition were non-Italian, were the only workers in Italy whose basic salaries were not stipulated in their national contracts. Attempts by the Italian state to sweep away the problem of the lettori undermined their civil rights, and above all their right to judicial redress. We note that the introduction of the Gelmini Reform in January 2011 explicitly 'extinguishes' the rights of the lettori to have their claims adjudicated in a court of law.

Croatian Serbs

The relationship between freedom of movement and democracy was implicitly accepted by the Croatian state authorities, and above all the central government and judiciary, recognizing that many of the rights enjoyed by ethnic Serbs hinged on their ability to return. Thus the discriminatory state sought to restrict the rights to freedom of movement.

Citizenship laws that provided for the acquisition of Croatian citizenship included residence requirements that displaced Serbs were unable to meet; property was repossessed while Serbs were in neighbouring states and unable to return; and judicial decisions were made in absentia. Authorities recognized that if the Serbs were allowed to return, then rights might follow. By denying ethnic Serbs the opportunity to settle in Croatia in the immediate aftermath of the war, the Croatian authorities prevented ethnic Serbs from accessing their economic, social and political rights in Croatia.

Although ethnic Serbs were able to return, thanks in large part to international pressure and the removal of hundreds of thousands of Serbs from host states, their return did not in itself advance democratic reform. As the above account records, there was extensive societal discrimination that undermined the reintegration of returning Serbs. There remains considerable social distance between Croatia's two largest ethnic groups. Serbs remain divided on the basis of property ownership, time spent abroad, family support, and access to social networks and community structures. Their situation stands in marked contrast to the ethnic Croat from Bosnia who was settled in Croatia and received Croatian citizenship immediately. The case of Croatia therefore illustrates two distinct patterns of migration and settlement that were structured according to ethno-centric policies and governmental programmes with profoundly undemocratic outcomes.

Internal Migrants in Russia

The scrapping of the propiska and the changes made to both the federal Constitution and national and regional laws (held out as indicators of democratic reform) have neither addressed the long-standing problems of mobility controls nor facilitated greater participation of large sections of the Russian public in the polity. As the above case study records, even with the cancellation of the propiska and its replacement with the system of registration, citizen rights have been routinely violated, including the rights to vote, establish residency, and access justice as well as the health and education systems.

The above account records just a selection of instances where Russian citizens have seen their civil rights abused by government authorities, police and the militia. We note that unregistered Russians have difficulty registering births and enrolling children in school and are unable to marry outside their hometown, unlike other citizens. In order to secure their status, internal migrants must call upon third parties, including employers and landlords, who must approve documents and engage with bureaucracies. For both employers and landlords, the lack of registration not only adds to their administrative burden but also leaves them vulnerable to exploitation by police and militia. Unregistered migrants are also unable to enjoy political rights, including the right to vote. Although this is permitted in law, in practice it is exceptionally hard to guarantee.

The case study of Russia also draws attention to many geographic disparities that expose considerable inequality of opportunity. Several of the participants interviewed described that while they were denied certain rights and privileges in one city, they were more successful in other cities – for example, when buying SIM cards for mobile phones. In other instances less fortunate migrants were forced to pay thousands of dollars to regularize their papers in order to receive essential medical care. Such irregular practices undermine the development of a culture of individual rights that applies equally to all Russians.

Other threats to democratization are described in the excessive bureau-cratization that several interviewees suggested invited greater corruption and increasing levels of authoritarianism, as experienced when dealing with law enforcement bodies, including the police and militia. In spite of the devolution of authority to sub-national governments and the growth of the private sector, the increase in regulations and intervention by state bodies undermined the quality of life available to non-registered migrants and further disabled them from exercising their constitutional rights. Participants also described how the use of registration controls increased social distance between Russian citizens. Just as the introduction of the propiska privileged populations in the large cities, the introduction of registration controls also created social hierarchies that left those non-Muscovites disadvantaged. Some participants therefore concealed their status and identities from associates.

One ironic feature of the problematic registration system was that in spite of the difficulties many internal migrants encountered, some were actively mobilized in protest against the unfair system. The testimonies of participants, including Galina and Kristina, record how some internal migrants chose to confront the authorities, including the police and militia, and engaged in sustained civic protest in defence of their democratic rights.

The Erased in Slovenia

The Slovenian case study records no positive relationship between freedom of movement and democracy. This research demonstrates instead that even as Slovenia engaged in democratic reforms by establishing multi-party elections and adopting a new Constitution as well as reforming its Parliament, banking and public administration systems, the state systematically undermined the rights of a substantial number of residents to access state services, participate in political life and enjoy personal security. The above account records that rather than promote a spirit of liberalism during the first two decades of its existence as an independent state, Slovenia's democratic institutions welcomed an ethno-centrism and xenophobia that was directed towards those identified with its Southern Balkan neighbours. The Erased became public enemies and several individuals spoke of growing social distance between family members and friends as a result of their change of status. Such behaviour reflects a pattern of ethno-centrism that is noted in the tradition of privileging ethnos over demos; we note that even ethnic Slovenes living in Austria, Italy and Hungary were considered co-nationals, in marked contrast to the Erased within their own borders.

FREEDOM OF MOVEMENT AND THE STATE

The relationship between the state and the right to freedom of movement is fundamental to this study. International human rights law, European Union law and the constitutions of all the countries investigated in this book provide the right of individuals to freedom of movement within the state. Yet many of the participants interviewed experienced multiple barriers to the enjoyment of this right. While some states worked to remove the blockages that prevented individuals from enjoying the right to freedom of movement, still others frustrated the participants' rights to free movement and settlement.

Spanish Doctors

The case study of Spanish doctors illustrates the ways in which states may facilitate the right to freedom of movement. The UK emerges as a direct recruiter of international specialist labour. While doctors trained in the European Union have exercised the right to practise in other EU member states for several decades as a result of specific directives, the United Kingdom is held out as an active recruiter, working through the Department of Health and Foreign Office (and through overseas embassies) to attract medical staff to the UK by means of the several schemes already described that also carry with them significant relocation packages.

The UK government is also identified as an indirect recruiter. We note that the doctors interviewed commented on the importance of public funding and its relevance to their professional and personal satisfaction. The highly publicized funding by the former Labour governments and the massive increase in NHS expenditure are cited as a source of attraction. In spite of these efforts we should note that the overall number of EEA nationals working in the British health system is just 6 per cent, as opposed to almost 25 per cent non-EEA nationals. Other explanations as to why medical staff are attracted to work in the UK should therefore be considered.

Foreign Language Teachers in Italy

The role of the Italian state is central in this story. While the Italian state promoted free movement in its recruitment of lettori, the above accounts also illustrate that it has equally frustrated opportunities for freedom of movement and especially settlement in Italy.

We note that the Italian state initially sought to recruit foreign nationals as university language teachers and introduced a specific law in 1980 that created the category of lettori. Although they were granted the right to work in Italy, the lettori had no rights to benefits, social security, national health insurance or pensions, and were considered to be 'autonomous workers'. Some 15 years later the Italian state moved to reclassify the lettori by means of a new law which designated them as 'collaboratori ed esperti linguistici' (linguistic experts), denying them security in the workplace as described above. It was only as a result of judgments from the Court of Justice of the European Union that the Italian state introduced Law 63 in March 2004, entitling the lettori to the minimum salary of tenured researchers and stipulating that their acquired rights were to be recognized from the first day of their employment. While this decision strengthened the lettori's rights associated with freedom of movement, we note that the government later reinterpreted this law with the introduction of the Gelmini Reform that extinguished their rights to have their claims adjudicated in a court of law.

Italian courts, however, have actively interpreted the right to freedom of movement as protected under Italian law. From 1987 onwards, when the lettori won their first case before a local employment tribunal in Verona and their employment status was guaranteed, courts have interpreted Italian law in a way that sought to correct the discriminatory practices established by law and by the actions of Italian universities. Two of the most significant judgments concerned the ruling in 1991 by the Pretura di Verona that found that the lettori enjoyed an indeterminate contract, and the subsequent judgment in January 1999 by the Venice Regional Tribunal that found that three British teachers had been illegally prevented from applying for a teaching post because of their nationality.

The European Union emerges from this story as the most influential actor in the defence of the right to freedom of movement. The judgments issued by the Court of Justice of the European Union in the cases of *Allué I* (1989) and *II* (1993) (ECJ C-33/88 and ECJ C-259/91) sought to reduce the possibility for nationality-based discrimination and the firing of non-nationals from their posts. The Court has more recently found that Italy has failed to uphold its Treaty obligations (C-212/99 and C-119/04) and established in the case of *Nancy Delay* (C-276/07) that non-nationals were entitled to equal treatment with national workers.

The European Parliament, as well as other parliamentary bodies, has played a key role in both publicizing the problems facing the lettori and calling upon states to respect their Treaty obligations to promote the free movement of workers and to respect their associated rights to establishment and settlement. For more than 20 years the European Parliament has assumed the role of the defender of the lettori. The UK Parliament has raised its concerns and has more recently initiated an initial investigation (see Home Office and Department for Work and Pensions 2013).

Croatian Serbs

For several years the Croatian state played a critical role in restricting the free movement of displaced people of Serb ethnicity. The Law on Temporary Take-Over and Administration of Specified Property (LTTP) of 1995 (Official Gazette NN 73/95, NN 7/96 and NN 100/97) was among the most significant pieces of legislation that saw the transfer of property fall into the hands of the state. Legal owners further saw their rights curtailed by the 1996 Law on Areas of Special State Concern, giving ethnic Croats private or state-owned property for their own use. Court hearings conducted in absentia also enabled the administration to dispossess tens of thousands of Serbs, as did corrupt housing commissions. By restricting other rights, such as access to state pensions, and by refusing to recognize periods of time spent in employment (through the process of convalidation), the Croatian government created further disincentives for displaced Serbs to return.

The introduction of construction schemes and legal reforms, including the Constitutional Law on National Minorities (CLNM) that introduced clauses regarding the representation of minority groups in the Parliament, helped to correct some of the barriers that had discouraged Serbs from returning. Other structural factors, however, including lack of economic opportunity, continued to make return an unattractive proposition. Many Serbs complained that persistent discrimination in public life, especially in the judiciary, further weakened the potential for long-term sustainable returns. By contrast governmental support to Bosnian Croats in the form of invitations, grants and aid made their settlement, transition and integration into the post-war state remarkably easy.

The European Union was instrumental in pressing Croatia to reform the discriminatory laws and institutions that prevented Serbs from returning and settling. We note that one of the pre-conditions to EU accession set by the European Council was the return and integration of ethnic Serbs; Croatia's neighbours and host states repatriated thousands of Croats and prompted a sequence of returns to Croatia. Further evictions of Croatian Serbs from Bosnia also compelled thousands to return to Croatia.

Internal Migrants in Russia

The role of the Russian state is paramount in both promoting and restricting free movement. On the one hand the introduction of a new Constitution in 2001 formally granted freedom of movement to Russian citizens, and indeed all who are lawfully present on the territory. In so doing the democratizing state stood in marked contrast to the previous Soviet system that had used the propiska to track the whereabouts of residents and served as part of a broader campaign of internal security. The fact that migrants interviewed have found opportunities to circumvent some of the requirements for registration (e.g. by working in the private sector, paying for health and education services, and using temporary permits) demonstrates the degree of reform that has taken place over the past 20 years.

On the other hand the Russian Constitutional Court has repeatedly ruled that the introduction of residency controls, including the practice of registration, violates the Constitution. Human rights monitors have independently recorded that federal municipal and regional governments have repeatedly frustrated the right to free movement by the introduction and administration of registration requirements. The above case study records that federal authorities refused to provide government services to unregistered individuals; the municipal government in Moscow, in addition to regional governments in Stavropol Krai, the North Caucasus and Voronezh, restricted the rights of migrants to settle. City authorities were condemned for extracting fees from migrants and refusing to register others.

The Erased in Slovenia

The erasure was the product of state decisions that undermined the mobility and associated rights of more than 25,000 people. This was a top-down action that found its origin in instructions drawn up by the Ministry of the Interior which were then served upon local civil servants to administer, which they did by destroying documents. The central state was therefore responsible for stripping people of their rights, expelling individuals to Bosnia, Croatia, Macedonia and Montenegro.

The most culpable layers of government include central ministries and the Parliament. We note that the Act Governing Citizenship of 1991, however liberal, nonetheless only provided non-ethnic Slovenes with a six-month period to apply for citizenship. The introduction of the Aliens Act of February 1992 designated new categories of non-citizens who later lost their residency rights as well as the social and economic privileges that came with residency status. The state's further attempts to amend these laws produced few gains for the Erased, and we note that both the 1999 Regulation of the Status of Citizens of Other Successor States to the Former SFRY in the Republic of Slovenia and 2002 amendments to the Act on Citizenship were contested by the Constitutional Court.

The Parliament played a particularly significant role and emerged as a voice of ethno-centrism. Although the government had made a gesture to reform the problems that arose from the erasure by means of the 2003 Technicalities Bill, we note that the National Council (upper chamber) voted against it and as such rejected the Constitutional Court decision that called upon the state to establish a legal framework for restoring the residency rights of those erased in 1992. More indicative of the xenophobia within the Parliament was the debate over the bill and the calling of a referendum in order to press the Interior Minister to abandon the practice of issuing corrective decrees to reinstate the permanent residency rights of the Erased, which he eventually did. The fact that 95 per cent of voters supported the referendum revealed widespread public resentment of the Erased and further stirred up ethno-centrist passions.

In this instance the Constitutional Court played a key role as a voice of censure and concern. In 1999 it decided that the erasure was unlawful and ruled that the 1991 Foreign Citizens Act violated the Constitution's principles of the rule of law and equality (see Constitutional Court Decision U-I-284/94). It also recorded that the erasure had violated the human rights of the Erased and ordered the state to introduce corrective legislative measures. Again in April 2003 the Court challenged the Act on the Regulation of the Status of Citizens of Other Successor States to the

Former SFRY and called upon the government to issue permanent residency permits retroactive from the date of the erasure (see Constitutional Court Decision 2003).

In addition to Slovene organizations we note that the European Parliament and Council of Europe both expressed concern over the slow progress in the reform of the discriminatory laws that disenfranchised the Erased. In addition the European Court of Human Rights ruled in 2012 in the case of *Kurić and Others v Slovenia* that 'the Slovenian authorities have failed to remedy comprehensively and with the requisite promptness the blanket nature of the erasure and its grave consequences for the applicants' and that Slovenia had violated the Erased's rights to family and private life (European Court of Human Rights 2012).

10. Conclusion

There is no Europe without freedom and solidarity.
(José Barroso, President of the European Commission, 2005)

The idea of freedom of movement as developed in both the history of inter-state relations and in the literature on migration is far removed from the practice of mobility. As this study records, the challenges facing migrants seeking to relocate operate not only between states, as commonly featured in contemporary accounts of immigration, but also within them. Developing Faist's (2000) transnational analysis of international migration, the case studies in this book identify multiple levels in which states, social networks and individuals influence mobility flows and thus determine the degree to which people are able to exercise their rights to freedom of movement. In this context, many of the claims made by scholars writing on inter-state migration apply equally to those seeking to relocate within states. For example, we note the relevance of Lee's (1966) writings on differentiated access and Sassen's discussion of the polarization of labour markets. While Sassen concentrates on the division of labour in service industries, the creation of occupational hierarchies is also born out of the studies included in this book, most notably in the accounts from Croatia, Italy and Russia. Where these studies differ, however, is in their focus on migrant identity as a factor which determines entry to protected labour markets.

The case studies included in this book chronicle in different ways the difficulties people have in migrating, settling and establishing their lives even when those rights are formally provided in law. In spite of national, international and specifically European Union provisions to protect the right to freedom of movement, the accounts of migrants seeking to relocate tell a very different story.

One unifying theme in the studies of Croatia, Italy, Russia and Slovenia is the overt discrimination against certain categories of 'outsiders'. Such discrimination cannot be reduced to capital- and class-based divisions, as suggested in the literature on dual labour market theory in Sassen's (1990) writings on labour markets in urban centres. Further, the notion of migrant opportunity warrants reconsideration. In contrast to classical economic arguments regarding the pursuit of opportunity as the

186

driving force for settlement, as included in Souffer's model (1940), we note that such opportunities are not easily calculated. In some instances the greatest challenge was not settlement but rather the prospect of 'returning', as recorded in the account of the Spanish doctors who were recruited to work in the North East of England and became locked out of the Spanish medical system.

The personal accounts and histories presented in this book expose the wide gulf between enumerated civil and political rights, including the right to migrate, and the enjoyment of substantive social, economic and cultural rights. With the exception of the Erased in Slovenia, for whom the loss of residency status resulted in total alienation, it was not that participants in this study were unable to move but that their opportunities to establish themselves and create meaningful lives were constrained by the state as well as by a wide range of organizations, a situation which does not feature in classical economic accounts of migration. The findings from this study are especially problematic for the European Union and associated institutions, including the Council of Europe, which have not only set out to defend the human rights of all on European soil but have also laid claim to champion the right to freedom of movement as a means of uniting the common market and reducing historic tensions between European states and populations.

In the context of the European Union, the principle of freedom of movement (the free movement of people) was expressed in the founding Treaties and has been reiterated in every subsequent treaty over the past 50 years. Yet until recently the idea of free movement was narrowly defined and (as discussed in Chapter 3) it was the introduction of the Citizenship Directive and the passage of a handful of Court rulings that expanded the right of freedom of movement beyond the rights of economically active migrants. The right to freedom of movement – for citizens – was a later development in the history of the European Union. Although freedom of movement is protected under the European Convention on Human Rights, in the case of the Council of Europe member states it has in practice been interpreted to protect people against expulsion. It also informs the right to non-discrimination, which applies equally to migrants. The recent decisions passed regarding the prohibition against torture (Art. 3) and the right to family life (Art. 8) suggest a new assertiveness from the Court that may further protect migrants' rights, including the right to freedom of movement when it affects the enjoyment of other rights.

In spite of these Europe-wide provisions, mobility rights are not universally respected in either the European Union or Council of Europe systems. Within the EU we note that nationals of new member states such as Croatia are excluded from entering other EU states to work or settle unless they meet stringent criteria. Moreover (also discussed in Chapter 3), those resident in the EU who do not have a family link to an economically active EU national and cannot meet the test of self-sufficiency (e.g. the elderly, the ill or those caring for children) are unable to enjoy the same mobility rights as EU nationals. Thus mobility remains a source of division among the citizens of Europe. These problematic areas will no doubt be further tested by future interpretation of relevant EU legislation, including Regulation 492/2011 and case law of the European Union and the Citizenship Directive.

The case studies included in this book have illustrated some of the contemporary barriers that prevent EU nationals from enjoying their protected rights to freedom of movement and settlement. For the Spanish doctors who enjoy full rights in the United Kingdom, the challenges affecting their potential return to Spain are rooted in the nature of the Spanish medical system. Their experiences as intra-European migrants stand in marked contrast to the Europeans working in the Italian university system who have seen their rights violated again and again for decades. In spite of judgments from the European Court of Justice affirming their rights to free movement and the prohibition against nationality-based discrimination, the lettori have been discriminated against, resulting in considerable material and personal loss.

The case studies of Croatia, Slovenia and Russia, three former Social-ist states that have since acceded to the European Convention on Human Rights (and in the case of Slovenia and Croatia, the European Union as well), also illustrate the many ways in which the rights to intra-state travel and settlement may be disrespected. Different discriminatory practices in all three states have conspired to undermine citizens' rights to settlement and establishment. In Croatia the introduction of exclusive citizenship laws and the repossession of property were facilitated by corrupt officials, housing commissions and a complicit judiciary that deterred ethnic Serbs from re-establishing their lives in post-war Croatia. Only pressure from the European Union successfully prompted reform. In Slovenia the cancellation of the residency status of the Erased resulted in them losing their economic and social rights as well as the right to state protection. In spite of this abuse of human rights, Slovenia still joined the European Union. And in Russia, where the introduction of new laws and a new Constitution heralded reform, the introduction of the registration policy has denied migrants the opportunity to establish themselves legally in Moscow, including access to state services.

The case studies also inform our understanding of the substance of freedom of movement. In the introduction to this book we note that the literature on freedom of movement largely concerns itself with the migration and rights of foreigners rather than with their settlement. The rights to freedom of movement and settlement, however, are part of the same logic. Arguably the failure to examine the nature of mobility and relate it to the wider context of personal freedoms has been misdirected by the evolution of discourses on immigration, sovereignty and border control. Yet the current fascination with state controls over immigration is by all accounts a modern twist. We note that the enumeration of mobility rights developed independently from classical writings on sovereignty and political authority, and that is why liberal scholars who support the idea of freedom of movement, such as Carens, Rawls and Sen, have been able to locate historical precedents for their claims in this ancient and early modern political thought. Communitarians like Walzer and others who are more critical of the right to free movement may find equally relevant sources for their arguments in the same canon. In the absence of consensus among liberal political theorists there has been little attempt to examine how the right to freedom of movement (that, aside from the open borders camp, unequivocally protects the rights of migrants to move within the state) aligns with the rights to non-discrimination and hence establishment and settlement. This study addresses this important omission and notes the problematic ways in which the right to freedom of movement may be undermined by the failure to uphold other civil, economic and social rights which determine opportunities for settlement.

As discussed in Chapter 9, Arendt's belief in freedom of movement as a condition for action is frequently contested in practice. It is not simply the exercise of mobility that may be frustrated by states but more often the barriers to establishment and settlement hinge on the degree to which migrants are able to access their rights in the face of discrimination and other structural barriers. We note that, in addition to the literature on freedom of movement, such issues are not adequately addressed by a legal or institutional reading of the right to freedom of movement as expressed in European Union Treaties, national laws and Constitutions. It is rather the experience of discrimination that exposes the challenges to the practical application of the right to free movement and the differential treatment of citizens.

The focus on discrimination among categories of migrants helps to mark out a line of continuity from Antiquity to the present day. We note from the historical review in Chapter 1 that the right to freedom of movement, understood in terms of the rights to migrate and settle, preceded what we may now understand as social, economic and cultural rights. The right to migration and settlement was further defined over

time by association with economic activity in Antiquity as in contemporary Europe. Yet the progressive development of mobility rights,
independent from social and economic rights, leaves open the possibility
for discrimination that in turn undermines the transformative power
associated with the right to freedom of movement as expressed in the
works of liberal theorists such as Sen and Carens. Freedom of movement
may be a pre-requisite to the enjoyment of other rights, but the idea that
it is a right that opens the door to other rights is too simplistic.

As evidenced in the above case studies, successful mobility, establishment and settlement is conditioned on migrants being received in a
rights-enforcing culture and by the removal of structural barriers that
undermine equality of opportunity. Structural considerations that affect
the enjoyment of one's freedom of movement include respect for political
and civil rights as set out in law. They also include the protection of
social and economic rights that emerge from this study as far more telling
indicators of successful mobility. Although many of the participants in
this study provided individualistic reasons for their migration (whether
internal or to another EU member state), their experiences record that
their successes, or more commonly their failures, in establishing their
lives elsewhere were determined by their ability to access the labour
market, enrol their children in school, and by the day-to-day living which
was influenced by their status. This book therefore reaffirms the conclusion by Condinanzi Lang and Nascimbene (2008) regarding the markers
of European integration. As recorded in the case studies, the areas of
residence, employment and social integration are among the greatest
challenges facing European migrants seeking to relocate internally as
well as between other EU member states.

The research findings also inform our understanding of open borders.
Successful entry into a state does not remove the hidden sources of
discrimination that frustrate the degree to which people are able to
establish themselves in the new setting. Moreover, they reveal the
limitations in Carens' argument in favour of open borders. Immigration
policies may protect unjust privilege but so do ethno-centric policies such
as citizenship legislation, residency controls and tolerated institutional
discrimination (as documented in the case of the foreign language
teachers in Italy). Relative inequality is not limited to levels of economic
development between states but, as World Systems theorists note, opportunities are also sharply delineated within states. In this study it is not
class which serves as the source of division but rather mobility status.

States influence the outcome of migration and settlement. They may
play a direct role as in Croatia and Slovenia, where the state authorities
undermine people's rights to move as well as their rights to remain. Yet,

beyond the central state, we note that sub-national actors, including regional and municipal governments and other organizations, are extremely influential in determining the outcome of internal relocations. In some cases collaborative efforts between state bodies and local organizations facilitate migrants' establishment in the new setting, as in the context of the Spanish doctors who relocated to Northern England. In other cases organizations may both replace and subvert the role of the state, as evidenced by the positive assistance of employers who enabled new migrants to settle in Moscow and by the negative actions of the Italian universities that undermined the foreigners' job security, pensions and related benefits. These findings therefore call into question the statist tendency in the literature on migration and citizenship studies that ignores the complexities of internal migration and the civic inequalities that may result from intra-state relocations. We further note that the statist model fails to recognize the many layers of conflict existing within the state that may be influenced by external parties, including the European Union. As the case studies from Croatia and Italy show, the great difficulty experienced by national governments and both domestic and international courts to hold offending actors to account and to impose the law reveals a pattern of intra-state and intra-European conflict around the rights of migrants to settle elsewhere. Arguably, the empirical findings in this book illustrate the potency of neo-pluralist approaches for our understanding of the ways in which conflict and competition among diverse groups, political institutions, and interests bear on successful migration and settlement.

The overriding conclusion of this book is that mobility status affects the substantive enjoyment of one's rights and hence undermines the idea of citizenship. While institutions of the European Union may be working through this dilemma, beyond academic studies of contemporary immigration there remains a noticeable gap in scholastic writing on this theme. If the concept of freedom of movement is to have any meaning, then the idea should be reconnected to the logic of personal freedom and the connection made between the rights to migration, settlement and establishment.

Bibliography

Abramson, Paul R., Susan Ellis, and Ronald Inglehart. 1997. 'Research in Context: Measuring Value Change.' *Political Behavior* 19 (1): 41–59.

African Commission on Human and Peoples' Rights. 1981. *African Charter on Human and Peoples' Rights.* http://www.achpr.org/instruments/achpr/. Accessed 10 January 2014.

Agence France Press. 2003. 'Croatia Renews Calls for Serb Refugees to Return.' Text. *ReliefWeb.* 16 June. http://reliefweb.int/report/croatia/croatia-renews-calls-serb-refugees-return. Accessed 10 January 2014.

Alexseev, Mikhail A. 2001. 'Decentralization versus State Collapse: Explaining Russia's Endurance.' *Journal of Peace Research* 38 (1): 101–6. doi:10.1177/0022343301038001006.

Alonso, William. 1976. *A Theory of Movements: I, Introduction.* Berkeley, CA: Institute of Urban and Regional Development, University of California.

Alonso-Rocafort, Victor. 2009. 'Freedom of Movement in Hannah Arendt.' *Revista de Estudios Politicos* 07/2009: 33–64.

Althusser, Louis. 1968. *For Marx.* London: Allen Lane.

Amnesty International. 1998. 'Croatia: Impunity for Killings after Storm.' 1 August 1998. EUR 64/004/1998. http://www.refworld.org/docid/45b9f4302.html. Accessed 22 April 2014.

Amnesty International. 2004. 'Europe and Central Asia: Summary of Amnesty International's Concerns in the Region: January–June 2004.' http://www.refworld.org/docid/45bf15ba2.html. Accessed 6 January 2014.

Amnesty International. 2005. 'Slovenia: Amnesty International's Briefing to the UN Committee on Economic, Social and Cultural Rights, 35th Session, November 2005.' http://www.refworld.org/cgi-bin/texis/vtx/rwmain?page=search&docid=43b2705c4&skip=0&query= Slovenia: %20Amnesty%20International%E2%80%99s%20Briefing%20to%20the %20UN%20Committee%20on%20Economic,%20Social%20and%20 Cultural%20Rights,%2035th%20Session,%20November%202005. Accessed 6 January 2014.

Andreev, Svetlozar. 2003. 'Making Slovenian Citizens: The Problem of the Former Yugoslav Citizens and Asylum Seekers Living in Slovenia.' *Southeast European Politics* 4 (1): 1–24.

Answers.Com. 2014. 'Propiska.' http://www.answers. com/topic/propiska. Accessed 1 April 2014.

Apap, Joanna, ed. 2002. *Freedom of Movement of Persons: A Practitioner's Handbook.* Alphen aan den Rijn, The Netherlands: Kluwer Law International.

Arendt, Hannah. 1993. *Between Past and Future: Eight Exercises in Political Thought.* London: Penguin Books.

Arendt, Hannah. 2004. *The Origins of Totalitarianism.* New York: Schocken.

Arnull, Anthony. 2006. *The European Union and Its Court of Justice.* Oxford: Oxford University Press.

Baker, Nicholas Scott. 2009. 'For Reasons of State: Political Executions, Republicanism, and the Medici in Florence, 1480–1560.' *Renaissance Quarterly* 62 (2): 444–78.

Balibar, Étienne. 2009. *We, the People of Europe? Reflections on Transnational Citizenship.* Princeton, NJ: Princeton University Press.

Baltic, Admir. 2005. 'On the Perceptions of the Socio-Cultural Integration, Including the Participants' Relation towards the Culture in the Narrow Sense, Language and Religiosity.' Email to the Author. 14 June.

Batchelor, Carol A. 1995. 'Stateless Persons: Some Gaps in International Protection.' *International Journal of Refugee Law* 7: 232.

Bauböck, Rainer. 2003. 'Towards a Political Theory of Migrant Transnationalism.' *International Migration Review* 37 (3): 700–723.

Bauböck, Rainer. 2009. 'Global Justice, Freedom of Movement and Democratic Citizenship.' *European Journal of Sociology/Archives Européennes de Sociologie* 50 (1): 1–31. doi:10.1017/S0003975609 00040X.

Bauböck, Rainer, and Sara Wallace Goodman. 2010. 'Naturalisation.' 2. EUDO Citizenship Policy Brief. European Union Democracy Observatory on Citizenship. http://eudo-citizenship.eu/docs/policy_brief_ naturalisation.pdf. Accessed 10 January 2014.

Bebler, Anton. 2002. 'Slovenia's Smooth Transition.' *Journal of Democracy* 13 (1): 127–40.

Bell, Martin, and Salut Muhidin. 2009. 'Cross-National Comparisons of Internal Migration.' Human Development Research Paper 2009/30. United Nations Development Programme. http://hdr.undp.org/fr/ content/cross-national-comparisons-internal-migration. Accessed 10 January 2014.

Benton, Meghan, and Milica Petrovic. 2013. 'How Free Is Free Movement?' https://emnbelgium.be/sites/default/files/publications/mpi europe-freemovement-drivers.pdf. Accessed 10 January 2014.

Berlin, Isaiah. 1969. *Four Essays on Liberty*. Oxford: Oxford University Press.

Bhagwati, Jagdish, and Koichi Hamada. 1974. 'The Brain Drain, International Integration of Markets for Professionals and Unemployment: A Theoretical Analysis.' *Journal of Development Economics* 1 (1): 19–42.

Biersteker, Thomas J., and Cynthia Weber. 1996. *State Sovereignty as Social Construct*. Cambridge: Cambridge University Press.

Blitz, Brad K. 1999. 'The Resistant Guild: Institutional Protectionism and Freedom of Movement in the Italian University System.' *South European Society and Politics* 4 (1): 27–47. doi:10.1080/13608740408 539558.

Blitz, Brad K. 2003. 'Refugee Returns in Croatia: Contradictions and Reform.' *Politics* 23 (3): 181–91. doi:10.1111/1467-9256.00195.

Blitz, Brad K. 2005. 'Refugee Returns, Civic Differentiation, and Minority Rights in Croatia 1991–2004.' *Journal of Refugee Studies* 18 (3): 362–86. doi:10.1093/refuge/fei036.

Blitz, Brad K. 2006. *War and Change in the Balkans: Nationalism, Conflict and Cooperation*. Cambridge: Cambridge University Press.

Blitz, Brad K. 2007. 'Decentralisation, Citizenship and Mobility: Residency Restrictions and Skilled Migration in Moscow.' *Citizenship Studies* 11 (4): 383–404. doi:10.1080/13621020701476277.

Blitz, Brad K. 2008. 'Democratic Development, Judicial Reform and the Serbian Question in Croatia.' *Human Rights Review* 9 (1): 123–35. doi:10.1007/s12142-007-0036-0.

Blitz, Brad K. 2010. 'Fractured Lives and Grim Expectations: Freedom of Movement and the Downgrading of Status in the Italian University System.' *Bulletin of Italian Politics* 2 (2): 123–40.

Bodin, Jean. 1992. *Bodin: On Sovereignty*. Cambridge: Cambridge University Press.

Bosniak, Linda. 2008. *The Citizen and the Alien: Dilemmas of Contemporary Membership*. Princeton, NJ: Princeton University Press.

Bourdieu, Pierre, and Jean-Claude Passeron. 1990. *Reproduction in Education, Society and Culture*. London; Thousand Oaks; New Delhi: Sage.

Bowles, Samuel, and Herbert Gintis. 1976. *Schooling in Capitalist America: Educational Reform and the Contradictions of Economic Life*. New York: Basic Books.

Boyd, Monica. 1989. 'Family and Personal Networks in International Migration: Recent Developments and New Agendas.' *International Migration Review* 23: (3) 638–70.

Brabandt, Heike, Lena Laube, and Christof Roos. 2012. *Liberal States and the Freedom of Movement: Selective Borders, Unequal Mobility.* Basingstoke: Palgrave Macmillan.

British Medical Association. 2012. 'The UK Medical Workforce.' http://bma.org.uk/-/media/Files/Word%20files/News%20views%20analysis/pressbriefing_uk%20medical%20workforce.doc. Accessed 6 January 2014.

Brouwer, Andrew. 2003. 'Statelessness in Canadian Context.' Geneva: UNHCR. http://www.unhcr.org/refworld/pdfid/405f07164.pdf. Accessed 6 January 2014.

Brown, Wendy. 2010. *Walled States, Waning Sovereignty.* Brooklyn, New York: Zone Books.

Brubaker, Rogers. 1996. *Nationalism Reframed: Nationhood and the National Question in the New Europe.* Cambridge: Cambridge University Press.

Brubaker, Rogers. 2009. *Citizenship and Nationhood in France and Germany.* Cambridge, MA: Harvard University Press.

Buchan, James. 2002. 'International Recruitment of Nurses: United Kingdom Case Study.' http://eresearch.qmu.ac.uk/18/. Accessed 6 January 2014.

Burrows, F. 1987. *Free Movement in European Community Law.* Oxford: Clarendon Press.

Cain, Glen G. 1976. 'The Challenge of Segmented Labor Market Theories to Orthodox Theory: A Survey.' *Journal of Economic Literature* 14 (4): 1215–57.

Caplan, Jane, and John C. Torpey. 2001. *Documenting Individual Identity: The Development of State Practices in the Modern World.* Princeton, NJ: Princeton University Press.

Carens, Joseph H. 1987. 'Aliens and Citizens: The Case for Open Borders.' *The Review of Politics* 49 (2): 251–73. doi:10.1017/S00346 70500033817.

Castells, Manuel. 1975. *Neo-Capitalism, Collective Consumption and Urban Contradictions: New Sources of Inequality and New Models for Change.* Los Angeles, CA: School of Architecture and Urban Planning, University of California.

Castles, Stephen, and Alastair Davidson. 2000. *Citizenship and Migration: Globalization and the Politics of Belonging.* New York: Routledge.

Castles, Stephen, Godula Kosack, and Institute of Race Relations. 1973. *Immigrant Workers and Class Structure in Western Europe.* Oxford: Institute of Race Relations/Oxford University Press.

Castles, Stephen, and Mark J. Miller. 2009. *The Age of Migration: International Population Movements in the Modern World*. Basingstoke: Palgrave Macmillan.

Cervantes, Mario, and Dominique Guellec. 2002. 'The Brain Drain: Old Myths, New Realities.' *Organisation for Economic Cooperation and Development. The OECD Observer*, no. 230: 40.

Chalmers, Damian, Gareth Davies, and Giorgio Monti. 2010. *European Union Law: Cases and Materials*. Cambridge: Cambridge University Press.

Chapman, Roger. 2000. 'General Practice in the United Kingdom: A New Dawn?' European Union of General Practitioners. http://www.uemo.org/natsec/uk.htm. Accessed 6 January 2014.

Cherepova, Olga. 1999. 'Freedom Online: Ethnic Discrimination and Discrimination on the Basis of Place of Residence in the Moscow Region.' http://freedom-online.narod.ru/ethdiscr.htm. Accessed 6 January 2014.

Clark, Burton R. 1977. *Academic Power in Italy: Bureaucracy and Oligarchy in a National University System*. Chicago: University of Chicago Press.

Codagnone, C. 1998a. 'The New Migration in Russia in the 1990s.' In Helma Lutz and Khalid Koser, eds., *The New Migration in Europe: Social Constructions and Social Realities*, 39–59. London: Macmillan. http://us.macmillan.com/thenewmigrationineurope/Khalid Koser. Accessed 6 January 2014.

Codagnone, C. 1998b. 'New Migration and Migration Politics in Post-Soviet Russia.' The Ethnobarometer Working Paper Series. Torpoint, UK: Centre for European Migration and Ethnic Studies (CEMES). http://www.ethnobarometer.org/wp-content/uploads/2013/03/wp02.pdf. Accessed 6 January 2014.

Commission of the European Communities. 2004. *Communication from the Commission Opinion on Croatia's Application for Membership of the European Union*. http://eur-lex.europa.eu/LexUriServ/site/en/com/2004/com2004_0257en01.pdf. Accessed 10 January 2014.

Commission on Human Security. 2003. *Human Security Now*. New York: Commission on Human Security. http://reliefweb.int/sites/reliefweb.int/files/resources/91BAEEDBA50C6907C1256D19006A9353-chs-security-may03.pdf. Accessed 6 January 2014.

Committee to Protect Journalists. 2002. 'Attacks on the Press 2001: Croatia – Committee to Protect Journalists.' 26 March. http://cpj.org/2002/03/attacks-on-the-press-2001-croatia.php. Accessed 6 January 2014.

Condinanzi, Massimo, Allessandra Lang, and Bruno Nascimbene. 2008. *Citizenship of the Union and Freedom of Movement of Persons.* Leiden: Brill.

Conversi, Daniele. 2000. 'Central Secession: Towards a New Analytical Concept? The Case of Former Yugoslavia.' *Journal of Ethnic and Migration Studies* 26 (2): 333–55. doi:10.1080/13691830050022839.

Council of Europe. 1963. *Protocol No. 4 to the Convention for the Protection of Human Rights and Fundamental Freedoms.* http://conventions.coe.int/Treaty/en/Treaties/Html/046.htm. Accessed 6 January 2014.

Council of the European Communities. 2004. *Council Directive 2004/83/EC of 29 April 2004 on Minimum Standards for the Qualification and Status of Third Country Nationals or Stateless Persons as Refugees or as Persons Who Otherwise Need International Protection and the Content of the Protection Granted.* http://eur-lex.europa.eu/LexUriServ/LexUriServ.do?uri=CELEX:32004L0083:EN:HTML. Accessed 6 January 2014.

Council of the European Communities, and European Parliament. 2004. *Directive 2004/38/EC of the European Parliament and of the Council of 29 April 2004 on the Right of Citizens of the Union and Their Family Members to Move and Reside Freely within the Territory of the Member States.* http://eur-lex.europa.eu/LexUriServ/LexUriServ.do?uri=CELEX:32004L0038:en:NOT. Accessed 6 January 2014.

Craig, Paul, and Gráinne De Búrca, eds. 2011a. *EU Law: Text, Cases, and Materials.* Oxford: Oxford University Press.

Craig, Paul, and Gráinne De Búrca. 2011b. 'Free Movement of Persons and Services.' In Paul P. Craig and Gráinne De Búrca, eds., *The Evolution of EU Law*, 499–545. Oxford: Oxford University Press.

Craig, Paul P., and Gráinne De Búrca, eds. 2011c. *The Evolution of EU Law.* Oxford: Oxford University Press.

Cranston, Maurice William. 1973. *What Are Human Rights?* London: Bodley Head.

Cremers, Jan. 2013. 'Free Provision of Services and Cross-Border Labour Recruitment.' *Policy Studies* 34 (2): 201–20.

Croatian Helsinki Committee for Human Rights. 2001. 'Media Report for July, August and September 2001.' Zagreb, October. http://www.greekhelsinki.gr/bhr/english/countries/croatia/chc_report.doc. Accessed 10 January 2014.

Croatian Helsinki Committee for Human Rights. 2004. 'Forced Evictions in the Republic of Croatia.'

Davidson, Scott. 1987. 'Free Movement of Goods, Workers, Services and Capital.' In Juliet Lodge, ed., *The European Community and the Challenge of the Future*, 111–28. London: Pinter.

Decision in Case No. U-I-246/02. 2003. Constitutional Court of the Republic of Slovenia.

Dedić, Jasminka, Vlasta Jalušič, Matevž Krivic, and Jelka Zorn. 2003. *The Erased: Organized Innocence and the Politics of Exclusion.* Ljubljana: Peace Institute, Institute for Contemporary Social and Political Studies.

Department of Health. 2002. 'International Recruitment of Consultants and General Practitioners for the NHS in England: Current Initiatives and Guidance to NHS Employers on an Infrastructure to Support International Recruitment.' London: Department of Health.

Department of Health. 2003a. 'Chief Executive's Report to the NHS 2002/03.' London: Department of Health.

Department of Health. 2003b. 'International Recruitment Global Scheme Recruitment Process.' London: Department of Health.

Deutsch, Karl W. 1969. 'The Concentration of Decisions: Sovereignty and Vulnerability in Political Systems.' In W.J. Stankiewicz, ed., *In Defence of Sovereignty*, 107–11. Oxford: Oxford University Press.

Deutsch, Karl W. 1972. *Nationalism and Social Communication: An Inquiry into the Foundations of Nationality.* The Massachusetts Institute of Technology: Technology Press.

Deutsch, Karl W. 1978. *The Analysis of International Relations.* Upper Saddle River, NJ: Prentice-Hall.

Diez Nicolas, Juan. 1996. 'Social Position, Information and Postmaterialism.' *Revista Española de Investigaciones Sociológicas* 96 (English Edition): 153–65.

Dokoza, Hrvojka. 2003. 'Report on Freedom of the Media – 2003', OSCE Memo. Unpublished.

Donnelly, Jack. 2002. *Universal Human Rights in Theory and Practice.* Ithaca, NY: Cornell University Press.

Doudeijns, Marco, and Jean-Christophe Dumont. 2003. 'Immigration and Labour Shortages: Evaluation of Needs and Limits of Selection Policies in the Recruitment of Foreign Labour.' http://www.oecd.org/migration/mig/15474016.pdf. Accessed 23 April 2014.

Dowty, Alan. 1989. *Closed Borders: The Contemporary Assault on Freedom of Movement.* New Haven, CT: Yale University Press.

Edwards, Chris. 1985. *The Fragmented World: Competing Perspectives on Trade, Money, and Crisis.* London: Methuen.

Ellis, Susan, and Sultan Barakat. 1996. 'From Relief to Development: The Long-Term Effects of "Temporary" Accommodation on Refugees and Displaced Persons in the Republic of Croatia.' http://www.academia.edu/1165572/From_Relief_to_Development_The_Long-term_Effects_of_TemporaryAccommodation_on_Refugees_and_Displaced_Persons_in_the_Republic_of_Croatia. Accessed 10 January 2014.

Eurofound. 2011. 'Non-Discrimination Principle.' IR term. 5 May. https://www.eurofound.europa.eu/areas/industrialrelations/dictionary/definitions/nondiscriminationprinciple.htm. Accessed 9 January 2014.

European Commission. 2007. 'Discrimination in the European Union.' 263. Special Eurobarometer, Wave 65.4 – TNS Opinion & Social. Brussels: European Commission. ec.europa.eu/public_opinion/archives/ebs/ebs_263_en.pdf. Accessed 6 January 2014.

European Commission. 2014. 'Fundamental Rights: Importance of EU Charter Grows as Citizens Stand to Benefit.' European Commission – IP/14/422, 14 April 2014. http://europa.eu/rapid/press-release_IP-14-422_en.htm. Accessed 22 April 2014.

European Commission against Racism and Intolerance. 1999. 'Second Report on Croatia.' Strasbourg, 9 November. http://hudoc.ecri.coe.int/XMLEcri/ENGLISH/Cycle_02/02_CbC_eng/02-cbc-croatia-eng.pdf. Accessed 10 January 2014.

European Commission against Racism and Intolerance. 2002. 'Second Report on Slovenia.' Strasbourg. http://hudoc.ecri. coe.int/XMLEcri/ENGLISH/Cycle_02/02_CbC_eng/02-cbc-slovenia-eng.pdf. Accessed 6 January 2014.

European Parliament. 1995. 'Human Rights – Resolution on Discriminatory Treatment on the Grounds of Nationality for Foreign Language Teachers ("lettori") at Verona University (Italy), in Violation of Article 48 of the EEC Treaty – B4-0968/95, Texts Adopted by Parliament. Final Edition.' 13 July. http://www.europarl.europa.eu/omk/omnsapir.so/pv2?PRG=CALDOC&FILE=950713&LANGUE=EN&TPV=DEF&LASTCHAP=12&SDOCTA=9&TXTLST=8&Type_Doc=RESOL&POS=1. Accessed 13 January 2014.

European Parliament and Council of the European Union. 1997. *Directive 96/71/EC of the European Parliament and of the Council of 16 December 1996 Concerning the Posting of Workers in the Framework of the Provision of Services.* http://eur-lex.europa.eu/LexUriServ/LexUri Serv.do?uri=CELEX:31996L0071:EN:NOT.

European Parliament/Legislative Observatory. 2010. Non-legislative basic document [document number] 2010/2273(INI), 13 July. http://www.europarl.europa.eu/oeil/popups/summary.do?id=1131084&t=e&l=en. Accessed 23 April 2014.

European Union Agency for Fundamental Rights. 2010. 'European Union Agency for Fundamental Rights Annual Report 2010.' Conference Edition. Vienna: European Union Agency for Fundamental Rights. http://fra.europa.eu/fraWebsite/attachments/AR_2010-conf-edition_en.pdf. Accessed 6 January 2014.

Evetts, Julia. 2002. 'New Directions in State and International Professional Occupations: Discretionary Decision-Making and Acquired Regulation.' *Work, Employment & Society* 16 (2): 341–53.

Faist, Thomas. 2000. *The Volume and Dynamics of International Migration and Transnational Social Spaces*. http://pub.uni-bielefeld.de/pub?func=drec&id=2465734. Accessed 6 January 2014.

Favell, Adrian. 2011. *Eurostars and Eurocities: Free Movement and Mobility in an Integrating Europe*. Oxford: John Wiley & Sons.

Federal Migration Service. 2013. 'Registration ("Федеральная Миграционная Служба России – Поиск").' 22 February. http://www.fms.gov.ru/search/?q=registration. Accessed 22 February 2013.

Findlay, Allan. 1995. 'Skilled Transients: The Invisible Phenomenon.' In Robin Cohen, ed., *The Cambridge Survey of World Migration*, 515–22. Cambridge: Cambridge University Press. http://scholar.google.co.uk/citations?view_op=view_citation&hl=en&user=DE-0qvgAAAAJ&citation_for_view=DE-0qvgAAAAJ:_FxGoFyzp5QC. Accessed 6 January 2014.

Fitzgerald, David. 2006. 'Inside the Sending State: The Politics of Mexican Emigration Control.' *International Migration Review* 40 (2): 259–93. doi:10.1111/j.1747-7379.2006.00017.x.

Garzon, Fernando Perez. 2014. 'General Medicine in Spain.' *European Union of General Practitioners*. http://www.uemo.eu/national-sections/12-spain.html. Accessed 22 April 2014.

Gazzetta Ufficiale n. 10 del 14 gennaio 2011 – Suppl. Ordinario n. 11. 2010. *Legge 30 Dicembre 2010, N. 240 – Norme in Materia Di Organizzazione Delle Università, Di Personale Accademico E Reclutamento, Nonche' Delega Al Governo per Incentivare La Qualità E L'efficienza Del Sistema Universitario (Gelmini Law). No 240.*

Gerber, T.P. 2005. 'Individual and Contextual Determinants of Internal Migration in Russia, 1985–2001.' http://www.researchgate.net/publication/228375599_Individual_and_Contextual_Determinants_of_Internal_Migration_in_Russia_1985-2001. Accessed 28 October 2013.

Gibney, Mark. 1988a. *Open Borders? Closed Societies? The Ethical and Political Issues*. Westport, CT: Greenwood Publishing Group, Incorporated.

Gibney, Mark. 1988b. 'Citizenship and Freedom of Movement: An Open Admission Policy?' In Mark Gibney, ed., *Open Borders? Closed Societies? The Ethical and Political Issues*, 3–40. Westport, CT; New York; London: Greenwood Publishing Group.

Gow, James, and Cathie Carmichael. 2010. *Slovenia and the Slovenes: A Small State and the New Europe*. London: Hurst.

Grossman, Gene M., and Elhanan Helpman. 1991. 'Quality Ladders in the Theory of Growth.' *Review of Economic Studies* 58 (1): 43–61.

Haas, Ernst B. 1968. *The Uniting of Europe: Political, Social, and Economic Forces, 1950–1957*. Stanford, CA: Stanford University Press.

Harris, John R., and Michael P. Todaro. 1970. 'Migration, Unemployment and Development: A Two-Sector Analysis.' *American Economic Review* 60 (1): 126–42.

Hedl, Drago. 2005. 'Croatia: Lora Retrial Eases Pressure on Sanader – Institute for War and Peace Reporting – P230.' *Balkans Crisis Report* no. 513. 21 February. http://iwpr.net/report-news/croatia-lora-retrial-eases-pressure-sanader. Accessed 30 October 2013.

Held, David. 1989. *Political Theory and the Modern State: Essays on State, Power, and Democracy*. Stanford, CA: Stanford University Press.

Hershey, Amos S. 1911. 'The History of International Relations during Antiquity and the Middle Ages.' *American Journal of International Law* 5 (4): 901–33.

Hinsley, F.H. 1986. *Sovereignty*. Cambridge: Cambridge University Press.

Höjdestrand, Tova. 2003. 'The Soviet-Russian Production of Homelessness: Propiska, Housing, Privatisation.' http://www.anthrobase.com/Txt/H/Hoejdestrand_T_01.htm. Accessed 6 January 2014.

Home Office and Department for Work and Pensions. 2013. *Review of the Balance of Competences, Internal Market: Free Movement of Persons, Call for Evidence*. https://www.gov.uk/government/uploads/system/uploads/attachment_data/file/200497/Free_Movement_of_Persons_-_Call_for_Evidence.pdf. Accessed 6 January 2014.

Hosein, Adam. 2013. 'Immigration and Freedom of Movement.' *Ethics & Global Politics* 6 (1). doi:10.3402/egp.v6i1.18188. http://www.ethicsandglobalpolitics.net/index.php/egp/article/view/18188. Accessed 17 June 2013.

Human Rights Ombudsman of the Republic of Slovenia. 2005. 'Ombudsman Calls on MPs Once Again to Tackle Problem of the Erased.' 14 July. http://www.varuh-rs.si/media-centre/work-and-news/news/detajl/ombudsman-calls-on-mps-once-again-to-tackle-problem-of-the-erased/?L=6&cHash=e0d24793da7f21841ca5b3f2b4cb2f1d. Accessed 6 January 2014.

Human Rights Watch. 1997. 'Moscow: Open Season, Closed City.' 9 October. Human Rights Watch. http://www.hrw.org/node/78319. Accessed 6 January 2014.

Human Rights Watch. 1998. 'The Residence Permit System (Propiska).' http://www.hrw.org/reports/pdfs/r/russia/russia959.pdf. Accessed 10 January 2014.

Human Rights Watch. 2001. 'Human Rights Watch and the World Conference against Racism, Racial Discrimination, Xenophobia and

Related Intolerance.' 22 June. http://www.hrw.org/legacy/campaigns/race/submission.htm. Accessed 6 January 2014.

Human Rights Watch. 2003. *Broken Promises: Impediments to Refugee Return to Croatia.* Human Rights Watch.

Human Rights Watch. 2006. 'Russia: Country Summary.' New York: Human Rights Watch. http://www.hrw.org/legacy/wr2k6/pdf/russia.pdf. Accessed 6 January 2014.

Human Rights Watch. 2011. 'Russia: Reported Roundup of Tajik Migrants.' 15 November. http://www.hrw.org/print/news/2011/11/15/russia-reported-roundup-tajik-migrants. Accessed 6 January 2014.

Inglehart, Ronald. 1971. 'The Silent Revolution in Europe: Intergenerational Change in Post-Industrial Societies.' *American Political Science Review* 65 (4): 991–1017.

Inglehart, Ronald. 1977. *The Silent Revolution: Changing Values and Political Styles among Western Publics.* Vol. 8. Princeton, NJ: Princeton University Press. http://familytoday.info/attachments/159_The%20Silent%20Revolution-Vom%20stillen%20Wandel%20der%20Werte.pdf. Accessed 6 January 2014.

Inglehart, Ronald. 1990. *Culture Shift in Advanced Industrial Society.* Princeton, NJ: Princeton University Press. http://books.google.co.uk/books?hl=en&lr=&id=ztYnOnSgs1EC&oi=fnd&pg=PR9&dq=inglehart+ronald&ots=vGU-5pwYUV&sig=bphNqPC5Zs_XJcqByREATOcI4b4. Accessed 6 January 2014.

International Conference of American States. 1948. *American Declaration of the Rights and Duties of Man.* https://www.oas.org/en/iachr/mandate/Basics/2.AMERICAN%20DECLARATION.pdf. Accessed 6 January 2014.

International Criminal Tribunal for the Former Yugoslavia. 2012. *Prosecutor v Ante Gotovina and Mladen Markač*, Case No. IT-06-90-A, 16 November 2012. http://www.icty.org/x/cases/gotovina/acjug/en/121116_judgement.pdf. Accessed 15 December 2013.

International Helsinki Federation for Human Rights. 2002. 'Slovenia–IHF Focus: Freedom of Expression and Media; Rule of Law and Independence of the Judiciary; Torture, Ill-Treatment and Police Misconduct; Right to Privacy; National Minorities; Citizenship; Intolerance, Xenophobia, Racial Discrimination and Hate Speech.' http://www.refworld.org/pdfid/469243630.pdf. Accessed 10 January 2014.

International Labor Organization. 2010. 'International Labor Migration Database.' International Labor Organization. http://www.ilo.org/public/english/protection/migrant/info/ilm_dbase.htm. Accessed 28 October 2013.

International Organization for Migration. 2012. 'Russian Federation.' May. http://www.iom.int/cms/en/sites/iom/home/where-we-work/europa

/south-eastern-europe-eastern-eur/russian-federation.html. Accessed 6 January 2014.

Ionescu, Ghita, ed. 1974. *Between Sovereignty and Integration: Introduction*. London: Croom Helm. http://onlinelibrary.wiley.com/doi/10.1111/j.1477-7053.1974.tb00874.x/abstract.

Iredale, Robyn. 2001. 'The Migration of Professionals: Theories and Typologies.' *International Migration* 39 (5): 7–26.

Ivanisevic, Bogdan. 2009. 'Broken Promises: Impediments to Refugee Return to Croatia.' http://dspace.cigilibrary.org/jspui/handle/12345 6789/17264. Accessed 6 January 2014.

Ivanisevic, Bogdan, and Jennifer Trahan. 2004. *Justice at Risk: War Crimes Trials in Croatia, Bosnia and Herzegovina, and Serbia and Montenegro*. Human Rights Watch.

Jackson, Robert. 2007. *Sovereignty: The Evolution of an Idea*. Cambridge: Polity.

Juss, Satvinder S. 2004. 'Free Movement and the World Order.' *International Journal of Refugee Law* 16 (3): 289–335.

Juss, Satvinder S. 2013. *International Migration and Global Justice*. Farnham: Ashgate Publishing, Ltd.

Karanja, Stephen Kabera. 2008. *Transparency and Proportionality in the Schengen Information System and Border Control Co-Operation*. Leiden: Martinus Nijhoff Publishers.

Katanian, Konstantin. 1998. 'Freedom of Movement in the Russian Federation Today.' *East European Constitutional Review* 7 (2). http://www1.law.nyu.edu/eecr/vol7num2/special/propiska.html. Accessed 6 January 2014.

Kavanagh, Dennis. 1974. 'Beyond Autonomy? The Politics of Corporations.' In Ghita Ionescu, ed., *Between Sovereignty and Integration*, 46–64. London: Croom Helm.

Khrushcheva, Nina L. 1999. 'Moscow's Boss under Fire.' *Project Syndicate*. 14 December. http://www.project-syndicate.org/commentary/moscow-s-boss-under-fire/english. Accessed 6 January 2014.

King, Russell. 2000. 'Generalizations from the History of Return Migration.' In Bimal Gosh, ed., *Return Migration: Journey of Hope or Despair*, 7–55. Geneva: International Organisation for Migration.

Komac, Miran. 2001. 'Forming a New Nation-State and the Repression or Protection of Ethnic Minorities: The Case of Slovenia.' In Stuart Nagel and Amy Robb, eds., *Handbook of Global Social Policy*, 267–92. New York: Marcel Dekker.

Komac, Miran, and Mojca Medvešek, eds. 2004. 'Perceptions of Slovenian Integration Policy (INV – Procesi Etničnega Razlikovanja v Sloveniji: Soočanje Percepcija).' Ljubljana, Slovenia: Institute of Ethnic Studies.

Kritz, Mary M., Lin Lean Lim, and Hania Zlotnik. 1992. *International Migration Systems: A Global Approach.* Oxford: Clarendon Press.

Lavenex, Sandra. 2006. 'The Competition State and Multilateral Liberalization of High Skilled Migration.' In Michael Peter Smith and Adrian Favell, eds., *The Human Face of Global Mobility: International Highly Skilled Migration in Europe, North America and the Asia-Pacific*, 29–54. New Brunswick, NJ: Transaction Publishers.

League of Nations. 1930. *Convention on Certain Questions Relating to the Conflict of Nationality Laws.* Vol. 179. Treaty Series 4137. The Hague: League of Nations. http://www.refworld.org/docid/3ae6b3b00. html. Accessed 8 January 2014.

Lee, Everett S. 1966. 'A Theory of Migration.' *Demography* 3 (1): 47–57.

Lenard, Patti Tamara. 2010. 'Culture, Free Movement, and Open Borders.' *Review of Politics* 72 (4): 627–52. doi:10.1017/S00346705 10000562.

Levine, Y., J. Rudnitsky, and M. Ames. 2006. 'Bribe to Live, Live to Bribe: An Exile Guide to Who Costs What in Putin's Russia.' *The Exile.* 24 March. http://www.exile.ru/print.php?ARTICLE_ID=807 7&IBLOCK_ID=35. Accessed 6 January 2014.

Light, Ivan Hubert, and Parminder Bhachu. 1993. *Immigration and Entrepreneurship: Culture, Capital, and Ethnic Networks.* New Jersey: Transaction Publishers.

Light, Matthew. 1995. 'Migration Controls in Russia since 1991: From Centralized Repression to Localized Anarchy.' Chapter 1, Doctoral Dissertation, Yale University. New Haven, CT: Yale University.

Lipp, Thomas. 1999. 'The Situation of General Practitioners in Germany in the Run-Up to the Year 2000.' European Union of General Practitioners.

Lobnikar, Branko, and Milan Pagon. 2002. 'Slovenian State Officials, Slovenian Citizens, and Refugees in Slovenia: How They Perceive Each Other.' *European Journal of Crime, Criminal Law and Criminal Justice* 10 (2): 192–201. doi:10.1163/157181702401475386.

Locke, John. 1993. *Two Treatises of Government.* London: Everyman Paperback.

Loiberg, M. 1998. 'Social Structure and Political Tenets of the New Branch of the Russian Regional Elite.' In V. Shlapentokh, C. Vanderpool and B. Doktorov, eds., *The New Elite in Post-Communist Eastern Europe*, 241–50. College Station: Texas A. and M. University Press.

Lowell, Lindsay B. 2002. 'Some Development Effects of the International Migration of Highly Skilled Persons.' 46. International Migration Papers. Geneva: International Labour Office. http://www.ilo.org/ public/english/protection/migrant/download/imp/imp46.pdf. Accessed 8 January 2014.

Lukšič, Igor. 2003. 'Corporatism Packaged in Pluralist Ideology: The Case of Slovenia.' *Communist and Post-Communist Studies* 36 (4): 509–25. doi:10.1016/j.postcomstud.2003.09.007.

Magaš, Branka. 1993. *The Destruction of Yugoslavia: Tracking the Break-Up 1980–92*. London: Verso.

Mahroum, Sami. 1998. 'Europe and the Challenge of the Brain Drain.' Institute for Prospective Technological Studies. http://ipts.jrc.ec. europa.eu/home/report/english/articles/vol29/SAT1E296.htm. Accessed 6 January 2014.

Mahroum, Sami. 2001. 'Europe and the Immigration of Highly Skilled Labour.' *International Migration* 39 (5): 27–43. doi:10.1111/1468-2435.00170.

Massey, Douglas S. 1987. 'Understanding Mexican Migration to the United States.' *American Journal of Sociology* 92 (6): 1372–403.

Massey, Douglas S., and Kristin E. Espinosa. 1997. 'What's Driving Mexico–US Migration? A Theoretical, Empirical, and Policy Analysis.' *American Journal of Sociology* 102 (4): 939–99.

Massey, Douglas S., Joaquin Arango, Graeme Hugo, Ali Kouaouci, Adela Pellegrino, and J. Edward Taylor. 1993. 'Theories of International Migration: A Review and Appraisal.' *Population and Development Review* 19 (3): 431–66.

Massey, Douglas S., Joaquin Arango, Graeme Hugo, Ali Kouaouci, Adela Pellegrino, J. Edward Taylor, et. al. 2005. *Worlds in Motion: Understanding International Migration at the End of the Millennium*. Oxford; New York: Oxford University Press.

Matthews, Mervyn. 1993. *The Passport Society: Controlling Movement in Russia and the USSR*. Boulder, CO: Westview Press.

Mau, Steffen, Heike Brabandt, Lena Laube, and Christof Roos. 2012. *Liberal States and the Freedom of Movement: Selective Borders, Unequal Mobility (Transformations of the State)*. London: Palgrave Macmillan.

McMahon, Joe, Adam Cygan, and Erika Szyszczak. 2006. 'II. EU Citizenship.' *International & Comparative Law Quarterly* 55 (4): 977–82. doi:10.1093/iclq/lei139.

Merriman, Peter. 2012. *Mobility, Space, and Culture*. London: Routledge.

Mesić, Milan, and Dragan Bagić. 2011. *Minority Return to Croatia: Study of an Open Process*. Zagreb: UNHCR.

Middleton, K.W.B. 1969. 'Sovereignty in Theory and Practice.' In W.J. Stankiewicz, ed., *In Defence of Sovereignty*, 132–59. Oxford: Oxford University Press.

Migration Policy Centre, European University Institute. 2013. 'MPC – Migration Profile Russia.' http://www.migrationpolicycentre.eu/docs/ migration_profiles/Russia.pdf. Accessed 23 November 2013.

Miklavic Predan, Neva. 1998. 'Human Rights Problems in Slovenia. Helsinki Monitor of Slovenia, Press Release Statement.' 11 February. http://webcache.googleusercontent.com/search?q=cache:jviwO1Bycb4 J:www.hartford-hwp.com/archives/62/473.html+&cd=1&hl=en&ct=cl nk&gl=uk&client=firefox-a. Accessed 6 January 2014.

Miklavic Predan, Neva. 1999. 'Human Rights Problems in Slovenia: Forced Evictions in Slovenia Under Way – Statement No. 6.' Ljubljana, Slovenia: Helsinki Monitor. http://community.fortunecity.ws/melting pot/iceland/363/Statement_No_6.htm. Accessed 6 January 2014.

Miller, David. 2007. *National Responsibility and Global Justice*. Oxford: Oxford University Press. http://www.oxfordscholarship.com/view/ 10.1093/acprof:oso/9780199235056.001.0001/acprof-9780199235056. Accessed 6 January 2014.

Miller, David. 2011. 'David Owen on Global Justice, National Responsibility and Transnational Power: A Reply.' *Review of International Studies* 37 (4): 2029–34. doi:10.1017/S0260210511000520.

Minority Rights Group International. 2003. 'Minorities in Croatia.' http://www.minorityrights.org/1005/reports/minorities-in-croatia.html. Accessed 30 October 2013.

Mitrany, David. 1966. *A Working Peace System*. Chicago: Quadrangle Books.

Moses, Jonathon W. 2006. *International Migration: Globalization's Last Frontier*. London: Zed Books.

Narodne Novine (Official Gazette). 1995a. 'Law on Temporary Take-Over and Administration of Specified Property (LTTP) Amended, NN 7/96.' Government of Croatia.

Narodne Novine (Official Gazette). 1995b. 'Law on Temporary Take-Over and Administration of Specified Property (LTTP) of 1995, NN 73/95.' Government of Croatia.

Narodne Novine (Official Gazette). 1996. 'Law on Areas of Special State Concern, No. 44/96.' Government of Croatia.

Narodne Novine (Official Gazette). 1998. 'Programme for Return and Accommodation for Displaced Persons, Refugees and Resettled Persons, No. 92/98.' Government of Croatia.

Neuman, Gerald L. 1996. *Strangers to the Constitution: Immigrants, Borders, and Fundamental Law*. Princeton, NJ: Princeton University Press.

Nordic Council of Ministers. 2012. *Freedom of Movement within the Social- and Labour-Market Area in the Nordic Countries: Summary of Obstacles and Potential Solutions*. Copenhagen: Nordic Council of Ministers.

Norwegian Institute of International Affairs, Centre for Russian Studies. 1997. *Residence Permits Ruled Unconstitutional by Constitutional Court*. Oslo: Norwegian Institute of International Affairs.

Norwegian Refugee Council. 2001. 'Briefing Paper.' Norwegian Refugee Council.

Norwegian Refugee Council. 2002. 'Slow Progress Reported in the Implementation of the Amnesty Law Amnesty.' Norwegian Refugee Council.

NUPI, Centre for Russian Studies. 1997. 'Residence Permits Ruled Unconstitutional by Constitutional Court'.

OECD. 2001. *International Mobility of the Highly Skilled*. Paris: Organisation for Economic Co-Operation and Development. http://www.oecd-ilibrary.org/content/book/9789264196087-en. Accessed 23 April 2014.

OECD Observer. 2002. 'International Mobility of the Highly Skilled.' *Policy Brief* 6.

Office for National Statistics, Surveys and Administrative Sources. 2013. 'International Passenger Survey (IPS).' Text. Office for National Statistics. 30 August. http://www.ons.gov.uk/ons/about-ons/get-involved/taking-part-in-a-survey/information-for-households/a-to-z-of-household-and-individual-surveys/international-passenger-survey/index.html. Accessed 28 October 2013.

Official Gazette. 2002. *Constitutional Law on the Rights of National Minorities*. http://www.vsrh.hr/CustomPages/Static/HRV/Files/Legislation__Constitutional-Law-on-the-Rights-NM.pdf. Accessed 10 January 2014.

Official Gazette of the Republic of Slovenia. 1991. *Aliens Act. ZTUJ-1-UPB1*. http://legislationline.org/documents/action/popup/id/3835. Accessed 6 January 2014.

Official Gazette of the Republic of Slovenia. 1999. *Act on the Regulation of the Status of Citizens of Other Successor States to the Former SFRY in the Republic of Slovenia*.

O'Leary, Siofra. 2011. 'Free Movement of Persons and Services.' In Paul Craig and Gráinne De Búrca, eds., *The Evolution of EU Law*, 499–545. Oxford: Oxford University Press.

Organisation for Economic Co-Operation and Development. 2002. *International Mobility of the Highly Skilled*. OECD Publishing.

Organisation for Economic Co-Operation and Development. 2013. 'OECD Health Data 2013.' Organisation for Economic Co-Operation and Development. http://stats.oecd.org/Index.aspx?DataSetCode=HEALTH_REAC. Accessed 13 January 2014.

Organization for Security and Cooperation in Europe. 2001. 'Internally Displaced Persons, Refugees and Return.' Organization for Security and Cooperation in Europe.

Organization for Security and Cooperation in Europe. 2002. 'OSCE Status Report No. 10, Assessment of Issues Covered by the OSCE Mission to the Republic of Croatia's Mandate since 12 November 2001.' 21 May 2002. http://www.osce.org/zagreb/13181?download= true. Accessed 22 April 2014.

Organization for Security and Cooperation in Europe. 2004. 'OSCE Croatia Mission Calls for More Profound Debate on Measures to Prevent Hate Speech and Assess Past Ideologies – OSCE Office in Zagreb.' 22 November. http://www.osce.org/zagreb/56980. Accessed 30 October 2014.

Organization for Security and Cooperation in Europe. 2011. 'Annual Report on OSCE Activities 2010.' Vienna. Organization for Security and Cooperation in Europe. http://www.osce.org/sg/76315? download=true. Accessed 14 November 2011.

Organization for Security and Cooperation in Europe (OSCE) Mission to Croatia. 2003. 'OSCE Status Report No. 13.' 18 December.

Organization of American States. 2014. *American Convention on Human Rights 'Pact of San Jose, Costa Rica.'* http://www.oas.org/juridico/ english/treaties/b-32.html. Accessed 10 January 2014.

OSCE Office in Zagreb. 2004. 'OSCE Croatia Mission Calls for Further Training on War Crimes Trials, Better Judicial Co-Operation between States.' 20 August. http://www.osce.org/zagreb/56616. Accessed 10 January 2014.

Owen, David. 2010. 'Global Justice, National Responsibility and Trans-national Power.' *Review of International Studies* 36 (Supplement S1): 97–112. doi:10.1017/S0260210511000118.

Parliamentary Assembly, Council of Europe. 2001. 'The Propiska System Applied to Migrants, Asylum Seekers and Refugees in Council of Europe Member States: Effects and Remedies.' Doc. 9262. For Debate in the Standing Committee. See Rule 15 of the Rules of Procedure. Council of Europe. http://assembly.coe.int/ASP/Doc/XrefViewHTML. asp?FileID=9539&Language=en. Accessed 6 January 2014.

Pécoud, Antoine, and Paul F.A. Guchteneire, eds. 2007. *Migration without Borders: Essays on the Free Movement of People.* Oxford; New York: Berghahn Books.

Permanent Court of International Justice. 1923. *Nationality Decrees Issued in Tunis and Morocco (French Zone) on November 8th, 1921, Great Britain v France*, Advisory Opinion, (1923) PCIJ Series B no. 4, ICGJ 271 (PCIJ 1923), 7th February 1923, Permanent Court of International Justice [PCIJ].

Peskin, Victor, and Mieczyslaw P. Boduszynski. 2003. 'Croatia's Moments of Truth: The Domestic Politics of State Cooperation with the International Criminal Tribunal for the Former Yugoslavia.' Berkeley Program in Soviet and Post-Soviet Studies Working Paper Series. http://iseees.berkeley.edu/bps/publications/2003_01-pesk.pdf. Accessed 22 April 2014.

Petras, Elizabeth. 1981. 'The Global Labor Market in the Modern World Economy.' In Mary M. Kritz, C.B. Keely and S.M. Tomasi, eds., *Global Trends in Migration: Theory and Research on International Population Movements*, 44–63. Staten Island: Centre for Migration Studies.

Petrie, David. 2010. 'Letter to Professor Enrico Decleva, 18 February 2010.' 18 February. http://davidpetrie.files.wordpress.com/2010/03/crui-en-web.doc. Accessed 6 January 2014.

Pilić, Damir. 1999. 'Chronicle of Brutal Torture of Captured Serbs in Military Prisons in Sibenik, Split and Zadar.' *Feral Tribune*, 27 September. http://www.ex-yupress.com/feral/feral102.html. Accessed 10 January 2014.

Pilkington, Hilary. 2002. *Migration, Displacement and Identity in Post-Soviet Russia*. London: Routledge.

Piore, Michael J. 1979. *Birds of Passage: Migrant Labor and Industrial Societies*. Cambridge: Cambridge University Press.

Piore, Michael J. 1983. 'Labor Market Segmentation: To What Paradigm Does It Belong?' *American Economic Review* 73 (2): 249–53.

Portes, Alejandro. 1998. *The Economic Sociology of Immigration: Essays on Networks, Ethnicity, and Entrepreneurship*. New York: Russell Sage Foundation.

Portes, Alejandro, and Rubén G. Rumbaut. 2006. *Immigrant America: A Portrait*. Berkeley, CA: University of California Press.

President of the Russian Federation. 1993a. *Law on the Right of Russian Citizens to Freedom of Movement, the Choice of a Place of Stay and Residence within the Russian Federation*. https://www.google.co.uk/search?q=Law+on+the+Right+of+Russian+Citizens+to+Freedom+of+Movement,+the+Choice+of+a+Place+of+Stay+and+Residence&ie=utf-8&oe=utf-8&rls=org.mozilla:en-US:official&client=firefox-a&channel=fflb&gws_rd=cr&ei=WAbQUo3BKrHd7QaS8IGQCg. Accessed 10 January 2014.

President of the Russian Federation. 1993b. 'Constitution of the Russian Federation.' 12 December. https://www.google.co.uk/search?q=Russian+Constitution&ie=utf-8&oe=utf-8&rls=org.mozilla:en-US:official&client=firefox-a&channel=fflb&gws_rd=cr&ei=cAfQUvmbFYrBhAeYx4HgBA. Accessed 10 January 2014.

President of the Russian Federation. 2004. 'Federal Law on the Legal Status of Foreign Citizens in the Russian Federation. No. 115-Federal Law (FZ).' http://moscow.ru/common/img/uploaded/useful_doc/FZ_o_pravovom_polozhenii_eng.doc. Accessed 10 January 2014.

Radio Free Europe/Radio Liberty. 2002. 'Balkan Report: September 6, 2002.' *Radio Free Europe/Radio Liberty*, 6 September, sec. Reports Archive. http://www.rferl.org/content/article/1341079.html. Accessed 30 October 2013.

Rakate, Phenyo Keiseng. 2000. 'The Shelling of Knin by the Croatian Army in August 1995: A Police Operation or a Non-International Armed Conflict?' *International Review of the Red Cross*. http://www.icrc.org/eng/resources/documents/misc/57jqta.htm. Accessed 30 October 2013.

Ramet, Sabrina P. 1996. *Balkan Babel: The Disintegration of Yugoslavia from the Death of Tito to Ethnic War*. Boulder, CO: Westview Press. http://www.getcited.org/pub/103295095. Accessed 6 January 2014.

Ramet, Sabrina P. 1998. 'The Slovenian Success Story.' *Current History* 97 (617): 113–18.

Ravenstein, Ernest George. 1885. 'The Laws of Migration.' *Journal of the Statistical Society of London* 48 (2): 167–235.

Rawls, John. 2005. *Political Liberalism*. New York: Columbia University Press.

Republic of Croatia, Bureau of Statistics. 2001a. 'Population by Ethnicity, by Towns/Municipalities, Census 2001.' http://www.dzs.hr/default_e.htm. Accessed 10 January 2014.

Republic of Croatia. 2011. 'Census of Population, Households and Dwellings 2011.' http://www.dzs.hr/default_e.htm. Accessed 10 January 2014.

Romer, Paul M. 1986. 'The Origins of Endogenous Growth.' *Journal of Economic Perspectives* 8 (1): 3–22.

Romer, Paul M. 1990. 'Endogenous Technological Change.' *Journal of Political Economy* 98 (5): S71–S102.

Rosenau, James N. 1974. *Citizenship between Elections: An Inquiry into the Mobilizable American*. Free Press.

Rousseau, Jean-Jacques. 1987. *Basic Political Writings*. Indianapolis, IN: Hackett Publishing Company.

Rubins, Noah. 1988. 'Recent Development: The Demise and Resurrection of the Propiska: Freedom of Movement in the Russian Federation.' *Harvard International Law Journal* 39: 545. http://www.nelegal.net/articles/oldpropiska.htm. Accessed 6 January 2013.

Rudolph, Christopher W. 1998. 'Globalization, Sovereignty, and Migration: A Conceptual Framework.' *UCLA Journal of International and Foreign Affairs* 3: 325.

Russian Life. 2006. 'Work Rules.' February. http://www.russianlife.com/ archive/backissue/params/Issue/2103108133/. Accessed 6 January 2014.

Salt, John. 2005. *Current Trends in International Migration in Europe.* Council of Europe. http://books.google.co.uk/books?hl=en&lr=&id=u YLZUq8EoOMC&oi=fnd&pg=PP9&dq=%22current+trends+in+inter national+migration+in+Europe%22&ots=HQDsWSaTdH&sig=CGM yvqgvi1bvGSbrHB0W5Qcx76o. Accessed 6 January 2014.

Salt, John, Allan Findlay, and Reginald Appleyard. 1989. 'International Migration of Highly Skilled Manpower.' *The Impact of International Migration on Developing Countries,* 159–80. Paris: OECD.

Salvatore, Dominick. 1977. 'An Econometric Analysis of Internal Migration in Italy.' *Journal of Regional Science* 17 (3): 395–408.

Sassen, Saskia. 1990. *The Mobility of Labor and Capital: A Study in International Investment and Labor Flow.* Cambridge: Cambridge University Press. http://books.google.co.uk/books?hl=en&lr=&id=frh QBVHW8ScC&oi=fnd&pg=PR7&dq=sassen&ots=iNpevSKiSV&sig= 5uDk8IAV9m4SBpg_m3v8JniBnvI. Accessed 6 January 2014.

Sassen, Saskia. 2000. 'Spatialities and Temporalities of the Global: Elements for a Theorization.' *Public Culture* 12 (1): 215–32.

Sassen, Saskia. 2001. *The Global City: New York, London, Tokyo.* Princeton, NJ: Princeton University Press. http://books.google.co.uk/ books?hl=en&lr=&id=PTAiHWK2BYIC&oi=fnd&pg=PR11&dq= sassen&ots=BS_JkmWkL3&sig=Pzi5DBSWt3kOeMlizAfMBvcR3Pw. Accessed 6 January 2014.

Sawyer, Caroline, and Brad K. Blitz, eds. 2011. *Statelessness in the European Union: Displaced, Undocumented, Unwanted.* Cambridge: Cambridge University Press.

Schaible, Damian. 2001. 'Life in Russia's "Closed City": Moscow's Movement Restrictions and the Rule of Law.' *New York University Law Review,* April. http://www.nyulawreview.org/issues/volume-76-number-1/life-russias-closed-city-moscows-movement-restrictions-and-rule-law. Accessed 6 January 2013.

Schmitter, Philippe C., and Terry Lynn Karl. 1991. 'What Democracy Is … and Is Not.' *Journal of Democracy* 2 (3): 75–88. doi:10.1353/ jod.1991.0033.

Schöpflin, George. 2000. *Nations, Identity, Power.* New York: New York University Press. http://www.getcited.org/pub/100337807. Accessed 6 January 2014.

Schwarzenberger, Georg. 1969. 'The Forms of Sovereignty: An Essay in Comparative Jurisprudence.' In W.J. Stankiewicz, ed., *In Defense of Sovereignty,* 160–96. Oxford: Oxford University Press.

Sen, Amartya. 2001. *Development as Freedom*. Oxford; New York: Oxford University Press.

SETimes.com. 2003. 'Croatian Government Urged to Step Up Refugee Voting Support.' 11 July. http://setimes.com/cocoon/setimes/xhtml/en_GB/features/setimes/features/2003/11/031107-SVETLA-001. Accessed 6 January 2014.

Shearer, David. 2004. 'Elements Near and Alien: Passportization, Policing, and Identity in the Stalinist State, 1932–1952.' *Journal of Modern History* 76 (4): 835–81.

Shevtsova, Lilia. 2006. 'Russia's Ersatz Democracy.' *Current History – New York then Philadelphia* 105 (693): 307.

Shevtsova, Lilia. 2010. *Putin's Russia*. Washington, DC: Carnegie Endowment.

Sircelj, M. 2003. *Religious, Lingual and Ethnic Composition of the Slovenian Inhabitants*. Ljubljana: Statistical Office of the Republics of Slovenia.

Sjaastad, Larry A. 1962. 'The Costs and Returns of Human Migration.' *Journal of Political Economy* 70 (5): 80–93.

Slovenia News. 2003. 'MPs Pass Technicalities Bill on Erased.' *Slovenia News*, 4 November, 39 edition. http://www.ukom.gov.si/en/media_relations/background_information/domestic_policy/the_erased/short_chronology_of_facts_related_to_the_erased/. Accessed 10 January 2013.

Spaak, Paul-Henri. 1956. 'Intergovernmental Committee on European Integration. The Brussels Report on the General Common Market (abridged, English Translation of Document Commonly Called the Spaak Report) [June 1956].' EU Other. http://aei.pitt.edu/995/. Accessed 6 January 2014.

Spiro, Herbert J. 1974. 'A Third Option between Sovereignty and Supranational Integration.' In Ghita Ionescu, ed., *Between Sovereignty and Integration*, 158–68. London: Croom Helm.

Stankiewicz, W.J., ed. 1969. *In Defense of Sovereignty*. Oxford: Oxford University Press.

Stark, Oded. 1993. *Migration of Labor*. Oxford: John Wiley & Sons.

Statistical Office of the Republic of Slovenia. 2002. 'Population by Ethnic Affiliation, Slovenia, Census 1953, 1961, 1971, 1981, 1991 and 2002.' http://www.stat.si/popis2002/en/rezultati/rezultati_red.asp?ter=SLO&st=7. Accessed 10 January 2013.

Stouffer, Samuel A. 1940. 'Intervening Opportunities: A Theory Relating Mobility and Distance.' *American Sociological Review* 5 (6): 845–67.

Straubhaar, Thomas, and Martin R. Wolburg. 1999. 'Brain Drain and Brain Gain in Europe: An Evaluation of the East-European Migration to Germany.' *Journal of Economics and Statistics (Jahrbuecher Fuer Nationaloekonomie Und Statistik)* 218 (5+6): 574–604.

Sznajder, Mario, and Luis Roniger. 2009. *The Politics of Exile in Latin America*. Cambridge: Cambridge University Press.

Tanner, Marcus. 2001. *Croatia: A Nation Forged in War*. New Haven, CT: Yale University Press.

The Moscow Times. 2014. 'Kremlin Aide Seeks 1 Million Migrants.' *The Moscow Times*. http://www.themoscowtimes.com/news/article/kremlin-aide-seeks-1-million-migrants/204053.html. Accessed 6 January 2014.

Thompson, Mark. 1999. *Forging War: The Media in Serbia, Croatia, Bosnia and Hercegovina*. Luton: University of Luton Press.

Todaro, Michael. 1980. 'Internal Migration in Developing Countries: A Survey.' In *Population and Economic Change in Developing Countries*, 361–402. Chicago: University of Chicago Press. http://www.nber.org/chapters/c9668.pdf. Accessed 8 January 2014.

Toft, Monica Duffy. 2000. 'Repatriation of Refugees: A Failing Policy.' Unpublished Paper. Cambridge, MA: John F. Kennedy School of Government, Harvard University.

Torpey, John. 1998. 'Coming and Going: On the State Monopolization of the Legitimate "Means of Movement."' *Sociological Theory* 16 (3): 239–59. doi:10.1111/0735-2751.00055.

Torpey, John. 2000. *The Invention of the Passport: Surveillance, Citizenship and the State*. Cambridge: Cambridge University Press.

Turack, Daniel C. 1968. 'Freedom of Movement and the Travel Document in Benelux.' *International and Comparative Law Quarterly* 17 (1): 191–206.

Ul Haque, Nadeem. 2007. 'Brain Drain or Human Capital Flight' (No. 11). Lectures in Development Economics. http://ssrn.com/abstract=987449. Accessed 6 January 2014.

UN General Assembly. 1948. *Universal Declaration of Human Rights*. 217A (III). United Nations General Assembly. http://www.refworld.org/docid/3ae6b3712c.html. Accessed 8 January 2014.

United Nations High Commissioner for Refugees. 1954. *Convention Relating to the Status of Refugees*. http://www.unhcr.org/3b66c2aa10.html. Accessed 10 January 2014.

United Nations High Commissioner for Refugees. 2005. 'UNHCR – Home Again, 10 Years after Croatia's Operation Storm.' 5 August. http://www.unhcr.org/42f38b084.html. Accessed 30 October 2013.

United Nations High Commissioner for Refugees. 2013. 'Return of Serb Minority Refugees to Croatia.' *UNHCR Croatia*. Accessed 30 October 2014. http://www.unhcr.hr/what-we-do/return-of-serb-minority-refugees-to-croatia. Accessed 30 October 2013.

United Nations Office of the High Commissioner for Human Rights. 1969. *International Convention on the Elimination of All Forms of Racial Discrimination.* http://www.ohchr.org/EN/ProfessionalInterest/ Pages/CERD.aspx. Accessed 10 January 2014.

United Nations Office of the High Commissioner for Human Rights. 1976. *International Covenant on Civil and Political Rights.* http:// www.ohchr.org/en/professional interest/pages/ccpr.aspx. Accessed 10 January 2014.

United Nations Population Division. 2009. 'International Migrant Stock: The 2008 Revision Population Database.' http://esa.un.org/migration/. Accessed 6 January 2014.

United States Department of State, Bureau of Public Affairs. 2005. 'Croatia: Country Report on Human Rights Practices 2004.' Human Rights Report. http://www.state.gov/j/drl/rls/hrrpt/2004/41675.htm. Accessed 30 October 2014.

US Committee for Refugees and Immigrants. 1999. 'Country Reports: Croatia.' US Committee for Refugees and Immigrants.

US Department of State, Bureau of Democracy, Human Rights, and Labor. 2003. 'Country Reports on Human Rights Practices 2002.' 31 March 2003. http://www.state.gov/j/drl/rls/hrrpt/2002/18388.htm Accessed 22 April 2014.

US Department of State. 2004. 'Croatia: Country Reports on Human Rights Practices 2003.' http://www.state.gov/j/drl/rls/hrrpt/2003/ 27831.htm. Accessed 30 October 2013.

US Department of State. 2014. 'Russia: Human Rights Report.' Human Rights Report on Country Practices 2013. http://www.state.gov/ documents/organization/204543.pdf. Accessed 10 January 2014.

Vaux, Roland De. 1997. *Ancient Israel: Its Life and Institutions.* Grand Rapids, MI: Wm. B. Eerdmans Publishing.

Velikonja, Mitja. 2002. 'Ex-Home: "Balkan Culture" in Slovenia after 1991.' In *The Balkans in Focus: Cultural Boundaries in Europe*, 189–208. Lund: Nordic Academic Press. https://getinfo.de/app/Ex-Home-Balkan-Culture-in-Slovenia-after-1991/id/BLCP%3ACN058915 917. Accessed 10 January 2014.

Vincent, Andrew. 1987. *Theories of the State.* Oxford: Basil Blackwell.

Viner, Jacob. 1937. *Studies in the Theory of International Trade.* New York: Harper & Brothers.

Vitkovskaya, G. 2002. *Forced Migration and Migrantophobia in Russia.* Budapest: Central European University.

Volčič, Zala. 2005. '"The Machine that Creates Slovenians": The Role of Slovenian Public Broadcasting in Re-Affirming and Re-Inventing the Slovenian National Identity.' *National Identities* 7 (3): 287–308.

Vučetić, Srdjan. 2004. 'From Southern to Southeastern Europe: Any Lessons for Democratization Theory?' *Southeast European Politics* 5 (2–3): 115–41.

Vuković, Marija Brajdić, and Dragan Bagić. 2004. *Croatia's Refugee Challenge*. OSCE Mission to Croatia.

Wallerstein, Immanuel Maurice. 2011. *The Modern World-System I: Capitalist Agriculture and the Origins of the European World-Economy in the Sixteenth Century*. Berkeley, CA: University of California Press.

Walzer, Michael. 1983. *Spheres of Justice: A Defense of Pluralism and Equality*. New York: Basic Books.

Weber, Cynthia. 1995. *Simulating Sovereignty: Intervention, the State, and Symbolic Exchange*. Cambridge, England; New York: Cambridge University Press.

Weissbrodt, David S. 2008. *The Human Rights of Non-Citizens*. Oxford University Press.

Westermann, William Linn. 1955. *The Slave Systems of Greek and Roman Antiquity*. American Philosophical Society.

Whelan, Frederick G. 1988. 'Citizenship and Freedom of Movement: An Open Admission Policy?' In Mark Gibney, ed., *Open Borders? Closed Societies?* 3–40. Westport, CT; New York; London: Greenwood Publishing Group.

White, Stephen. 2003. 'Rethinking Postcommunist Transition.' *Government and Opposition* 38 (4): 417–35.

Wilhelm, Kathryn. 2010. 'Freedom of Movement at a Standstill? Toward the Establishment of a Fundamental Right to Intrastate Travel.' *Boston University Law Review* 90: 2461–95.

Yablokova, Oksana. 2014. 'Kremlin Aide Seeks 1 Million Migrants.' *The Moscow Times*. http://www.themoscowtimes.com/news/article/kremlin-aide-seeks-1-million-migrants/204053.html. Accessed 10 January 2014.

Young, Ruth, Jenny Noble, Ann Mahon, Mairead Maxted, Janet Grant, and Bonnie Sibbald. 2010. 'Evaluation of International Recruitment of Health Professionals in England.' *Journal of Health Services Research & Policy* 15 (4): 195–203.

Zolberg, Aristide R. 1989. 'The Next Waves: Migration Theory for a Changing World.' *International Migration Review* 23 (3): 403–30.

Zorn, Jelka. 2005. 'Ethnic Citizenship in the Slovenian State.' *Citizenship Studies* 9 (2): 135–52. doi:10.1080/13621020500049093.

Zorn, Jelka. 2011. 'From Erased and Excluded to Active Participants in Slovenia.' In Brad K. Blitz and Maureen Lynch, eds., *Statelessness and Citizenship: A Comparative Study on the Benefits of Nationality*, 66–83. Cheltenham, UK; Northampton, MA, USA: Edward Elgar Publishing.

Index

acceptance 108, 128, 162, 165
  and integration 110–11
accession to European Union 49, 52, 55, 146, 176
acquired rights 81, 142, 166, 171, 181
administrative courts 95, 159
adventure 71, 74, 172–3
advocacy groups 127, 134
AFSJ (Area of Freedom, Security and Justice) 51
agreements 47, 50, 52, 65, 81
Albanians 144, 150
alienation 126, 147, 156, 162
  Russia 131–3
Amnesty International 101, 151, 155–6
annual contracts 78, 80
anxiety 135, 170
Apap, Joanna 33
apartheid 84
Appleyard, Reginald 75
arbitrariness 135, 138, 153
  lettori 83–4, 93
  Russia 126–9
Area of Freedom, Security and Justice (AFSJ) 51
Arendt, Hannah 19–20, 34–5, 167, 169, 189
assistance 43–4, 48, 105, 112, 115
  reconstruction 106
  social 34, 47, 49, 171
asylum 2, 4, 12, 15, 19, 42, 50–51
  seekers 12, 14, 51, 163
Australia 9–10, 73
Austria 10, 147–8, 180
authority
  devolution of 128, 137, 179
  political 8, 129, 162, 189
autochthonous minorities 148–9
autonomy 12, 14, 19–21, 61, 74, 76, 171

personal 71, 116, 168
avoidance, Russia 135–7, 139

banks 129–30, 170
Barcelona 58, 68–9
Bauböck, Rainer 3, 14, 21–2
Belgrade 99, 113, 145, 147
benefits 31, 33, 39–40, 45, 47–8, 50, 112–13
  retirement 33, 92
Bhachu, Parminder 30
birth 3, 131, 137, 141, 144, 151, 160
Bodin, Jean 6
bonded labour 5
borders
  internal 22, 51, 175
  open *see* open borders
Bosnia 104–5, 108, 113–17, 160, 164, 175–6, 183–4
Bosniak, Linda 33
Bosniaks 102, 147–8, 150–51, 156, 159, 166
Bosnian Croats 104–5, 109, 115–17, 173, 183
Brabandt, Heike 33
brain drain 12–13, 27, 29, 31
bribes 123, 137–9
Britain *see* United Kingdom
Buynaksk 141

capital 26, 31, 37, 99, 186
  human 27, 29, 58, 60, 74–5, 175
Carens, Joseph 19–21, 34–5, 189–90
case law 24, 33, 39, 42, 44, 54, 188
casualization, *lettori* 84–7
Celje 142, 156–63
Central Italy 77–8, 82–4, 86–7, 89, 91
Chester-le-Street 66